Monsters

Genre Fiction and Film Companions

Series Editor: Simon Bacon

MONSTERS

A Companion
Edited by Simon Bacon

PETER LANG
Oxford • Bern • Berlin • Bruxelles • New York • Wien

Bibliographic information published by Die Deutsche Nationalbibliothek. Die Deutsche
Nationalbibliothek lists this publication in the Deutsche Nationalbibliografie; detailed
bibliographic data is available on the Internet at http://dnb.d-nb.de.

A catalogue record for this book is available from the British Library.

Library of Congress Cataloging-in-Publication Data
Names: Bacon, Simon, 1965- editor author.
Title: Monsters : a companion / [editor] Simon Bacon.
Description: Oxford ; New York : Peter Lang, 2020. | Series: Genre fiction
   and film companions, 26318725 ; 5 | Includes bibliographical references.
Identifiers: LCCN 2020012239 (print) | LCCN 2020012240 (ebook) | ISBN
   9781788746649 (paperback) | ISBN 9781788746656 (ebook) | ISBN
   9781788746663 (epub) | ISBN 9781788746670 (mobi)
Classification: LCC P96.M6 M64 2020 (print) | LCC P96.M6 (ebook) | DDC
   809/.9337--dc23
LC record available at https://lccn.loc.gov/2020012239
LC ebook record available at https://lccn.loc.gov/2020012240

Cover design by Peter Lang Ltd.

ISSN 2631-8725
ISBN 978-1-78874-664-9 (print) • ISBN 978-1-78874-665-6 (ePDF)
ISBN 978-1-78874-666-3 (ePUB) • ISBN 978-1-78874-667-0 (mobi)

© Peter Lang AG 2020
Published by Peter Lang Ltd, International Academic Publishers,
52 St Giles, Oxford, OX1 3LU, United Kingdom
oxford@peterlang.com, www.peterlang.com

Simon Bacon has asserted his right under the Copyright, Designs and Patents Act, 1988, to
be identified as Editor of this Work.

All rights reserved.
All parts of this publication are protected by copyright.
Any utilisation outside the strict limits of the copyright law, without
the permission of the publisher, is forbidden and liable to prosecution.
This applies in particular to reproductions, translations, microfilming,
and storage and processing in electronic retrieval systems.

This publication has been peer reviewed.

Contents

Acknowledgements ix

Sherry C. M. Lindquist
Foreword: Culture's Monsters: *Monster Marks* (Lindquist 2018) xi

Simon Bacon
Introduction 1

PART I   Home

Angela M. Smith
Madness: *The Babadook* (Kent, 2014) – Monsters of Mental Illness 15

Simon Bacon
Domestic Abuse: *The Invisible Man* (Whannell, 2020) – Domestic Monsters 23

Phil Fitzsimmons
Paedophilia: *The Nightingale* (Kent, 2018) – Monsters of Abuse 31

Agnieszka Kotwasińska
Immigrants: *The Lure* (Smoczyńska, 2015) – Monstrous Outsiders 41

PART II   Society

John Edgar Browning
The Mask: Slasher Cinema (1978–1998) – Teaching the Monster   51

Lauren Rosewarne
The Cyberbully: *Cyberbully* (Binamé, 2011) – Monsters of Cyberspace   69

Anthony Curtis Adler
Lady Gaga: Stefani Joanne Angelina Germanotta (1986–present) –
Monsters of Celebrity   77

Alexandra Heller-Nicholas
The Slit-Mouthed Woman: *Carved* (Shiraishi, 2007) – Monsters of
Urban Legend   85

W. Scott Poole
Melmoth: *Melmoth* (Perry, 2018) – Monsters of War   93

PART III   Cultural Intersections

Benjamin Baumann
Phi Krasue: *Inhuman Kiss* (Mongkolsiri, 2019) – Thai Monsters   101

Inés Ordiz
La habitación del desahogo (2012) – Mexican Monsters   111

Gail de Vos
Baba Yaga: *Hellboy* (Mignola, 1997–2004) – Russian Monsters   119

Contents

Partha Mitter
Deumo: *Indiana Jones and the Temple of Doom* (Spielberg, 1984) –
Monsters of Colonialism   129

Yasmine Musharbash
The Hairies: *Cleverman* (Griffen, 2016–2017) – Aboriginal Monsters   137

PART IV   Gender

Eddie Falvey
Satan: *The Witch* (Eggers, 2015) – Patriarchal Monsters   149

Emily Brick
Warlocks: *AHS Apocalypse* (Murphy and Falchuk, 2011–present) –
Monsters of Masculinity   157

Craig Ian Mann
She-Wolves: *When Animals Dream* (Arnby, 2014) – Monsters of
Femininity   167

Daniel Sheppard
Serial Killers: *Bates Motel* (Ehrin, 2013–2017) – The Queer Monster   175

Murray Leeder
The Skeleton: *Game of Thrones* (Benioff, 2011–2019) – Monsters of
Death   183

PART V Futures

Leah Richards
Clones: *Orphan Black* (Manson and Fawcett, 2013–2017) – Monsters of Reproduction ... 193

Dahlia Schweitzer
The Master: *The Strain* (del Toro and Hogan, 2014–2017) – Monsters of Contagion ... 201

Carl H. Sederholm
The Ecomonster: *Megalohydrothalassophobia* (Abhorrence, 2018) – Monsters of the Anthropocene ... 209

Gerry Canavan
Aliens: *District 9* (Blomkamp, 2009) – Monsters of Hybridity ... 217

Elana Gomel
Zombie: *The Girl with All the Gifts* (Carey, 2014) – Posthuman Monsters ... 225

Patricia MacCormack
Afterword: Becoming Monstrous and the Monster Becoming: *Hannibal* (Fuller: 2013–2015) ... 233

Bibliography ... 245

Notes on Contributors ... 267

Index ... 275

Acknowledgements

Many thanks to Laurel Plapp and the team at Peter Lang for all their help and assistance, the always helpful suggestions of friends and colleagues along the way and particularly all those at the Horror Studies SIG FB group and the invaluable comments made by Reviewer No. 2. As always, I cannot thank my wonderful Mrs. Mine enough for her continual help, support and encouragement, and our two little monsters, Elbi and Majki, who are always "helpful" by just being themselves. I na koniec, bardzo dziękuję Mam i tacie za wsparcie… i "sernik Magdy".

Figure 1. Wangechi Mutu (1972–), Untitled, 2004, mixed media collage on paper, 93.345 cm x 66.04 cm x 5.08 cm. Collection of Dr James Patterson. Photo: Jason Miller. Reproduced with permission.

Sherry C. M. Lindquist

Foreword: Culture's Monsters: *Monster Marks* (Lindquist 2018)

The charismatic being – part-human, part-animal, part-machine – in an untitled collage by Wangechi Mutu embodies Jeffrey Jerome Cohen's thesis that monsters announce category crisis, that they resist 'any classification built on hierarchy or a merely binary opposition', that they are 'full of rebuke about traditional methods of organizing knowledge and human experience' (Cohen 1996: 7). This work was shown at an exhibit I curated at the Art Museum of the University of Memphis (AMUM) in 2018 entitled *Monster Marks* (Lindquist 2018). It hung in the largest gallery, which, to commemorate the fiftieth anniversary of the assassination of Dr Martin Luther King Jr in Memphis, was dedicated to the theme of how contemporary artists use the visual vocabulary of monstrosity to address issues of race and racism. It could as easily have been placed in the gallery dedicated to feminism and posthumanism, and it is certainly in dialogue with the historical works in the third gallery, which interrogated the relationships of monstrous themes to the power of rulers in the dominant art historical narrative. The exhibit itself had a monstrous quality, since it resisted traditional ways of organizing historical and contemporary art, bringing together works of different media, historical periods, and geographical origins made by canonical, established, emerging, and student artists. *Monster Marks* takes its cue from Fred Wilson's landmark exhibit, *Mining the Museum*, at the Maryland Historical Society in 1992. Fred Wilson mined the collections of a single museum to expose the hierarchies and ideologies built into traditional museum displays purporting to be both neutral and true (Corrin 1994). *Monster Marks* mined the culturally significant objects gathered in the collections of a single city – Memphis – to explore how the themes of monstrosity and the uncanny surfacing in them might (re)shape identity and make new meanings when considered together. Wangechi Mutu has said that 'Every little bit of culture can be used to investigate almost any other bit of culture' (*Cultural Cutouts* 2015: 9:24–9:27). In dialogue with other bits of culture in the Memphis exhibit and in this volume, Mutu's collage is revealing about both the perils and the possibilities of our monstrous imaginations.

The collage exhibited in *Monster Marks* is representative of Mutu's work, which expresses themes of violence, colonization, overconsumption, and cultural annihilation, as well as human interconnectedness and resilience. Here, as in her other early collages on paper, Mutu uses ethereal watercolour washes to fit together body parts snipped from popular magazines. She has said that 'there's a kind of violence to breaking up an image – if one looks at collage technique. Cutting is violent' (Schoonmaker 2013: 115). And indeed, her works frequently show wounded, dismembered beings as well as splatters that suggest bodily fluids, like the bloody red tendrils dripping from the mushroom on which the woman-Holstein hybrid is perched. The mushroom is a clue to the being's status and identity. For Mutu, 'Fungus was one of those things that played into my sense of the grotesque'; a mushroom is phallic-looking, but also resembles a little stool, structure, or 'a little man in a hat' (Enright 2008). In pondering a colony of mushrooms in her shed, she thought 'they were almost like a migrant culture that exists in the most decrepit parts of the city, and what emerges are these fascinating people and interactions. They're also in-between … a little alien family found in the middle of these two massive kingdoms' (Enright 2008). The mushroom, like the human/animal/cyborg it supports, is not one thing or another, and the liminal world it evokes calls into question the normative cultural categories defined by elite and majority populations.

It is not easy to know what to make of the arresting protagonist inhabiting the non-place conjured up by Mutu's uprooted fungus. The figure here is infused with nervous energy, having just nimbly landed on the spongy surface. Clipped from fashion or pornographic magazines, her composite hands-as-feet are bent at right angles, and her long neck is arched. The tendrils on her back seem to undulate, and her tail forms a question mark. Perhaps the artist's decision to give this being a bovine body evokes the Kenyan agricultural shows that fascinate Mutu, fairs that feature the 'biggest cow and the most plump cabbage', and which 'have a circus freak side to them. That's where you can see something like a double-headed calf or a bearded woman' (Willis 2014). The animals in the show seem analogous to the models in fashion magazines: both are selected for physical qualities and put on display to provide visual pleasure, whether for the price of admission, or to sell products. Mutu's works forces viewers to confront biological realities obscured by the sanitized, sexualized staging of women's bodies in popular culture. There are, for example, recurrent themes of suckling in Mutu's works, which may be related to the melding here of woman and cow (e.g. *The Bourgeois is Banging on My Head*, 2003). Her other works bring in even more explicit imagery from anatomy books and pornographic magazines. The in-between beings exemplified by the one in this untitled collage are once centred and marginal, isolated and engaged, seductive and discomfiting, too real and surreal, energized and poised, glamorous and abject.

Mutu has said of her use of glossy magazines, 'I really got to vandalize the original narrative to make something dignified, beautiful, unreal and to me attractive about these things that kind of bothered me' (*Inside My Studio* 2018, 4:14–4:27). Mutu's figure is aware she is being looked at, which is part of the exploitative narrative of her origins: her seductive smoky eye, plump lips, and glittering accessories were designed for visual consumption. This is true also of the featured engine part fused to her forehead – its polished, customized copper surface fetishized in magazines for motorcycle enthusiasts. And yet, this being's hybrid nature and unfamiliar surroundings undermine the Western consumerist narrative. The motorcycle part evokes an elegant African-style headwrap, read as a sign of exoticism in the Eurocentric magazines she plunders. As Mutu notes, they 'portray women as perfect and idealized and often very homogenous in the kinds of women they have' (*Inside My Studio* 2018, 3:55–4:03). Mutu transforms this clichéd, photoshopped brand of glamor into unrecognizable, no longer human, beings, like this one, who radiate an insistent, powerful presence. These beings undercut strict gender binaries; she describes them as 'female-ish' (Moos 2010, 99). She has said,

> I believe our bodies are only a single part of the many dimensions of our identity and, in some ways, the body becomes a trap in the understanding of the whole. We can invent, transform, re-imagine ourselves through manipulating our outer appearance and, thus, 'conquer' adversity through our physicality; or we can become subjugated ... often there may not be a choice. (Moos 2010, 99)

Mutu identifies the human body as a battleground that can be colonized, conquered, and subjugated, but also as a protean origin for multiple possible futures. The fiction of a normal human body serves as a foil for Mutu's enigmatic beings, just as it creates the 'monster culture', identified by Cohen and other recent theorists of monstrosity.

When we encounter Mutu's fantastic beings in their perplexing habitats, when we are outnumbered them as in an exhibit, or a catalogue of her work (e.g. Schoonmaker 2013), our notions of normativity, difference, otherness, and monstrosity must shift. Who are we in relationship to them? Mutu's objects create meanings in a different way when they are exhibited with the works of other artists, as was the case with this single collage in the 2018 exhibition in Memphis. It shared a gallery with artists whose works addressed racism in myriad ways.

Visitors viewed the works on the walls through the elements of the striking installation in the centre of the main gallery, made especially for the exhibit by Memphis artist Le Marquee la Flora. La Flora's sculpture, *The Old Landmark*, consists of upside-down nooses that seem to rise to the ceiling of their own volition, invoking the ghostly presence of the African-American lives cut short by lynchings. He used lighting effects to place his work in dialogue with a series of large-format Polaroid prints by the photographer William Christenberry, whose *Metamorphosis (4 Works)*, shows the horrifying transformation of a wholesome-looking ragdoll into a Klansman.

Christenberry had written of these and his other Klan-themed works that, as a white southerner, he felt obligated to address the atrocities resulting from white southern culture, to 'deal with evil' and 'to reveal what we might call a strange and secret brutality, the Ku Klux Klan' (Ferris 2013: 188). By lighting the nooses so that they cast unnerving shadows between Christenberry's disturbing images of another inanimate, uncanny, dreadful object, La Flora underscores the culpability confessed by

Figure 2. Installation photo of *Monster Marks*. The Art Museum of the University of Memphis, curated by Sherry C. M. Lindquist (25 March–28 July 2018). Photo: Jason Miller. Reproduced with permission.

Christenberry's photographs. And yet, La Flora graced these nooses with gold leaf, and in some cases gold-coloured nails. These details, along with the seeming upward movement of the nooses and the work's title after a heartening gospel song, suggest a narrative of forgiveness and redemption. From its place in the centre of the gallery, *The Old Landmark* encourages viewers to make connections among themes evident in the works on the walls: of trauma and survival, woundedness and resilience, guilt and forgiveness. In this context, Mutu's collage links the experiences and aspirations of the global African diaspora it addresses with other, specifically American horrors and hopes at a poignant moment and place: Memphis on the anniversary of the assassination of Dr Martin Luther King.

The hybrid denizen of Mutu's stark fungal landscape shares its postapocalyptic, Afrofuturist aesthetic with a painting by Memphis artist Roger Cleaves, which was shown next to Mutu's collage in the main gallery.

Cleaves's renderings of a traumatized people named 'Forget Me Nots' are oil paintings, not collages, but they still look as though they have been cut up and put back together. Barely surviving in an inhospitable underwater environment, this Forget Me Not is under attack: stabbed by swords, bitten by a shark, weighed down by balls and chains. Even though the Forget Me Nots belong to a much larger fictional world constructed by Cleaves, his imagery nevertheless refers to motifs identifiable with slavery and Jim Crow in our world – not only the leg irons, but also the

Figure 3. Installation photo of *Monster Marks* featuring details of Le Marquee La Flora (1993–), *The Old Landmark*, 2018 (rope, gold leaf, nails, collection of the artist), and William Christenberry (1936–2016), and *Metamorphosis (4 Works)*, 1984 (large-format Polaroid prints, 86.36 cm x 109.22 cm, collection of Dr James Patterson). Photo: Jason Miller. Reproduced with permission.

Figure 4. Roger Cleaves (1980–), *You Can't Drown a Shark*, 2017 (oil on canvas, collection of the artist, 122 cm x 152 cm). Photo: Jason Miller. Reproduced with permission.

lynching victim that sprouts from a plant on a miniature island formed by the Forget Me Not's hand. The 'afroglyphic' in the lower left corner – with its obvious references to Egyptian writing – affirms the diasporic connection between African-Americans and their mother continent. Side-by-side, these works by Cleaves and Mutu reinforce each other, and together they ask their Memphis audience to consider the issues of race and racism addressed in the gallery with a diasporic global perspective.

Noticing such affinities can be powerful and revelatory. In the Memphis exhibit, the Afrofuturist aesthetic of Cleaves and Mutu links the themes of race and racism in the main gallery to those of feminism and posthumanism on display in an ancillary gallery. There, Saya Woolfalk's video, *Chima TEK: Hybridization Machine* also presents an alter world that creates hybrid humans.

Figure 5. Saya Woolfalk (1979–), Still from *Chima TEK: Hybridization Machine*, 2013 (single-channel video loop with sound by DJ Spooky). Collection of Dr James Patterson. Reproduced with permission.

In Woolfalk's imagined future, an industry arises to enable humans to create designer hybrid selves by merging with plants. Their liminality is voluntary rather than violent and seems to celebrate a multicultural, posthuman future. Even so, Woolfalk's Utopia has its dark side: the Hybridization Machine may be creating catastrophic environmental damage. In common with other works shown in this gallery (by Cindy Sherman, Yasumasa Morimura and others), Woolfalk's groovy-looking video considers the promise and perils involved when we, in Mutu's words, 'invent, transform, re-imagine ourselves' (Moos 2010: 99). This process can turn us into monsters for better or worse.

Like the fictional, privileged customers of Chima TEK, those who are able to effect beneficial self-transformations, to transcend accepted norms, to leverage the power of the monstrous for their own advantage, are most often the wealthy and powerful. Thus, these contemporary works resonate with the historical works featured in the exhibit. In the latter images, rulers may incorporate fearsome monstrous characteristics to project strength, as shown in samurai armour and images of Mayan kings morphing into hybrid jaguar deities, but monstrous imagery may also be used to dehumanize the other. A sixteenth-century map of Africa by Abraham Ortelius designates the site of the legendary kingdom of Prester John, thought to rule over a land of wondrous beasts and monstrous hybrid peoples. European conquerors hoped to find this mythical Christian ally, to help them stake a claim to the wealth of the continent and to subdue the Africans, whom they imagined as semi- or non-human, hybrid monstrosities. By bringing together these disparate manifestations of the monstrous in art and visual culture, *Monster Marks* contemplates the power and multivalence of monsters and monstrosity in the past, present, and hypothesized futures.

The being in Mutu's collage is frozen in a moment in time, and we don't know her story. In fact, in her more recent work, Mutu ponders the future of the traumatized, prepossessing, 'female-ish', characters of her early collages. It is a question that arose for her when making 'a film that felt like the collages had come alive' (*The End of Eating Everything* 2015, 0:40–0:43). The film was *The End of Eating Everything*, in which the singer Santigold channels one of Mutu's collage characters presented as a 'planetary persona' (*The End of Eating Everything* 2015, 1:49). At once strangely beautiful and repulsive, she floats in an ominous sky devouring a flock of birds, snake-like tresses undulating behind.

Her hulking body, glittering with day-glow tumours and shiny machine parts, is animated by human arms and spinning wheels. About this creature, Mutu has said,

> I didn't go out of my way to make her look grotesque ... My thing was that she was going to evolve into something that was quite familiar but at the same time was obscene – obscene in the sense that, you know, it's like encountering a dirty lake or a dump, you know,

Foreword xix

Figure 6. Wangechi Mutu (1972–), screenshot from *On the End of Eating Everything*, 2013 (taken from the video interview with Wangechi Mutu, *On the End of Eating Everything* (Louisiana Channel, 2015)).

a big dump with garbage. Is it grotesque or is it magnificent, or is it just absolutely sad? … I was going for something that would change her from something we could understand to something that made absolutely no sense. (*The End of Eating Everything* 2015, 3:09–4:01)

Mutu's monstrous beings, like all monsters, are not supposed to be reasonable. They are contested. They are commandeered by one constituency and another. They are confusing. They make us wonder. Wangechi Mutu's refusal to make sense of the grotesque, magnificent, obscene, hybrids – like the one that challenges us in this early collage – is why they have the ability to unsettle us, to make us different, to make us change how things are. To subvert.

Simon Bacon

Introduction

Monsters. The etymological roots of 'monsters' illustrate how monsters are supposed to tell us something: 'monstrum' and 'monēre' mean 'omen' and 'warning' respectively, establishing monsters as harbingers of change and facilitating the realization of the fragility of the world we live in. Jeffrey Jerome Cohen notes that monsters are born from very particular cultural moments (Cohen 1996: 4) and provide something of a road map to the cultures that have produced them (Cohen 1996: 3). This does not mean an infinite supply of newly created monsters appearing one after the other to express every new twist and turn of unravelling history, but rather monsters that 'return in slightly different clothing, each time to be read against contemporary social movements, or a specific determining event' (Cohen 1996: 5). It should come as no surprise that Cohen was talking about a particular kind of monster when describing an eternally transforming entity: the undead – it is worth noting that 'undead', although commonly understood as referring to vampires and/or zombies, is a category that can cover any entity that continually returns, exceeds the normal in some way, and embodies a threat, often existential, to humanity. In relation to a particular expression of the undead, Nina Auerbach wrote that each generation gets the vampire it needs (Auerbach 1996: 9) and Jack Halberstam, in noting the non-universalism of a specific monster – in this case Dracula (Halberstam 1993: 335) – described how a monster evolves, or rather carries the marks of its birth with it into the future as it changes and mutates (Halberstam 1993: 349). 'Birth' here denotes the kind of 'determining event' that Cohen spoke of earlier and is largely situated around a point of crisis that is often about difference or resistance to categorization. Difference, as Cohen further notes, is centred around culture, politics, race, economics, and sexuality, and categorization more often involves a change in what was previously considered acceptable or normal but equally implies terms such as recognition, misrecognition (wilfully recognized as something it's not), or non-recognition. Much of the anxiety around the figure of the monster is its resistance to being categorized or contained within current cultural parameters, thus forcing a reconfiguration of some sort. Cohen sees the monster as providing a catalyst of sorts to resolve the clash of extremes – thesis, antithesis, and eventual synthesis – and, quoting Marjorie Garber, sees it as way of questioning binary thinking.[1] Similarly, Elaine Showalter sees the monster (Dracula) as offering a third alternative or more specifically a place/space outside, or beyond, normativity (Showalter 1992: 164). The space of the monster is worth considering more closely, but first it is worth unpacking a little of what has been said in relation to the specific objectives of this companion.

Halberstam, Auerbach, and Cohen all mention the monsters of the nineteenth century – Frankenstein's Monster, Dr Jekyll and Mr Hyde, and Count Dracula – partly because of their importance within Western, English-language literature, but also because they are considered seminal within the Gothic genre. *Dracula* is often pinpointed. Halberstam writes of the vampire count being 'birthed' from the intersection of homophobia, anti-Semitism, xenophobia, and misogyny that typified a certain moment in the late Victorian period in general, and the 1890s, in particular, when Bram Stoker put pen to paper. The traces or scars Halberstam subsequently describes are those that remain latent in all later incarnations of the count from Transylvania, or indeed figures/monsters based upon Dracula. However, *Dracula* was not created from a void and it is obvious that Stoker knew of earlier works in the genre, such as J. Sheridan Le Fanu's *Carmilla* (1874), and John Polidori's *The Vampyre* (1819). In fact, although Stoker invented some characteristics of the vampire that were unique, most came from earlier literary or folkloric sources. The vampire panic of the early 1700s is a case in point: reports of people returning from the grave to feed on the living spread from the Eastern outposts of civilized Europe into the newspapers and salons of London, Paris and Vienna and arguably created the popular awareness that Byron ('The Gaiour' 1813), Coleridge ('Christabel' 1797) and even Polidori would respond to. This was before popular iterations such as *Varney the Vampire* (Prest and/or Rhymer, 1845–7), and *Carmilla* (Le Fanu, 1872) brought further scar tissue with them.

1   Garber 1992: 11.

Count Dracula, then, was already an evolving monster, a point upon a trajectory that brought the fears of outsiders, ignorance, and the old world with it before adding the specific points of crisis that came with the end of the nineteenth century in Victorian England.

It is important to note that in 1897 the vampire did not just take the form of a bisexual, blood-sucking immigrant from Eastern Europe. In the same year as *Dracula* was published, Florence Marryat, in *Blood of the Vampire*, saw her vampire as a young girl travelling to Europe from the Caribbean, but as a daughter of miscegenation she drains the life energy out of all those she loves, and H. G. Wells, in *War of the Worlds*,[2] saw vampires as creatures from Mars that were dependent upon machinery and driven by a need to consume the Earth and human blood to survive. Unsurprisingly all these different representations contain many of the same points of crisis – the fear of reverse colonialism, miscegenation, and cultural degeneration – yet the differences in representations illustrate how certain characteristics of monsters become foregrounded whilst others regress, with the monsters' subsequent popularity or obscurity revealing how, for parts of a society, certain 'scars' remain fresh and raw, whereas others heal and become barely noticeable.

Obviously the lasting popularity of a text like *Dracula* points to an ongoing resonance not only within the cultural moment in which it coalesced – the word 'coalesce' most aptly suggests the conglomeration of anxieties that come together at a moment in time to produce a specific monster – but also its ongoing relevance, or stickiness, within popular culture as an ever-changing phenomena. Something similar could be said about *War of the Worlds*, except that the literal vampirism of Wells' original is downplayed in favour of the metaphorical vampire of colonial consumerism, which is brought into sharper focus. Count Dracula rather interestingly shows how a monster can remain quite similar in its appearance over time yet represent very different things to different generations. That said, it is worth noting that various aspects have been changed during that evolution with the result that the Transylvanian count with bushy eyebrows and moustache in Stoker's late Victorian work changed into the evening dress-wearing, debonair, aristocrat from Europe with the

---

2   Whilst the novel of *War of the Worlds* was published in 1898, it was first serialized the year before.

distinctive accent by the 1930s in America – a monster created to encourage American isolationism, showing that even sexy, mysterious Europeans were dangerous and should be kept over there and not over here. By the twenty-first century, this particular monster can be seen to have fragmented into a myriad of monstrous shards that include teenaged sparkly boys who promote abusive relationships and suave businessmen who will do anything to recapture the love of their eternal soulmate.[3] Count Dracula is a useful example, especially for an author such as myself who researches such things, but the same is true for a range of well-known monsters, such as werewolves, zombies, Satan, Phi Krasue (from Thailand), or Baba Yaga (from Russia), all of which will be discussed in this companion. In this sense, as Cohen also notes, all monsters will go away, but more often than not they return. The problems, or crises, that produced them are rarely solved (resolved) for good and inevitably re-emerge, slightly changed, at a later date. This throws up two further points that require looking at in this introduction as they are important aspects of this companion: space and meaning (interpretation).

Space, or place, with the latter intimating a more focused area of interaction, is vital not just in relation to the form of the monster, but also to the levels of disturbance it creates. As described above, the monster is created by, and in, a specific cultural moment but tends to interact on a much more intimate scale. So, although all monsters are arguably culturally produced, their actual space of operations can range from the most intimate to the societal or beyond. This can be seen in the scale of monster activity from the childhood monster under the bed – an invasion of an especially vulnerable and intimate place – to the Godzilla that can destroy cities and the societies connected to them. Of course, monsters often act within multiple areas at once; an interesting example of this can be seen in the film *It Follows* (Mitchell, 2014). The monster in this film, although focused on the most intimate of places, sexual contact, acts on a cultural, almost global, level, as the monster is able to follow its chosen victim anywhere – the victim is chosen by the previous victim, who passes their curse on before the monster can kill them. This growing chain of (potential) victims – once the monster kills one, the curse

---

3   Edward Cullen (Robert Pattinson) in *Twilight* (Hardwicke, 2008), and Jonathan Rhys Meyers' count in *Dracula* (Haddon, 2013–14).

reverts back to the one who passed it on – could, in theory, include hundreds of people, yet the monster is amazingly individual in that only the cursed person can see it. Although those around the victim can see the physical effects of the monster at work – things being knocked over, etc. – to all purposes, it is invisible. As Jeffrey Weinstock notes, it can become anyone or anything; it is literally everywhere at once (Weinstock 2017: x).

Just as importantly, the monster from *It Follows* invades the mind of the victim, so it is as much a product of an individual's consciousness as it is of the culture around them – indeed, even more so, given that society is largely unaware of the monster in its midst. This departs from the view of Marina Levina and Diem-My T. Bui, who see the current age as inherently monstrous and believe that the pace of change in contemporary life and its associated technologies constantly creates new and continually changing monsters. *It Follows* suggests that monsters are actually more relative in their nature: what is an existential threat to one individual is just a plastic table and chairs being knocked over for those around them. This, of course, is equally true on a larger scale: what one culture calls a monster is seen as funny or ridiculous by another – Chinese green, hairy, and hopping vampires being a case in point.[4] With that in mind, it can be seen that monsters, or at least aspects of them, have certain effects in particular spaces, be they private or public, which can be global, societal, or limited to a city/town, the home and/or the individual. Count Dracula is again a useful example here as he has provoked very different responses to his monstrousness in different spaces of interaction. On one level, he is configured as a threat from outside, endangering England and the British Empire on an ideological level, though he also causes very real fear and panic in the countryside around his lair, corrupting the sanctity and the refuge of hearth and home, while eliciting deep sexual responses from his victims.[5] In a sense, this also addresses aspects of the notion of living in times of monstrosity as, not unlike Joseph Campbell's 'Hero with a thousand faces', the same monster will show differing versions of itself to those looking at it, even within the same historical moment.

4 Unless one has seen *Rigor Mortis* (Mak, 2013).
5 This should be qualified as not all the count's victims receive the same level of personal attention.

This leaves the interpretation or meaning of monsters. Halberstam calls them 'meaning machines'; as noted above, this says as much about us as humans – 'what it means to be human, our relations to one another, and to the world around us, [and] our conception of our place in the greater scheme of things' (Weinstock 2017: x) – as it does about the monsters themselves. By and large, what the construction of the monsters says about humanity can be interpreted on a psychoanalytical level as transgressive acts and/or desires that are repressed. On a social level, this conforms more to Mary Douglas' idea of 'Purity and Danger' (1966) and Julia Kristeva's notion of the abject (1980). Douglas, in particular, with extensive nods to Michel Foucault, sees the idea of social taboo as a way for society to keep itself 'pure' from outsiders and controlling, unruly insiders. Kristeva envisions a similar outcome through a more personal, psychoanalytical approach. Of course, much of this utilizes a theoretical sleight of hand that automatically equates the cultural with the individual consciousness, something even Sigmund Freud was wary of until *Moses and Monotheism* (1939). Consequently, most readings of monsters perform a curious act of balancing things that transgress the ideological mores of a given culture and the individual psychic responses to them, as well as personal fears, phobias and prejudices. Arguably, then, the effectiveness of the monster is predicated on how closely the societal and the individual mesh, so that the 'best' monsters become self-regulating, which sees the separate members of society reinforce the points of abjection that are ideologically required to monsterize the unwanted and transgressive (Foucault 2008).

Necessarily, and indeed appropriately, some monsters will foreground particular interpretations or readings for the times within which they appear, many of which will be touched on in this collection. Of note is the idea that a cultural or national consciousness has a memory, which is assumed to work in a very similar way to that of an individual, so that the (re)appearance of monsters connects to the memories of any of their earlier manifestations in that culture/nation – obviously cultural 'memory' is temporally longer than the memory of individual humans. These memories or echoes of previous manifestations recall Halberstam's idea of traces, which could further be equated with a sense of an undead memory that sees the monster rise again from the cultural subconscious – the grave, as such – bearing the scars and traces of its earlier self in each new resurrected form.

Whilst discussing monsters through a psychoanalytical lens, it is worth touching on what might be termed our undead desire for them, for even though we do our best to repress or remove them from our conscious mind – the real world – without any kind of resolution, synthesis, or reparation, they will eventually destroy us and what we might become. Desire, here, does not automatically imply a sexual element, although sexual transgression is often present within the body of the monster, but it certainly implies an irresistible pull towards that which is made abject and monstrous. Kristen Wright talks of the tension between disgust and desire in relation to the monster and how something that purposely causes such extreme emotions does not necessarily hold them as Manichaean opposites, but rather as equal points of excess that can switch or bleed into each other (Wright 2018: vii). Ernest Jones has an interesting take on this idea. A relatively early exponent of Freudian theory on the supernatural and 'nightmares', he notes, in relation to vampires and revenants, that only those who are loved are brought back from death (Jones 1951: 104–9), that it is our desire for monsters that brings them back from the grave (the subconscious). Vampires are an obvious case in point, but it does suggest a not unsurprising correlation between sex and death (the death drive, in particular, at least symbolically) and the desire to recreate (the synthesis of thesis and antithesis) society and ourselves anew. Consequently, this companion, whilst noting the different individual and cultural spaces that the monster operates in, will conclude with examples of human/monster becoming, illustrating ways in which humanity (culture) evolves into something other than what it is now.

Monsters, Traces, and Portents

The companion itself will be comprised of twenty-six original essays, including a Foreword, 'Culture's Monsters', by Sherry C. M. Lindquist to set the scene for what follows and an Afterword, 'Becoming Monster and the Monster Becoming', by Patricia McCormack, which, whilst bring the thematic of the volume to a conclusion, also suggests what is to come in the ongoing evolution of our (humanity's) monsters. The remaining essays are divided into five thematic parts, in an inside-to-outside trajectory, exploring the various places/spaces that we as humans inhabit and the kinds of monsters we have created to express our ongoing relationships and our anxieties about them. The five parts, 'Home', 'Cultural Intersections', 'Society', 'Gender', and 'Futures', each feature a contemporary or recent example of a monster, which is then used as a lens through which to examine the historical evolution of that manifestation and the individual and/or cultural anxieties that produced it. 'Home' centres on the most intimate of places: places we consider as home in some way, which can include our own mental space, our home and relationships, and our 'home' society/nation and those that are seen to endanger it. Accordingly, the first chapter by Angela M. Smith, on 'Monsters of Mental Illness', looks at madness in the film *The Babadook* (Kent, 2014) and the kinds of monsters that are created to express fears regarding the state of madness itself, as well as those deemed to suffer from it. Simon Bacon looks at 'Domestic Monsters' and specifically abusive relationships through the main character in *The Invisible Man* (Whannell, 2020), which describes the processes of violence and gaslighting that feature in such situations. Thereafter, Phil Fitzsimmons considers 'Monsters of Abuse' in *The Nightingale* (Kent, 2018), in which both the home and societal space are invaded by colonial monsters. The last piece in Part I, by Agnieszka Kotwasińka, concerning 'Monstrous Outsiders', is a more general, and topical, invasion of the space of the 'home' nation, as seen in the film *The Lure* (Smoczyńska, 2015) through the body of the mythical immigrant from the sea, the mermaid.

Part II, 'Society', remains in what can be considered as the space of the 'home' nation and looks at the ways in which monsters are used as an ideological tool or to represent certain focus points of anxiety within society. It begins with John Edgar Browning's chapter on 'Teaching the Monster', in which the Slasher film provides an educational framework for examining what lies behind the mask of contemporary ideology. The next chapter, by Lauren Rosewarne, on 'Monsters of Cyberspace', looks at a related area of interaction, that of cyberspace and a recent manifestation of the Monster, the Cyberbully, as portrayed in the eponymous film, *Cyberbully* (Binamé, 2011). Following this, Anthony Curtis Adler considers a further related area of social media and the modern manifestation of 'The Celebrity Monster', as exemplified in the figure of Lady Gaga (1986–present), who is especially apt as she uses the notion of 'the monster' as part of her celebrity status. Alexandra Heller-Nicholas takes the use of social media and popular culture even further in the creation and contagion of 'Monsters of Urban Legend', where unreality becomes real, even deadly, as seen in the figure of the Slit-Mouthed Woman in *Carved* (Shiraishi, 2007). The last chapter in Part II looks at the deadliest of social realities, which becomes almost imaginary in its monstrosity, as explored by W. Scott Poole in *Melmoth* (Perry 2018).

Part III stays with the idea of the 'home' nation, but in different cultural settings. The chapters in this part illustrate how other cultures have created and evolved their own monsters, though often in ways that have become transcultural or have evolved in resistance to, or in line with, colonial appropriation. Benjamin Baumann considers a resolutely 'Thai Monster' in the figure of Phi Krasue, as seen in the film *Inhuman Kiss* (Mongkolsiri, 2019), a monster that has a long history in its homeland but rarely travels. Inés Ordiz takes the figure of La Llorona, a 'Mexican monster' that is getting more and more attention in a transcultural sense and is evolving from straightforward monstrosity to a symbol of female agency. Gail de Vos shifts to a more European location and considers a figure, Baba Yaga, a 'Russian Momster', that also has a wider influence, as evidenced by its appropriation in *Hellboy* (Mignola, 1997–2004). Transculturalism is replaced with colonial appropriation in Partha Mitter's chapter on 'Monsters of Colonialism', in which Mitter considers the continual misrecognition and misuse of the Indian deity Deumo since the time of early European adventurers up to the present, as seen in the relatively recent *Indiana Jones and the Temple of Doom* (Spielberg, 1984). Yasmine Musharbash brings this part to a close with an example of colonial resistance, as seen in the 'Aboriginal Monsters' of the Hairies in the television series *Cleverman* (Griffen, 2016–17).

Part IV turns to more existential concerns, which, although expressed within a particular cultural setting, are global in character. Non-normative gender positions have often manifested within the body of the monster and never more so than in times when gender is considered an individual choice rather than an ideological, patriarchal given. Appropriately then, the first essay on 'Satan' by Eddie Falvey looks at the Christian world's Big Bad through the lens of *The Witch* (Eggers, 2015), which is portrayed as inherently male and bestial. The problematics of unquestioned male dominance are further explored in a chapter on 'Monsters of Masculinity', in which Emily Brick considers *AHS Apocalypse* (Murphy and Falchuk, 2011–present) and male resistance to sexual equality and religious ignition in the twenty-first century. Craig Ian Mann shifts the perspective to feminine resistance in his chapter on 'Monsters of Femininity', which considers *When Animals Dream* (Arnby, 2014), in which the she-wolf represents a necessarily bloody, hairy manifestation of the historical monsterization of femininity. Daniel Sheppard queers these perspectives to focus on a monster that refuses to accept or conform to simplistic binary positions whilst demanding the right to sexual expression. Murray Leeder concludes the section by looking at a figure beyond or outside of gender, yet oddly suggestive of many, if not all, available positions, as seen in the skeleton in his chapter on 'The Monster of Death', which uses *Game of Thrones* as a lens through which to consider its subject (Benioff, 2011–19).

The final part explores what might be thought of as twenty-first-century or future monsters. Highlighting manifestations of humanity's current position in the world in terms of science, ecology and human evolution, and how the monsters of today reveal the hopes and fears of tomorrow and even ask the question of whether there will be a tomorrow. It begins with Leah Richards' consideration of 'Monsters of Reproduction' and the economics of science and identity, as seen in the series *Orphan Black* (Manson and Fawcett, 2013–2017). The next chapter shifts to a related topic: that of disease and contagion, an ongoing fear in an increasingly connected world. Dahlia Schweitzer considers 'Monsters of Contagion', as represented in *The Strain* (del Toro and Hogan, 2014–17), configuring both biological and ideological viruses. Contagion can also be read through an ecological lens. The relationship between humanity and the planet is picked up on by Carl H. Sederholm in his chapter on 'Monsters of the Anthropocene', which considers the album *Megalohydrothalassophobia* (Abhorrence, 2018), in which soundscapes communicate the insignificance of mankind in the larger order. Whilst humanity is often subsidiary to the future of the earth, Gerry Canavan begins to describe ways forward in his chapter on 'Monsters of Hybridity', in which contamination and miscegenation, as seen in *District 9* (Blomkamp, 2009), offer paths towards human evolution and becoming. Elana Gomel concludes the section with a chapter on 'Posthuman

Monsters', in which the monsters of the future combine both fauna and flora and humanity is rejoined to the planet in an ongoing symbiotic union, as in *The Girl with All the Gifts* (Carey 2014). The companion ends with Patricia McCormack's discussion of the series *Hannibal* (Fuller, 2013–15), in which the human is recognized as its own monstrous self, but in which the aestheticized stuff of humanity is an ongoing momento mori to its beautiful insignificance. In this world the eternal traces of our monsters will be the only monument to our passing.

Part I

Home

Angela M. Smith

Madness: *The Babadook* (Kent, 2014)

Gothic and horror have long conflated madness with monstrosity, evil, and murderous violence. From the villainous Manfred and his 'tempest of mind' in Horace Walpole's *The Castle of Otranto* (1764), to the 'lunatic' Bertha Mason of Charlotte Bronte's *Jane Eyre* (1847), to perpetual asylum escapee Michael Myers in the *Halloween* films (1978–2018) and The Beast in *Split* (dir. M. Night Shyamalan, 2016), horror's mad monsters offer sensationalistic portraits of mental illness as a demonic or pathological threat to normalcy (Zimmerman 2003, Phillips 2012, Gupta 2017, Hovitz 2017). But the genre also aligns viewers with sympathetic mad victims who experience trauma and distress due to forces outside their control. Such representation can exceed understandings of mental illness as a pathology located only in certain devalued bodyminds, vividly rendering mental illness as a real and painful experience common to human experience.[1]

A recent example is Jennifer Kent's Australian horror film *The Babadook* (2014). Through its mad monster and sympathetic mad victim, the film invokes shifting historical and cultural views of psychological disturbance: as demonic possession, innate and visible deviance, and socially shaped experience. In combining these perspectives, *The Babadook* renders as monsters not its mad characters but the stigma and isolation that intensifies their pain. It thus engages principles of disability studies and mad studies that recast ostensible 'defects' in terms of human variation while emphasizing the harms of systemic oppression and exclusion.[2]

The Babadook initially positions viewers in a realist mode, seeming to associate the beliefs of childhood, folklore, and superstition with madness.

---

1 'Bodymind'. See Price 2011: 240.
2 On mad studies, see Price 2011, LeFrançois and Menzies 2013, LeFrançois et al. 2016, Russo and Sweeney 2016, and Aho et al. 2017.

The film follows Amelia (Essie Davis), whose husband, Oskar (Benjamin Winspear), was killed in a car accident as they drove to the hospital for their son's birth. Amelia's high-strung 6-year-old son Samuel (Noah Wiseman) discovers in his room a handmade children's pop-up book entitled *Mister Babadook*, which promises, 'If it's in a word or it's in a look, You can't get rid of the Babadook'. The Babadook thus appears as a folkloric figure meant to frighten children and govern their behaviour: his name echoes that of the English/American 'boogeyman', Italian 'Babau', and Russian 'Babayka' (see Warner 1999: 42–3, Bane 2016: 50, 65, 327) and that of the Big Bad Wolf, also glimpsed in Sam's book *The Three Little Pigs*. Sam becomes obsessed with the Babadook: a charcoal-sketched figure with black top hat and cloak, shaggy hair, wild eyes, gaping mouth, and pointed fingers.

He builds weapons to fight the monster and blames him for shards of glass in soup and a defaced photo of his parents. When he 'sees' the Babadook, he shrieks himself into a febrile seizure. Despairing, Amelia begs a doctor to prescribe her son sedatives until he can visit a psychiatrist. Sam's belief in monsters is marked as aberrant, even for a child, and a matter for medical intervention: Amelia's sister declares, 'It's not normal for a kid to carry on with this rubbish'.

The film thus reflects a contemporary worldview in which apparently irrational beliefs, exemplified by Sam's hallucinations or paranoia, are best understood as pathologies requiring medical treatment. But as Ernst Jentsch and Sigmund Freud point out in their studies of the uncanny, our ostensibly rational selves, especially when confronted by 'the articulations of most mental and many nervous illnesses', remain haunted by superstitious understandings of the world and our own psyches (Jentsch 1906: 225, Freud 1919: 243).

As *The Babadook* proceeds, it exploits this psychological uncertainty, undermining Amelia's and viewers' disbelief in the supernatural. The monster becomes audible, creaking and knocking

Figure 7. The Babadook. *The Babadook*, directed by Jennifer Kent (Entertainment One, 2014).

around the house. His book mysteriously returns from the trash, now with gruesome images of Amelia killing her dog, Samuel, and herself. Eventually, the Babadook becomes visible to Amelia and viewers. He lurks in the neighbour's living room, a pale-faced man with blackened lips and dark hat and overcoat, and later takes the form of a large black shape that skitters across the bedroom ceiling before lurching downward into Amelia's open mouth.

His omnipresence is accentuated by a frequent background buzzing and chittering that occasionally rises to a screeching volume, along with the startling rasping shriek of his own name: 'Ba-ba-Dook-Dook-DOOK'! Amelia's eventual acceptance of the monster's reality corresponds to her growing recognition of her own psychological distress and debility; in the same way, viewers' acceptance of the Babadook's on-screen reality aligns with their sympathetic belief in the reality and difficulty of Amelia's mental illness. In this way, the film functions like the speculative fictions considered by disability scholar Sami Schalk, 'representing a variety of differing realities' to 'critique the denial of individual experiences of reality without suggesting that mental disability is not real and without denying that different experiences of reality can be painful, frightening, or otherwise difficult' (Schalk 2018: 67).

Before proffering a contemporary view of mental illness, however, *The Babadook* invokes older understandings of madness. In the monster's plunge into Amelia, the film foregrounds ancient and medieval concepts of demonic possession and humoral imbalance. As Sander Gilman explains, 'maniacs' were thought to suffer 'an excess of black bile' that signalled the 'infiltration of the evils of the world and the flesh into the purity of the soul' and was 'perceived as the possession of the individual by actual demons'. Treatment required exorcism, as in early visual depictions where 'the possessed is portrayed with arms askew, head tilted back, the demon fleeing from his open mouth' (Gilman 1982: 21–2). *The Babadook* invokes these tropes. Once 'inhabited' by the monster, Amelia exhibits seizures, sleepwalking, increased strength,

Figure 8. The Babadook. *The Babadook*, directed by Jennifer Kent (Entertainment One, 2014).

levitation. She insults and threatens her son and strangles the family dog. Sam ties his mother up and exhorts her to 'get it out'! Her body contorts, she tries to strangle Sam, and her head tosses back and forth at superhuman speed before she vomits out a pool of black liquid. *The Babadook* thus recalls the assertion by *The Exorcist* (Friedkin, 1973) of the reality of supernatural possession in a modern and secular age, but also marks the enduring potency of Gothic and supernatural horror as modes of representing madness.

The film also recognizes the displacement of such medieval notions of madness by the Victorian era's more medicalized views. The Babadook's appearance specifically invokes nineteenth-century efforts to taxonomize madness in 'deviant' facial or physical forms. In 1806, for instance, Scottish physician Charles Bell described the physiognomy of the 'outrageous maniac' as 'strong and muscular', 'his features sharp; his eye sunk', 'his hair sooty, black, stiff, and bushy', and 'his colour ... a pale sickly yellow', while his 'Burning eyen [eyes]... stared full wide' (Gilman 1982: 90). This view of madness, as discernible pathology in singular and defective bodies, resurfaces in the Babadook's tall form, dark-rimmed or 'sunk' eyes, bristling hair, 'wide' eyes, and 'pale sickly' skin. His top hat and coat – which at one point drop emptily down the chimney into Amelia's bedroom – also link him to the hat- and cape-wearing mad monsters of Victorian Gothic texts such as Robert Louis Stevenson's *The Strange Case of Dr. Jekyll and Mr. Hyde* (1886), Oscar Wilde's *The Picture of Dorian Gray* (1890), and Bram Stoker's *Dracula* (1897).

The Babadook thus participates in a Victorian medical and Gothic tradition that consolidates horror and madness in a monstrous and threatening non-normative figure. His staring and dark-ringed eyes, wild hair, and fixed facial expressions mimic early horror-film monsters in *The Cabinet of Dr. Caligari* (Wiene, 1920); the *Jekyll and Hyde* adaptations of Robertson (1920), Mamoulian (1932), and Fleming (1941); *Nosferatu* (Murnau, 1922); *The Phantom of the Opera* (Julian, 1925), glimpsed on Amelia's TV in *The Babadook*; Tod Browning's *London after Midnight* (1927); *The Man Who Laughs* (1928); and Browning's *Dracula* (1931). These movies employ madness as a monstrous spectacle that shocks and thrills viewers. They do so via racist iconographies: anti-Semitic motifs of beaked noses and long, grasping fingers inform *Nosferatu*'s Count Orlok, Barrymore's Hyde, and, arguably, the Babadook, while the darkened skin and broadened nose of

Fredric March's Hyde in Mamoulian's *Dr. Jekyll and Mr. Hyde* suggest anti-Black stereotypes.³ They also perpetuate ableism and sanism, insofar as these characters' seizures, collapses, extreme or deficient emotional expressions, sickliness, and/or acts of violence confirm physical and psychological disability as threatening deviance (Smith 2011). These characterizations persist in contemporary film, absorbing notions of 'psychopathy' and 'psycho killers', to generate mad monsters such as Norman Bates, Michael Myers, Jason Voorhees, Freddy Krueger, Hannibal Lecter, and the Beast in M. Night Shyamalan's *Split* (2016).

At the same time, Gothic representations of mad monstrosity persistently undercut medical efforts to explain and contain madness in singular diseased bodyminds. From Mary Shelley's *Frankenstein* (1818) onward, horror texts often present scientists and doctors as themselves mad, indicting medical figures for creating the boogeyman of the mad monster, asserting the prevalence of madness, and depicting mental illness as profoundly influenced by social context: Stevenson's Hyde, for example, can be read as a product of and scapegoat for a repressively heteronormative society.⁴

The Babadook thus constitutes a culturally familiar icon of monstrous madness that registers the uncanniness of our opaque psyches *and* the disabling social structures that intensify suffering due to illness or disorder. In particular, he powerfully manifests for viewers Amelia's unresolved trauma and grief, signalled also by the film's opening nightmare, in which Amelia relives the car accident that killed her husband. Because Amelia has been unable to confront and process her loss, Samuel never gets to celebrate his birthday, Oskar's things remain locked in the basement, and Amelia lives in a twilight state signified by the house's dusty blues and greys and her exhausted affect. Amelia's mental distress is manifested in part by her wide-eyed spectatorship of silent supernatural films, including scenes from George Meliès' *The Magic Book* (1901) and *The Infernal Cake-Walk* (1903) into which the Babadook suddenly inserts himself.

---

3   For readings of the racial dynamics of Gothic and horror monsters see, for instance, Halberstam 1995, Wexman 1988, Young 2008, and Means Coleman 2011.

4   For queer readings of Stevenson's novel see, for instance, Showalter 1990, Halberstam 1995, and Sanna 2012.

These demonic spectacles link the Babadook's appearance to Amelia's dissociative experiences; indeed, the film suggests not only that *she* put the glass in the soup and defaced the photo, but also that she created the Babadook book, since she mentions her earlier life as a writer of 'kids' stuff'. Accordingly, viewers have consistently interpreted Amelia's behaviour in relation to conditions such as depression, PTSD, and traumatic bereavement (Ingham 2015, Jacobsen 2016, Riggs 2018).

Figure 9. Expressionistic monster. *The Babadook*, directed Jennifer Kent (Entertainment One, 2014).

As the creator of the Babadook book, Amelia is aligned with another tradition in Gothic madness: that of the woman author whose psychological distress is represented in relation to traumatic experiences and oppressive patriarchal structures. In her 1831 introduction to *Frankenstein*, for instance, Mary Shelley depicts both her book and its monster, her 'hideous progeny', as reworkings of her mother's post-partum death and her own experiences of pregnancy- and child-loss. Charlotte Perkins Gilman's *The Yellow Wallpaper* (1892) compellingly depicts not only post-partum depression but also the harms of a patriarchal 'cure' that suppresses female expression and creativity. Critics have read such stories as entries in a powerful 'female Gothic' tradition, generating feminist readings that interpret 'mad' behaviours as acts of social and gendered resistance (Moers 1974, Gilbert and Gubar 1979, Creed 1993, Smith and Wallace 2004, Wehler 2010, Kungl 2010).

The Babadook, a female-authored and -directed film, thus acknowledges the gendered social structures that constrain women's grappling with distress and loss. Amelia is unable to grieve her husband's death with what Jennifer M. Poole and Jennifer Ward term a 'good grief' that is 'quiet, tame, dry, and controlled' (Poole and Ward 2013: 95), focused on 'moving forward, progressing through, and returning to a state of normalcy and productivity' (Poole and Ward 2013: 97). She is repeatedly castigated, disbelieved, or dismissed: by her sister, her son's principal and teacher, a doctor, an angry stranger, and social workers. Lacking supportive spaces in which to explore her 'mad grief', Amelia creates *Mister Babadook*, a tale of rage and violence so inadmissible she keeps her authorship secret even from herself, while nonetheless undertaking 'a resistant practice that allows, speaks, names, affords, welcomes, and stories the subjugated sense of loss that comes to us all' (Poole and Ward 2013: 95).

The book's production enables Amelia to confront her trauma. Once exorcized, the Babadook throws Samuel against a wall and then appears as Amelia's husband, compelling her to re-live the fatal accident. Left sobbing and groaning, Amelia manages to articulate a protective maternal rage, screaming, 'If you touch my son again, I'll fucking kill you'! The Babadook rises to monstrous size, caped arms raised like a giant bat, but collapses, moaning, into a pile of clothes, before ricocheting downstairs and into the basement, where Amelia locks him in. In the film's concluding scenes, Amelia feeds the Babadook worms from her garden. Now an invisible presence, he looms frighteningly over her before her reassurance – 'It's all right. It's all right' – returns him whimpering to the shadows. Out in the garden's sunshine, Amelia reports to Sam that the creature was 'quiet today'. Sam performs a magic trick that appears real, summoning an actual dove, and Amelia contentedly embraces her son.

Figure 10. Exorcized of the monster. *The Babadook*, directed by Jennifer Kent (Entertainment One, 2014).

In this concluding sequence, *The Babadook* makes several claims about mental illness that coincide with mad studies approaches. First, it centres the perspective of those with mental illness and insists on the reality of their experience without eliding its horrific and painful aspects, vividly impressed on viewers by the Babadook's monstrous attacks. Second, the film rejects stigmatization, isolation, or exclusion as modes of 'treating' mental illness and emphasizes the inadequacy of existing medical and social supports for Amelia and Sam's psychological needs. Third, *The Babadook* presents interpersonal love and connection as necessary sustenance for those in mental distress. The film particularly embraces a mad, queer, and/or 'crip' family constituted not only of Amelia, Sam, and the Babadook but also their supportive elderly, disabled neighbour Mrs Roach, whose name, referencing the cockroaches Amelia hallucinates, signals the integration, rather than expulsion, of madness.[5] Fourth, the film affirms the commonplaceness of mental illness and the possibility of pragmatic adaptation to it. The conclusion particularly glimpses mental illness as what Gordon Warme calls 'an expression of ordinary humanity' and 'a social practice'; it models learning to 'live with unsteadiness and uncertainty' while 'coming up with new and imaginative responses to human suffering' (Warme 2013: 213). Sam's act of magical creation constitutes such a response, reminding viewers that top hats and capes are also the costume of stage magicians, and that, as affirmed in Sam's magical mantra, life is both 'treacherous' and 'wondrous'. Finally, in keeping with the 'female Gothic' tradition, *The Babadook* celebrates horror as a genre wherein female rage, madness, artistry, and abjection can find expression.

---

5   On 'crip' as a defiant reclamation of a stigmatizing term, see Sandahl 2003 and McRuer 2006.

Simon Bacon

Domestic Abuse: *The Invisible Man* (Whannell, 2020)

The Invisible Man is not a character that is necessarily connected to the domestic space and yet, as this chapter explores, it is within intimate spaces that his 'power' has its most physically and emotionally violent repercussions. This chapter will look at how the changing representations of his invisibility on screen do not so much hide the responsibility for his actions from the world around him, but rather, as shown in *The Invisible Man* (Whannell, 2020), increasingly see him as a mirror reflecting the acceptance of violence and abuse in the society around him. Consequently, the chapter will not show the Invisible Man as a brilliant, if dangerously unstable, scientist, but will rather cast him as the abusive, domestic monster he has always been.[1]

Invisibility is not uncommon in Western mythology, with objects such as caps (the Helm of Hades),[2] or capes (King Arthur's 'Mantle of Invisibility')[3] being able to bestow the power on their respective wearers. H. G. Wells' story of *The Invisible Man* (1896) uses the mythological tale of the Ring of Gyges, as retold in Plato's *Republic*, which made its wearer invisible. In that tale a shepherd finds the ring and effectively invades the home of the King, bedding/raping the Queen, then killing the monarch himself. Plato used the story to warn against the dangers of giving in to one's appetites, but he also intimated that the site of the greatest danger in regard to the Invisible Man is the domestic one. Part of the Invisible Man's power is being able to escape the regulating gaze of society, which in Plato's and Wells' hands allows a freedom from accountability that can only end in madness. However, both Plato and Wells only saw this freedom in relation to wider society, never as a tool of

---

1   Many thanks to Craig Ian Mann for coming up with the idea for this article.
2   See Hansen 2004.
3   In 'Chulwch ac Owen' [Chulwch and Owen], *c.* 1100.

systematic and destructive abuse within the domestic sphere. Subsequent interpretations of Wells' story, as discussed below, have begun to address this discrepancy, shifting the focus of the story away from that which we cannot see and on to the bruises, cuts, and emotional trauma that the Invisible Man leaves in his wake.

Wells' novel centres on a brilliant scientist, Griffin, who becomes increasingly unhinged as the realization of the power he now commands in being invisible affects his mental state. He rapidly transitions from scaring his landlady to announcing a 'Reign of Terror' across Britain. Whilst his threat is constructed as one aimed at wider society, outside in the world he is at his most vulnerable – he is naked, open to the weather, leaves tracks and, unsurprisingly, it is there that he is eventually killed. In contrast, his monstrosity is at its most powerful indoors. In enclosed spaces his presence is everywhere, violence can explode from any place, or any direction. His invisibility makes him seem virtually omnipresent even when he is no longer there. The 1933 film by James Whale follows the novel with Dr Jack Griffin (Claude Rains) shown as a largely malevolent figure filling domestic spaces with a predominantly malignant presence.

Figure 11. The Invisible Man's violent energy barely contained by his bandages. *The Invisible Man*, directed by James Whale (Universal Pictures, 1933).

He seems to 'possess' the room he rents and when his former fiancé visits he soon attempts to blame her for his increasingly extreme actions declaring 'I did it all for you' (Whale, 1933). The only thing that seems to contain him are the bandages he wears, wrapped tightly around his head, with tufts of hair shooting out between them visibly representing social regulation that is unable to hold him. Once the bandages are off, he literally explodes into the space around him, as seen when he enters the bar below his lodging where literally bursts into the town meeting sending bottles, objects and townspeople smashing into walls, doors and windows.

Curiously, in the many sequels that followed, *The Invisible Man Returns* (May, 1940), *The Invisible Woman* (Sutherland, 1940), *Invisible Agent* (Marin, 1942), and *Abbott and Costello Meet the Invisible Man* (Lamont, 1951) invisibility is shown as a largely positive tool in solving crimes or spying for the government. In fact, post-Second World War and into the Cold War period American series often portrayed invisibility, and more specifically the American science associated with it, as an asset in espionage-oriented outings such as *The Invisible Man* (Smart, 1958–8), *The Invisible Man* (Bennett, 1975–6), *Gemini Man* (Stevens, de Souza and Telford, 1976–6), and even the later *The Invisible Man* (Greenberg, 2000–2). Often in these stories invisibility is accidental or occurs as the result of an experiment and rarely involves the scientist themselves as the protagonist. Resultantly, the positive attributes are brought to the fore with the occasional hint to the voyeuristic possibilities.

In this vein *Memoirs of an Invisible Man* (Carpenter, 1992) is a good example because being a more light-hearted movie it uses many ways to render the character safe and non-threatening. Invisibility is bestowed upon him by accident and not only does he not see himself as invisible – in scenes from his view point we can see him, whilst the other characters cannot – but when he actually wears make-up to make himself visible, he actually looks like his former self. This is even more so when with his love interest in the film, this in itself being a change as he actually has emotional attachments to others rather than just power over them he makes himself 'visible' or non-threatening thereby safeguarding some of his humanity.

However, most of these versions are predicated on the Invisible Man being a good person, or at least not a sociopath or sexual predator, before the

Figure 12. Chevy Chase made visibly harmless by looking like himself. *Memoirs of an Invisible Man*, directed by John Carpenter (Warner Brothers, 1992).

procedure takes place. In Wells' story Griffin is always a driven person with huge sense of his own worth above others, and invisibility just makes him even more himself. As such, the threat of physical violence is an easy recourse to get his own way. Griffin remains totally unaware of himself and what he is becoming, bemoaning the response of the world around him to his increasingly violent responses: 'What was I to do? And for this I had become a wrapped-up mystery, a swathed and bandaged caricature of a man'! (Wells 1896: 279). Wells' Griffin, like Whales', is contained by the bandages he wears to stop him from escaping social proscription; however, the Invisible Man, Sebastian Caine (Kevin Bacon), from Paul Verhoeven's *Hollow Man* (2000) requires no such constraints as he embodies society itself.

Verhoeven's film is a critique of toxic masculinity with the Invisible Man being its apotheosis. Although it largely centres around a laboratory, its occasional forays into domestic areas reinforce the feeling of the invasion of personal space and the inescapability of male sexual violence. Caine is a brilliant scientist and part of a research team investigating how to make organic life invisible. The team is evenly balanced between men and women, but Caine's presence engenders a toxic masculinity that aggressively sexualizes the female members of the team. This becomes even more so when Caine becomes invisible. Whilst under observation in the lab his first action is to sexually molest one of the female scientists who has fallen asleep, fondling and sucking her breast without her consent. Caine, though supposedly under constant surveillance, is largely free to move around the facility leaving all the female staff on edge, to the point where one of them declares to the gathered team 'it gives me the creeps. I can't take a piss without wearing my thermals' (Verhoeven, 2000). Not long after this, one of the male staff, Carter (Greg Grunberg) is seen looking at the centre-fold in a porn magazine commenting loudly 'I'd suck the tits right off you' (Verhoeven, 2000), framing the sexual abuse performed by Caine as a male fantasy made real.

This is shown with even more starkness later in the film after Caine escapes the facility and returns to his own apartment only to invade the home of the woman living opposite him, brutally raping her. Indeed, the film sees almost all the interior spaces as being Cain's 'home'. He moves seamlessly between his apartment, his neighbour's apartment, the laboratory and 'possesses' all of them with his presence. On returning to the lab Carter asks Caine if he had done 'anything' with his new ability, obviously implying sexual or titillating activity with women. Caine guffaws and says 'some' as Carter gives him a congratulatory smirk. The invisible Caine embodies male privilege and arrogance through its correlation of rock music, fast cars, sex and self-gratification as unbridled male excess. Indeed, rape and sexual violence seem casual and imminent occurrences, leaving the strong, professional female characters constantly on edge and in fear for their safety. This sense of omnipresent sexual violence is also signified by the look of the Invisible Man here. In Whale's film, as mentioned above, the bandages on Griffin barely contain the ball of aggression he has become, with tufts hair from his wig in 'curious tails and horns' (Wells 10–11), forcing their way out between the wrappings, but with Caine it is a bland latex skin, an Everyman kind of covering revealing nothing within it. Thus, sexual violence he embodies is literally faceless and can be anyone, or everyone. More disturbingly, Caine was formerly friends with all his female victims in the lab – one was even his fiancé – giving substance to the shocking statistic that women are far more likely to be molested and/or raped by someone they know.

More than its precursors *Hollow Man* intersects with narratives around sexually violent spirits or demons and much of what Caine does is exactly like that seen in films such as *The Entity* (Furie, 1982) or *Lovely Molly* (Sanchéz, 2011) where a malignant 'male' ghost victimizes and violently sexually abuses

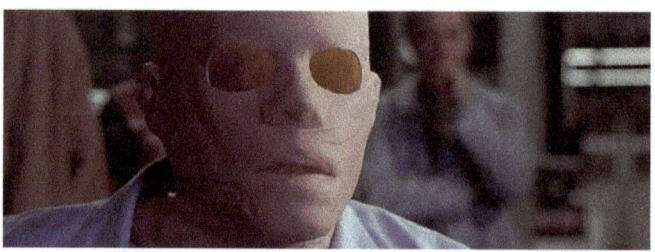

Figure 13. The Invisible Everyman and the bland face of sexual violence. *Hollow Man*, directed by Paul Verhoeven (Sony Pictures, 2000).

a female victim in their own home. *Lovely Molly* in particular shows a newly married woman being continually and viciously abused by the ghost of her father following her even into her workspace. The immateriality of the spirit means its presence invades every aspect of its victim's life, leaving all interior spaces as imminently dangerous.

The denouement of the film especially exemplifies how difficult it is to rid yourself of such a monster – Caine's former fiancé, Linda (Elizabeth Shue), who has already moved on from their relationship, is repeatedly attacked by him. Most of the team are already dead and Linda is trying to escape the facility with her new boyfriend, when Caine continually kicks and punches her trying to prevent her leaving. Even after it appears, she has killed him, he still comes back from the dead to try and drag her down with him, becoming a literal malignant weight on her back until she finally drops him down a lift shaft to be free. Verhoeven's Invisible Man is then the product of a time of toxic masculinity, showing an environment of ambient male sexual violence. At one-point Linda is even shown fantasizing/dreaming of Caine on the cusp of raping her reinforcing a kind of patriarchal belief in that it is what women secretly want. Much of this is picked up in the most recent version of the story by Leigh Whannell which re-envisions the Invisible Man story for the post-#MeToo era.

In some respects, the most important feature of *The Invisible Man* (2020) is that the main protagonist is his ex, Cecilia Kass (Elizabeth Moss). Consequently, the film is not about the Invisible Man but explicit about the effects he has on those around him. The story begins with Cecilia in a relationship with a wealthy scientist Adrian Griffin (Oliver Jackson-Cohen). However, he is a psychopath who wants to control every part of her life. Finally, getting the courage to leave she runs away with the help of a friend. Not long after she discovers Griffin is dead, apparently committing suicide, but has left her a large amount of money, though on the proviso that she is deemed mentally competent by the time the cash is due to be collected by her. This intimates what is going to happen next as with Griffin believed dead, he begins bullying and abusing Cecilia in an attempt to 'gaslight' his former lover so that the world believes that she is insane. With the world around Cecilia believing that Griffin is dead, her escalatingly erratic behaviour is first put down to grief or memories of her former partner 'haunting' her, but then soon becomes a belief in her mental collapse. More importantly, it also shows how even in the time of post-feminism and post-#MeToo, society does not believe or support the abused, expecting them to assert their own agency or be undeserving of any kind of help or sympathy.

Griffin himself is much more spectral in this film compared to the ones discussed above, never really having a form to reveal his presence – no bandages or latex masks to pretend he is normal. Indeed, one only knows he is around by what happens to Cecilia, either through her seemingly bizarre actions or expressions of total fear on her face. Consequently, the overriding image of the Invisible Man in this film is not of the bandages, masks or special effects showing his appearing or disappearing body, but the face of Cecilia herself. This reveals a victim left largely alone in the face not only of ongoing abuse but societal disbelief, or victim shaming and blaming, in what is happening to her and viewing it as being internal to herself. Simultaneously, she is viewed as someone who will not help herself but is also mentally unhinged and/or the perpetrator of 'gaslighting' herself, and neither state is deemed worthy of help other than constraining her for the protection of wider society.

Not unlike *Hollow Man*, *The Invisible Man* in 2020 manifests the overarching ideology of the society around him. In 2000 this was a world still dominated by men; one where strong, independent women were still largely treated as objects of male desire and violence. In 2020, although this has shifted, the results are not as dramatically different as they should be. The Invisible Man has always been a monster and wealth and privilege

Figure 14. The visible face of the Invisible Man in 2020. *The Invisible Man*, directed by Leigh Whannell (Universal Studios, 2020).

have provided the means for his abuse to spill out of the home and into wider society. However, whilst that society can clearly see the evidence of his physical abuse in the face of his victim, they still refuse to see him for the monster he is.

Phil Fitzsimmons

Paedophilia: *The Nightingale* (Kent, 2018)

Acting as a reflective foil revealing the true depth and nature of the worst of humanities traits which become embedded in personal and cultural memory, the monster has been in human narratives as long as there have been humans to tell stories. They have been our ubiquitous shadows just as much as those cast by the sun, moon and luminescence of our own making. In both a visual and psychical sense, they cling to our touch points on the earth and arc out to the surroundings we inhabit. While our body-casts dissolve with shifts in causal light, removing the dark silhouettes of our physical form that never realign in the same way, so too the narrative monster once named dissolves reappearing again in different forms. The reason for this is that the human condition is slow to learn and even slower to change. 'Monsters are the patron saints of our blissful imperfections' (Moreno, 2018).

Having said this, I want to begin this chapter by arguing that as well as the monsters that can be teased out in our texts: there are also the uber-monstrous or the *deprime monstrare*. These are not 'blissful imperfections' rather they vehemently resist even the simplest overtures of being named or cinematically framed. They remain deep within both psychical self of an individual and a culture. In bringing these to the fore, these monsters leave a trail of narrative stains of 'absences, slippages and silences' (Blake 2008: 20).

This chapter deals with one such current cinematic uber-monster and the precursory string of narrative stains in previous films, that point to what Halbertsam believes is the causal artefacts of monstrosity: 'The monster is the product of and the symbol for the transformation of identity into sexual identity through the mechanism of failed repression' (1995: 9).

A caveat needs to be stated at this point. To paraphrase Benn Michaels, these are not representations per se as 'the scuffs and stains on a wall aren't representations of the people who leaned against it; they're traces left by their bodies' (Benn Michaels 2015: 40). These body stains are traumatic cultural memories, 'relational histories' acting 'as multidirectional memory' (Rothburg 2009: 225). This stain of ultra-otherness has been lurking in the spectrum of Australian film for some time and has only recently has begun to emerge, albeit discursively and exophorically. Only in the newly emerging cinematic thread of *Tassie Noire* (Cooper 2019) and its predecessors, does paedophilia fleetingly surface: an axiological beast that has long 'been shoved deep down in the closets of our society' (Dove 2002: 1).

Tassie Noire and the Complexities Explicated

As the name implies *Tassie Noire* films are set on the island of Tasmania, with its dark Gothic-like forests and constant sense of foreboding. The British mindset mitigated this fear of Tasmania to some degree by falsely construing it to be a 'wasteland' (Lawson 2014: 120). And so, they raped, pillaged and destroyed all the Aboriginal clans on this island, and believed the mostly white convicts under their control to be on the same social footing as the indigenous tribes they eradicated.

The Nightingale is set in this 1825 colonial context of Tasmanian non-being, with the narrative swirling around Clare Carrol, a young Irish convict. Because of her looks and singing voice, a British Lieutenant Hawkins had set her free from incarceration. While allowed to marry he refuses to sign off on her ticket of leave forcing her to serve as an attendant to Hawkins and sing to his constantly drunken garrison.

Clare is well aware that the Lieutenant has ulterior motives in freeing her and keeping her under his control. The precise location of the garrison is not clear, as is Clare's age. Placeless and stateless, clearly at best she is in her mid-teens although her exact age is also not given. With her husband constantly reminding her that she is not totally free, and Hawkins reminding her he gave her early release, the movie then pivots when Hawkins and his sergeant brutally rape her. A soldier also kills her baby, as it will not stop crying during the attack. She survives, and while the movie then embarks on her journey of revenge through the Gothic-like forest, it this rape scene of this young woman

Figure 15. Clare serving the garrison. *The Nightingale*, directed by Jennifer Kent (IFC Films, 2018).

that acts as a psychosocial allegorical pinnacle of 'the masculine authority that saturated the colonial worldview' (Dwyer and Nettlebeck 2018: 14).

Clare is raped in the central space of power, which is sparse in the extreme. Shown as brown and filthy it is in direct contrast to the verdant bush land and pastures surrounding the building beyond the small colonial space. Thus, this British outpost, with their supposed advanced knowledge of morals, truth and purity is cast as being directly opposite to the fecundity of the life giving rich brown earth on which it is situated. Desperately afraid of the wilderness the soldiers were also afraid that they, along with the convicts, were also to be exiled in the forests of Van Diemen's Land.

In raping Clare, Hawkins' forced penetration is representative of entering the 'dark tunnels and underground passages of Gothic edifices, a descent into the unconscious, away from the socially constructed self and toward the uncivilized, the primitive' (Clemens 2009: 7). As representative of 'Mother

England' his rape of a mother who collapses into a catatonic state after the event is in Gothic literature indicative of the total death state already existing in the perpetrators.

This contrast in human care, and the environment with its Gothic nature is also emblematic of aspects of the psychology of fear and repression that pervaded the colonial power. Hawkins' is obviously fearful of being simply being consigned to this wilderness outpost by the officer above him despite his claim he has cleared some of the land for farming and eradicating the aborigines. On the other hand, Clare is a captive but not afraid to deal with soldiers who make sexual advances towards her. Indeed, she knocks a drink into the lap of on who lewdly licks his tongue at her. Clare also fights of Hawkins' sexual advances, much to his chagrin, as he believes he has the right to simply take her with the same attitude as he had done in clearing land for pasture.

However, as demonstrated in this movie, the hybrid monster of paedophilia and colonial excess is not only soul destroying for the victim but is far worse for the perpetrator. In what Banivanua-Mar (2007: 33) terms the 'colonial mirror effect' the destruction of the environment and the humanity under colonial control has a self-defeating socio-psychological effect. Just as paedophilia rarely leaves the victim's consciousness, so it is for the colonizer. It remains a permanently repressed collective memory in which the underpinning institutional elements eventually rape themselves into destruction: 'civilization sniffs out the enemy, uses smell against itself in an orgy of imitation' (Taussig 1992: 67). Australia is only now emerging painfully from the monstrous stain of colonialism.

Two years before the release of *The Nightingale*, *The Kettering Incident* aired on Foxtel's Showcase to a high degree of Australian interest. This eight-part series set in Kettering, an actual small logging town in the Tasmanian wilderness, focused on Dr Anna Macy, who returns to her childhood home of Kettering after working as a medical consultant in a London hospital. Suffering from blackouts and lapses in consciousness for extended periods she is unable to continue working and returns to the place where fifteen years before she had also experienced unconsciousness. Cycling with her best friend Gillian in what was considered a supernatural forest surrounding Kettering both girls disappeared only for Gillian to be found dead with Anna alive but covered in blood.

Figure 16. The supernatural Kettering forest. *The Kettering Incident*, created by Victoria Madden and Vincent Sheehan (Showcase, 2016).

On her return Anna finds Kettering is racked by disagreements between environmentalists and loggers, with the latter the economic and social mainstay. The majority of the townspeople meet her with mistrust and outright hostility. When another young girl, Chloe, disappears and is found murdered in an abandoned farm within the forest Macy is once again blamed for another girl's murder. In a clear connection to the Gothic surrounds, Chloe's body is found in a circular dam that has been recently and inexplicably drained on a supposedly haunted farm.

As a consolidating figure linking the previous female disappearance and the investigation in Chloe's demise is Brian Dutch. The lone detective in Kettering, his place in this series continues the masculine thread of Hawkins in *The Nightingale* as his groping and intimate contact in his initial contacts with Macy makes his sexual intentions abundantly clear. However, it is not these overtures that eventually alarms her

As the institutional power figure in Kettering, he is aided by Fergus, the local constable in now searching for Chloe and her killer. As 'Dutch' questions Macy about her relationship to both the murders she realizes that he is also a drug importer and Chloe was one of his dealers. Anna also concludes that he has also been having sex with her. There are also inferences that there are other underage girls he has also been involved with. He has been highly successful in hiding his paedophile behaviour.

As with *The Nightingale*, the monster as 'male enacted paedophilia' is linked to the notion of 'centrality in Gothic spaces and its relationship to the feminine body' (Halberstam 1995: 156). Such spaces typically represent menstruation and birth, spaces of abjection from a male perspective. However, Chloe's body is finally found, while also linked to a dam recently emptied of water, and so her dead body and this circular space become signifiers of her waters breaking before giving birth and being consumed by the earth as she dies. Thus, the entire site appears to allow a gaze into her 'innermost being', that feminine space that is 'desirable and terrifying, nourishing and murderous, fascinating' (Kristeva 1982: 54). It is clear from his walk around this area and from his facial expressions that his dealings with Chloe and his sexual interactions with this young girl has placed her in this circle, adding to his rising fears that there is supernatural interference in Kettering. As well, his monstrous stain has been physically crystallized into the environment.

Indeed, from a mythic perspective this is a visual metaphor of monstrous 'mirroring doubling' (Parkin-Gounelas 2001: 7), often seen as a full moon reflected in the ocean or body of water representing the epitome of monstrous *coincenditia oppistorum*. Rather than being a place of stability and peace, it coded as relational dislodgement and disruption of social norms. The moon is a constant focus in this series, and here it is represented as circular pit and with ocean drained. As is often the case, it fits into a horizontal and vertical axis, coded as a conflation or 'doubling' (Botting 1995: 7) of universal liminality, or a totally unstable site captured between two crisis events.

The empty pond and the emptied life call are a crossroads marker, as the: 'prohibition exists to demarcate the bonds that hold together that system of relations we call culture, to call horrid attention to the borders that cannot – must not –be crossed' (Cohen 1996: 13).

Australian Noire and the Precursory Stain

Several decades prior to the emergence of *Tassie Noire*, *Picnic at Hanging* generated international praise, at a time when Australia was once again considering its national identity and its colonial ties. The tropic and mythic elements of this film made it clear that *Picnic at Hanging Rock* represented the oppressive nature of British colonization. In discussing the female centre of this movie, Josephine May make the comment: 'The nation as feminine is an innocent girl killed by Empire, with the colonizer's desire to remake the colonial object in its own image leading to death' (85).

As the briefest of summaries, *Picnic at Hanging Rock* deals with a Valentine's Day outing to Hanging Rock by a group of boarding schoolgirls in 1900. This

1975 movie shifted away from the 'all too mundane national culture and its archive of myths and symbols' (O'Regan 1996: 92), eliminating aspects of the Australian outback masculinity and mateship. These were replaced by a dark mythic imaginary, a feminine erotic emphasis and understated horror. As the day on which this event takes place there are within the confines of the school subtle hints of lesbian love, attraction and possible sexual exploration amongst some of the girls. As Hood states, this movie is contained within an 'aura of incipient sexuality and brooding menace' (1994: 4).

Leaving for their picnic all the girls are dressed in white and having arrived at the rock they are warned not to explore. However, four girls wander off. Higher up the monolith, with its rocky pinnacles clearly marked as phallic images, three of the group remove the colonially enforced educational trappings of gloves, hats and shoes.

As they climb higher, the pinnacle begins to merge into tight clefts and meandering caverns, clearly suggestive of vaginal penetration. Finally, they enter a final cleft and disappear. Two never return but one of them, Irma, is found a week later but without her corset. However, she is deemed to be 'intact' but then next appears dressed in bright crimson red.

While researchers have recognized that the entire movie is enmeshed in clear references to colonial repression and repression of woman, what has been ignored is the significance of the primitive supernatural and all consuming paedophilic masculine force of the rock. The girl's climb clearly indicates some form of predatory calling and transgression. Irma's transformation from a white to red dress clearly indicates the there was penetration of a threshold. This entire concept of a devouring and penetrating male force both resonates with and inverts Creed's concept of vampirism. Firstly, it is evident that this 'narrative constitutes a patriarchal discourse that legitimizes sexual aggression and rape within the confines of an erotic and forbidden sexual encounter' (2017: vii). While it is certainly

Figure 17. The girls climbing Hanging Rock. *Picnic at Hanging Rock*, directed by Peter Weir (British Empire Films, 1975).

the case that any 'monster is a threshold figure' (2017: v) the following conditional clauses of her description need to be paraphrased given the voracity of the *deprime monstrare* in *Picnic*: 'The monster is a threshold figure – both emphatically of this world and a portal to another. Once consumed, the victim (particularly if a virgin) is never energized, but joins a deadly circle, and guaranteed of a non life' (Creed 2017: v).

The Long Road Back

Monsters never truly die and the forces that make them do not simply dissipate but transform. As noted by Halberstam:

> We wear modern monsters like skin, they are us, they are on us and in us. Monstrosity no longer coagulates into a specific body, a single face, a unique feature; it is replaced with a banality that fractures resistance because the enemy becomes harder to locate and looks more like the hero. What were monsters are now facets of identity; the sexual other and the racial other can no longer be safely separated from self. But still, we keep our monsters ready. (Halberstam 1995: 163)

The paedophilic monster embedded in the Australian metanarrative as exemplified in the films briefly discussed in this chapter will again rise staining the national character, but rise it must. In doing so its end will be assured.

Figure 18. *The Lure*. *The Lure*, directed by Agnieszka Smoczyńska (Kino Świat, 2015).

Agnieszka Kotwasińska

Immigrants: *The Lure* (Smoczyńska, 2015)

'All monstrous bodies come as questions', writes Patricia MacCormack (2012: 258), and the two syrenas, Silver and Golden, from Agnieszka Smoczyńska's musical horror movie *The Lure* (2015) are no exception. Their hybrid bodies, half-human, half-fish, trouble both normative understandings of female corporeality and more general dichotomies organizing Western subjectivity, such as human/non-human, urban/rural, native/foreign. While Robert Bolesto's script brings into focus the two young mermaids' coming-of-age stories and trans-species sexual difference, their coiled fish tailed-bodies, living and breathing question marks, probe the limits of (human) hospitality in relation to immigrants. The fact that the two mermaid sisters stay in the big city could be read as a commentary on the rural/urban divide in Polish society and the frailty of Polish middle-class identity (see Kotwasińska 2017). The so-called refugee crisis in Europe and the Polish government's xenophobic response to it calls for more attention to be given to how immigrants and refugees are cast as monstrous in hegemonic media discourses and the ways in which *The Lure* complicates the concept of monstrous immigration via its emphasis on sexuality and sex politics.

The figure of a monstrous immigrant was mobilized perhaps most in/famously in the late 1890s in Bram Stoker's *Dracula* at a time when imperialist fears of the so-called reverse colonization and the revenge of the colonized overlapped with racially motivated anti-Semitism in Western Europe (Arata 1990; Halberstam 1995; Beller 2015). Still, fears of immigrants have emerged in twentieth- and twenty-first-century horror and Gothic scholarship only in few prominent contexts, such as H. P. Lovecraft's racist loathing of non-WASP immigrants, transnational horror (in the case of Guillermo del Toro and Robert Rodríguez, and Latin American horror cinemas), eugenics and enfreakment discourses in horror cinema, and finally, the figure of a zombie, especially in its current ultra-fast and super-massive incarnation.[1] Nevertheless, the critical tides might be turning, as proven by how North American anti-immigrant rhetoric is mentioned with increased regularity in the works on recent horror production (McCollum 2019).

Notwithstanding particular examples of movies and TV shows in which monstrous immigration and xenophobia take the spotlight in more or less direct terms, the cultural production of monstrosity can also be observed at work in Western discourses on groups migrating from the Global South to the Global North. It is hard to ignore the ways in which recent migrant bodies have been made monstrous in ways painfully similar to the Foucauldian 'human monster':

> It could be said that the monster's power and its capacity to create anxiety are due to the fact that it violates the law while leaving it with nothing to say. [...] When the monster violates the law by its very existence, it triggers the response of something quite different from the law itself. It provokes either violence, the will for pure and simple suppression, or medical care or pity. (Foucault 2003: 56)

The two reactions, virulent xenophobia and, to a lesser extent, sympathy and pity, reverberate through media accounts on the European migrant crisis (2015–9). Immigrants are transformed into monstrous others through dehumanizing and demonizing language and insistent references to (1) diseases, infections, and bacteria (Reisigl and Wodak 2001; Musolff 2000 and 2015), (2) natural disasters (Charteris-Black 2006), (3) animals (Santa Ana, 1999), and increasingly, (4) water-based metaphors (Kainz 2016; Murphy 2018).[2]

---

[1] For more on the history of eugenics and horror cinema see Smith (2011). For a comprehensive introduction to the contemporary refugee-as-zombie trope see Crofts and Vogl (2019).

[2] Importantly, I am using 'immigration' and 'immigrant' to discuss the concept of monstrous immigration, as these are the most commonly used designators in the European migrant crisis discourses, but the majority of people migrating to continental Europe over the Mediterranean Sea and through Turkey are actually Syrian and Afghan refugees and asylum seekers. The prevalent use of the 'immigrant' with its connotations of economic motivation and personal choice makes the existing anti-immigrant sentiments more easily manipulated by right-wing nationalist politicians and public figures.

Carole Murphy writes about the Mediterranean becoming a Sea of Bodies: 'The bodies in question, those of refugees, are most often represented in the media as an amorphous mass, a hungry beast, devouring all in its path. This trope draws on both ancient fears of the sea as the repository of unknown monsters and more recent fears of the perceived threat of 'refugee-as-invader' and "consumer of homes, jobs and benefits' (Murphy 2018: 154). I want to argue that not only is the discourse on immigrants Gothicized through notions of alterity and monstrosity, but the reverse is also true, and the profusion of such negative metaphors in daily language influences the way fictional monsters in horror cinema are now received. For instance, uber-fast zombies in *World War Z* are made more easily recognizable as monstrous immigrants through the CGI images that transform them into an unstoppable wave of infected liquid. Similarly, paying attention to the Polish anti-immigrant discourse and specifically, its gendered aspects, complicates Silver and Golden's status as immigrants even further.

Even when not engaging fears triggered by racist or xenophobic rhetoric and when not embodying them directly via particular tropes or imagery, every monster is always already deeply invested in illegal border-crossings. By transgressing boundaries inaccessible to others – inaccessible because of law, biological restriction, or cultural taboos – '[t]he monster prevents mobility (intellectual, geographic, or sexual), delimiting the social spaces through which private bodies may move' (Cohen 1996: 12). Monsters' radical mobility is thus met, in equal measure, with resistance and awe, an uneasy alliance perhaps best exemplified by the monstrous mermaids in *The Lure*.[3] After all, as sea creatures, they live above (or perhaps, more appropriately, below) maritime borders and their freedom of movement is nearly absolute. Closely related to Greek *Nereids* and *undines*, Slavic *rusalkas*, Northern European *selkies*, and a

---

Obviously, the very distinction between 'a refugee' and 'an immigrant' is in itself an imperfect one as it divorces a (vaguely defined) survival from material needs, economic opportunities, historical and socio-political context, which directly impact human life and its quality.

3   Even though sirens and mermaids are two different mythological species, they began to merge in medieval bestiaries, and a number of European languages use now the Latinized form 'sirena' to refer both to sirens and mermaids. For more on sirens and mermaids see Wood (2018), Bacchilega and Alohalani Brown (2019).

host of other water spirits (not necessarily female), mermaids are invariably associated with impossible sexuality and treacherous singing voice that leads enamoured human males to their doom.

While the Polish title, *Córki dansingu* [*Daughters of a Dance Bar*], and various promotional materials conceal the protagonists' fish tails, the English title, *The Lure*, together with an international poster presenting a naked fish-tailed girl in a bathtub, banks on the mermaids' recognizability as a sexually magnetic non-human monster. The original Polish marketing constructs *The Lure* as a whacky musical about two teenage ingénues, adopted by a sleazy 1980s dance bar in communist Warsaw, whereas the Western distributor and media outlets saw *The Lure*, first and foremost, as a 'Polish cannibal horror mermaid musical', as a quick Google search makes abundantly clear.[4]

Figure 19. Opening titles. *The Lure*, directed by Agnieszka Smoczyńska (Kino Świat, 2015).

On the one hand, these two frameworks point to how the East and the West imagine the mermaid sisters' roles in *The Lure* (uncouth immigrants and monstrous females, respectively), but, on the other, a more careful reading reveals the two narratives co-habiting the same story and, perhaps cannibalistically,

---

4 As Smoczyńska recalls, the Polish distributor did not want to reveal that *The Lure* was actually a horror movie about monstrous mermaids and instead wanted to market *The Lure* as 'a Polish *Chicago*', which rather unsurprisingly backfired with viewers walking out of the theaters disgusted and disappointed with a horror musical rather than just a musical. See Gingold (2017).

feeding upon each other. This tension is already visible during the opening titles, which drag the audience to a dark, dank cave inhabited by man-eating female monsters.[5] And yet, the first scene of the movie moves away from their monstrosity by showing how it is Silver who is first lured to the shore by a young man's (siren) song. The mermaids ask the boy, Mietek, and his father to help them ashore as there is 'no need to fear, we won't eat you, my dear', which links their monstrosity to vampirism – it seems they need to be invited onto land by humans. The mermaids speak Polish, which they learnt in a Bulgarian beach resort, Golden Sands (also known as an Eastern Block Riviera), and soon the viewers learn of the sisters' plan of going to the US. The only acceptable direction of travel, East to West, with Poland being the last Eastern stop (still Eastern but already undergoing aesthetic and economic Westernification) before the final swim over (under) the Atlantic, marks them as hopeful immigrants.[6]

Clearly, in contrast to actual Poles dreaming of the American Dream in the 1980s, Silver and Golden do not require dollars, visas, or smugglers to get them to the West, as they can cross international waters any time they want. What keeps them in Warsaw are their failed attempts to secure male love and respect; namely, Silver's unrequited love for Mietek and Golden's attempts at winning the approval of their father Triton. Interestingly, Triton is another immigrant figure, one who, in contrast to the two sisters, had successfully adapted to the new environment by capitalizing on his monstrosity through a punk-rock artist persona. At the very least, Triton is capable of 'passing off' his monstrous origin as part of his stage act, whereas the sisters either refuse to do this (Golden cannot restrain her appetite for male human flesh) or are unable to fit in (Silver undergoes a botched surgery to become a human girl from the waist down, losing her voice in the process).[7]

Following Halberstam's argument that '[t]echnologies of monstrosity are always also technologies of sex' (Halberstam 1995: 88), the two mermaids are marked as foreign (non-human) and sexualized at the same time. While

5   The animation is based on painter Aleksandra Waliszewska's works. See Kay (2016).
6   Smoczyńska supports this reading in an interview from 2016. See also Ramji (2016). For more on the pre-transformation 1980s Poland, see Pyzik (2014).
7   Directly linking to the story of *The Little Mermaid* by Hans Christian Anderson.

their tails easily transform into human legs on land, the two mermaids remain 'smooth as Barbie dolls' (rendered in Polish as 'empty as Barbie dolls'), which pushes them outside a heteronormative economy of human sexuality – one that revolves around penetrative vaginal sex. In other words, they are treated as monstrous not because they are non-human but because their femininity is inaccessible and impenetrable to human males. Of course, as a typical postmodern horror mash-up, *The Lure* deploys monstrous feminine imagery not only as a source of the abject but also as an ironic commentary on female bodies and femininity. For instance, in a pastiche of a glamorous *Playboy* magazine photo shoot, the two sisters are shown wearing fishnet stockings over their grotesquely enormous tails and black bunny ears. A running joke throughout the movie concerns a fishy smell which, of course, refers to the mermaids' fish-like bodies, but also to female sexuality as such, and, on a meta-level, to the 1980s vodka drinking rituals that customarily involved herring and pickles.

In fact, it is through the sisters' non-normative sex – understood here both as a physical act and also a sexed body – that they approximate the figure of a monstrous immigrant who, by their very existence, threatens to destabilize the Western patriarchal system of control over female bodies. Mermaids' parasitic sexuality 'represents a bad or pathological sexuality, non-reproductive sexuality' (Halberstam 1995: 16–17) and, just like vampiric parasitism, was linked to monstrous Jewishness in 1890s Europe. Today's Islamophobic responses to the so-called refugee crisis in Poland lean heavily on anti-Semitic discourses centered on the parasitic and/or infected body.[8] At the same time, the portrayal of the sisters' non-human sexuality cannibalizes a particular strand of anti-immigrant rhetoric, which is based on racist and misogynist fears of miscegenation and the loss of 'white' Europe. This metaphor of Europe-in-distress is constructed in popular media through images of white female bodies being violated by dark-skinned male others, but in *The Lure* it is actually the white female bodies who endanger unsuspecting white men. Indeed, Golden's nasty appetites and murderous tendencies can be read as revenge on behalf of the abused immigrant women, tired of (s)exploitation in sleazy bars, constant prodding, and male hands probing their non-human skin and orifices. In this

---

8   The most infamous Islamophobic media coverage include reports by Polish weeklies *Gazeta Polska* (June and July 2017) and *wSieci* (September 2015 and February 2016). For more on Polish Islamophobia see Bobako (2017) and Jaskułowski (2019).

sense, Golden turns monstrous not because it is in her nature to be monstrous (as Triton seems to suggest), but rather because the very process of migration is in fact monstrous and dehumanizing. The conditional hospitality with which the mermaids are met in Warsaw is predicated on the accessibility of their bodies, their compliance to male demands, and ability to generate profits.

Figure 20. Krysia's erotic fantasy. *The Lure*, directed by Agnieszka Smoczyńska (Kino Świat, 2015).

Initially, they are welcomed into the family of musicians. Krysia, the family's matriarch, reacts with empathy and pity when she suspects the two girls have been molested by the club owner. Eventually, rage trumps pity and Krysia's maternal concern is replaced by erotic fascination and jealousy, as evidenced by a sexual fantasy in which she imagines herself as a mermaid mother breastfeeding two little mermaids. The fantasy is interrupted by a fishy smell she notices on her husband's fingers; his assurance that he only ate some herring only further enrages her. As the mermaids soon discover, human hospitality turns into hostility very easily, and when their adoptive human family learn of the sisters' murderous proclivities, they knock the girls unconscious and unceremoniously throw their bodies into the river. The ease with which their bodies are disposed of and thrown back whence they came from suggests a level of desensitization, not unlike the one discernible in today's anti-immigrant rhetoric. Looking at *The Lure* not just through the monstrous feminine, but also through the concept of monstrous immigration reveals a contemporary technology of monstrosity that generates images of immigrants as non-human others. But mermaids turn out to be slippery creatures and their monstrosity might just be a natural response to the abuse they suffer as immigrants.

Part II
Society

John Edgar Browning

The Mask: Slasher Cinema (1978–1998)

Behind the Eyes: Some Notes on Teaching Slasher Cinema

'Nobody ever lost money scaring the American public', aptly quipped narrator Rob Lowe in the iconic documentary TV mini-series *The '80s: The Decade That Made Us* (Rudd, 2013). And how very American indeed was Slasher cinema during its prime in the 1980s. Despite the subgenre's famously popular appeal among young audiences, however, teaching Slasher cinema in a classroom setting remains very messy work, something I often find myself telling students. Maybe that is because it is a messy subgenre, not in a bloody, gory sort of way – though that is certainly true as well. Rather, Slasher is conceptually, psychically, and, above all, psychosexually messy because it stirs in all of us, like no other genre before it or since, at once the parts we tend to keep most hidden from ourselves and others, and the parts we seem less able to explain or perhaps even understand. Slasher serves as a kind of Rosetta stone for peering into and laying bare, as best as one can, not only the primitive or *caveman* portion of our brain, but the *morally socialized* portion as well, as I will explain momentarily. Yet even after thirty years of scholarship on the topic, Slasher remains for even the most astute among us a code we have not fully cracked – getting to know Slasher is, in many ways, like getting to know oneself, and how few of us truly know ourselves? With the recent release of *AHS: 1984* (Murphy and Falchuk, 2019), now at least marks a good time to try.

What follows is a distillation of some of the major points of interest I have worked through while teaching Slasher cinema over the years in the university classroom. I begin first by trying to flesh out a stable structure for defining Slasher, followed then by a retrospective on the origins of Slasher.

Afterwards, I provide what I term 'The "Safe" List', a filmography (alphabetically and chronologically organized) of the Slasher titles that meet the criteria I outline in the sections prior to it. And finally, I offer a week-by-week schedule of selected classroom readings and accompanying screenings. All of this I do in the hopes of offering guidance to educators as they attempt to navigate in the classroom the intricacies of Slasher cinema and the flood of meanings harbored behind its masks and faces. Due to spatial constraints, however, I do not include Slasher titles from the 2000s or 2010s or discussion thereof, though the new millennium almost assuredly comprises a new, and important, fourth wave in Slasher history.

Each of us wears a mask, some of us several even. It could be that Slasher cinema is an indictment of that practice, though which masks precisely, that is to say which behaviours, I leave with the readers' judgement.

As Dr. Loomis carefully phrases it in *Halloween II* (1981), "we're all afraid of the dark inside ourselves.

Body(s) of Evidence; or, Towards a Definition of Slasher

On the one hand, Slasher plays into our collective, primordial fear, as viewers, of being stalked, hunted, and rendered prey, and on the other, it plays into our collective moral conditioning. Yet, despite these and other recurring thematics, arriving at a consensual definition of Slasher still proves no easy task. Indeed, the subgenre is both imaginatively complex and expansively varied, in spite of its relegation by critics to a status just above pornography.[1] It is perhaps fortuitous then that Slasher's singular consistency is one which lends itself to the task of tracing the subgenre's cultural endurance: its structural regularity.

I routinely tell my students that the central monster of a non-Slasher horror film, particularly or especially before the new millennium, largely occupies two spaces simultaneously in the narrative: that of social deviant (i.e. the 'sinner')

---

1 See Linda Williams, 'Film Bodies: Gender, Genre, and Excess', *Film Quarterly* 44, no. 4 (Summer, 1991): 2–13.

and physical or mental anomaly (Count Dracula, I remind my students, is not only physically *other* but also morally transgressive). In Slasher cinema, however, according to the classification I have deduced from over 150 films, the monster generally commits few or no other sinful or unlawful acts beyond using close-quarters weapons to police (i.e. murder) the film's otherwise 'normal' characters who have now absorbed the role previously occupied by the monster of social transgressor. Thus, the physically or mentally anomalous Slasher kills off one by one, i.e. for their 'sins', the film's socially transgressive protagonists, the very characters with whom adolescent viewers are supposed to identify, albeit only in part. Indeed, as I have noted elsewhere it is this particular feature that 'categorically distinguishes Slasher cinema within the horror genre'.[2] Curiously, *what* Slashers do is no less important than *why* they do it in the first place.

Jason Voorhees in *Friday the 13th* (1980), Michael Myers in *Halloween* (1978), the maniacal Second World War veteran in *The Prowler* (1981), etc., etc. – consistently the Slasher villain has exhibited in his or her[3] respective narrative what I term an originary traumatic moment, conflict, or history, one which has previously left them physically and/or psychologically scarred or disabled. This trauma subsequently induces the killer's practice of wearing a mask, that is, if some disfiguring accident or genetic malformation has not already rendered his face mask-like, either scenario serving to hide his inner (or outer) trauma.[4] Here is yet another fundamental component of Slasher cinema, for it is this key moment (or 'unresolved pain', to use famed horror actress Barbara Steele's useful phrasing about a different but similar topic)[5] that motivates the villain's repeated policing of socially transgressive behaviours (e.g. fornicating, adultery, drugs, rape, emotional and physical abuse, hazing,

2   Browning 2015: 178.
3   Hereafter I will use the masculine pronoun when referring to the Slasher, though there is certainly a handful of female Slashers as well; however, the change in the Slasher's sex from male to female – or even gender, from masculine to feminine – often has a simple yet markedly profound effect on the narrative, one which the scope of this essay has not the space to treat of adequately.
4   In some cases, the Slasher may even conceal his previously disfigured face behind a mask. Or, alternatively, the film may simply anonymize the killer by relegating his identity to the shadows until some big reveal at the end of the film.
5   Jones 1997: 130.

Figure 21. *Watch Me When I Kill*, directed by Antonio Bido (Elis Cinimatografica, 1977).

professional misconduct, manslaughter, etc.), behaviours which, coincidentally, visually or conceptually echo the killer's traumatic past. Thus, the Slasher is essentially a deranged moral vigilante, avenging some trauma the film often reveals through flashbacks or monologue by the Slasher. Perhaps it is at this juncture that we, as viewers, in part come to sympathize with the killer, even, to some degree, identify with him.

Michael Meyers wears a mask, in part, to blend in on Halloween, but its meaning doesn't end there. For the mask (or 'the Shape', as it is termed in John Carpenter's script) also allegorically hides the Slasher's traumatic past, anonymizes the dark deeds he or she must perform to satiate that trauma, and provides a canvas that we, each of us, form to our terror's desire. Through the subgenre's characteristic I-camera or POV shots, we as audience members at once watch ourselves being punished through the transgressive protagonists while living vicariously, if anonymously, as Norman did in *Psycho*, through the masked Slasher's eyes: watching, doting over, and punishing transgressive acts; we are the punished and the punisher. As punisher, we are exonerated through the Slasher's originary trauma; as punished, we pay penance for own guilty conscience. In the end, without sin there can be no retribution, so what the Slasher cinema needs next is a place.

The protagonists in Slasher cinema – the subgenre's ubiquitous social transgressors – always find themselves in particular situations (i.e. at camp, a party, a house where they are left alone and unsupervised) in which they are

Figure 22. *Friday the 13th: Part 2*, directed by Steve Miner (Georgetown Productions Inc. and Sean S. Cunningham Films, 1981).

most themselves; or, to use John Carpenter's prescient epigraph in his pre-*Halloween* student short film *Captain Voyeur* (1969): 'in [their] quiet hours, when the mask is off ... and when [we] put [our] mask on'.[6] Thus, the mask – or anonymity in some other form – in turn gives us, as viewers, à la Norman Bates's peephole in *Psycho* (1960), permission to watch whatever it is they do in secret in those places. A Slasher film's central setting becomes the other side of Norman's peephole, what I like to call the loco peccatum ('place of sin'), representing either a forbidden place, or a place where certain behaviours are forbidden, or both. And if 'horror can get there', remarked John Carpenter about *Halloween*'s suburban locale, 'it can get anywhere'.[7]

Horror Comes Home and the End of America's Innocence: Getting at a Genealogy of Slasher

It is no exaggeration to say that harder than even defining Slasher cinema is arriving at agreement about which film(s) helped to birth the subgenre. While that much may be true, Slasher's primogenitor is hardly in dispute, nor when, nor where.

The 1950s, as declared by many who lived it, was a 'good time', an innocent time, and Ed Gein, of Plainfield, Wisconsin, took that away – nay, *exposed* it for the deception it turned out to be, and he did so with a shovel, some scissors, and a little needle and thread. Gein, wrote journalist Dion Henderson at the time, 'had two faces. One he showed to the neighbors. The other he showed only to the dead. I think there was a third face to Gein also – the one he showed only to those he was going to kill. That would have been the worst face of all.'[8]

In 1957, Gein confessed to murdering two women and afterwards fashioning their bodies, as well as a number of other bodies, also female, that he exhumed from local cemeteries, into various trinkets made from skin and

---

6   *Captain Voyeur*, written and directed by John Carpenter (University of Southern California, 1969). Student film.
7   Jones 1997: 64.
8   Henderson 1957: 18.

Figure 23. Waushara County Sheriff Arthur ('Art') Schley holds up a sketch of evidence in the case against serial killer Ed Gein (1906–84), Plainfield, Wisconsin, 20 November 1957. The sketch appears to be a face, possibly a dead skin mask. (Photo by Francis Miller/The LIFE Picture Collection via Getty Images.)

bones, including, most gruesomely of all, several female skin masks, a mammary vest, and leggings, all of which he reportedly donned himself. Appropriately enough, Robert Bloch, who would author the Gein-inspired suspense novel *Psycho* in 1959, observed of *The Phantom of the Opera*'s (Julian, 1925) title villain that he 'masked himself to disguise a hideous face. ... a man who was ashamed of his own sexuality, who conceals his monstrous desire ... under a mask'.[9] But Gein did not haunt the Paris underground or hale from some distant castle in Transylvania; he haunted America's Heartland.

Joseph Stefano, who wrote the screenplay for Alfred Hitchcock's adaptation *Psycho* (1960), said of his treatment, 'I tried to make everything terribly ordinary, and even once you got inside Norman Bates house, it wasn't a dark alley, it wasn't all you had seen before. I was kind of bringing murder home.'[10] Hitchcock's *Psycho*, together with Michael Powell's *Peeping Tom* (1960), is often attributed to the Slasher's teratogenesis. Both films brought horror into the safety of the home, but they were not Slasher films proper, not yet at least. Even still, they and a handful of other films that followed shortly after helped to supplied the subgenre with several crucial conventions. Together they helped form the basis for a wave of called 'proto-Slashers' (some of which double as Italian *giallo* films), that would include *Blood and Black Lace* (Bava, 1964), *The Psychopath* (Francis, 1966), *The House That Screamed* (Serrador, 1970), *Hatchet for the Honeymoon* (Bava, 1970). While Slasher proper began to germinate with these early proto-Slashers, it took the Vietnam War and the 'new horror' of the early 1970s to help flesh out the subgenre more fully. Aiding the subgenre as well was a subset of films I like to call 'transitional Slashers' (i.e. something structurally and aesthetically in-between) that included *Schizo* (Walker, 1976), *Alice, Sweet Alice* (Sole, 1976), *Massacre at Central High* (Daalder, 1976), *Watch Me When I Kill* (Bido, 1977), *Rituals* (Carter, 1977), *The Toolbox Murders* (Donnelly, 1978), *Eyes of Laura Mars* (Kershner, 1978), *Someone's Watching Me!* (Carpenter, 1978).

The conventions established in 1960 and in the proto- and transitional titles thereafter – targeted 'punishment'-killings, masks and anonymity, the

---

9   *The Horror of It All*, directed by Gene Feldman, Suzette Winter (Wombat Productions, 1983).
10 Quoted in Jones 1997: 25.

marked adolescence of the killer, close-quarters weapons, deviant or transgressive sexual subtexts, etc. – much of which derives, directly or indirectly, from Gein's story, culminate in the Slasher subgenre's first installment with Carpenter's *Halloween* (1978). *Halloween* combined recognizable features from the proto- and transitional periods to such effect that the film achieved overwhelming financial success, affording the subgenre its template, the *locus classicus* of Slasher cinema.

The 'Safe' List: A Slasher Filmography

The following list comprises films that most comfortably (or safely) belong in the Slasher subgenre. The list is by no means complete and hinges solely upon my ability to watch or research adequately the films it includes. Notable omissions include, unfortunately, a number of non-English foreign Slashers whose inclusion is barred by my own ignorance of their language. Readers will also note the omission of film titles that, while generally categorized as Slasher, do not meet the specific criteria in any substantive detail; perhaps a future categorization for them might be termed 'off-Slasher' or 'hybrid Slasher'.

However, conspicuously present among the films below, even though it does not meet what is perhaps the subgenre's most important criterion, is Wes Craven's *A Nightmare on Elm Street* (1984; and sequels); readers will recall that Freddy Krueger's originary traumatic history (his being set alight by angry parents) is the result of his own social and moral transgression of murdering (as well as, albeit left unspoken, sexually assaulting) the children of Elm Street.

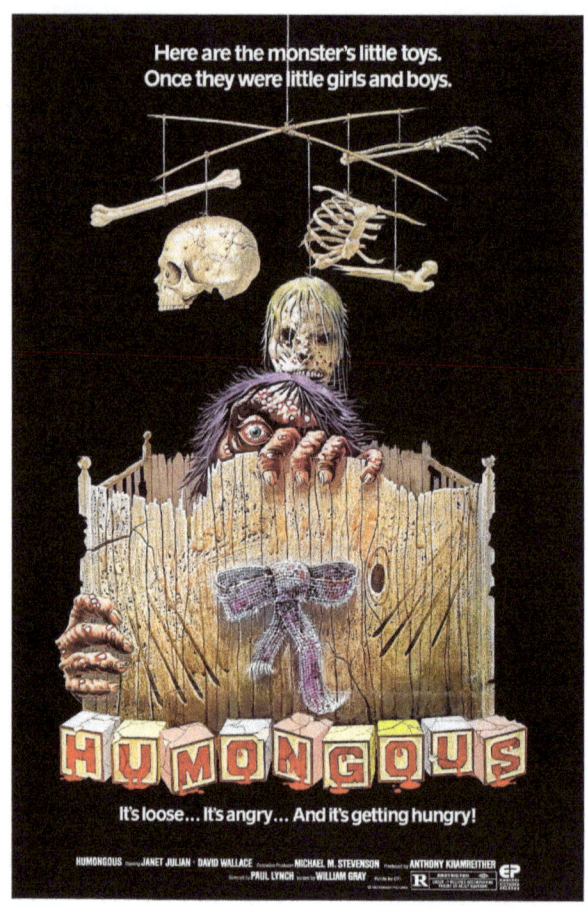

Figure 24. *Humongous*, directed by Paul Lynch (Humongous Films, in association with Manesco Films, 1982).

A Chronological Filmography[11]

Halloween (Carpenter, 1978)
Don't Go in the House (Ellison, 1979)

---

11 This list is limited to film titles I can verify with reasonable certainty and should not be deemed definitive.

Silent Scream (Harris, 1979)
Tourist Trap (Schmoeller, 1979)
Christmas Evil (Jackson, 1980)
Cruising (Friedkin, 1980)
Demented (Jeffreys, 1980)
Don't Answer the Phone! (Hammer, 1980)
Dressed to Kill (De Palma, 1980)
Friday the 13th (Cunningham, 1980)
Funeral Home (Fruet, 1980)
He Knows You're Alone (Mastroianni, 1980)
Maniac (Lustig, 1980)
New Year's Evil (Alston, 1980)
Nightmares (Lamond, 1980)
Patrick Still Lives! (Landi, 1980)
Prom Night (Lynch, 1980)
Schizoid (Paulson, 1980)
Terror on Tour (Edmonds, 1980)
The Prey (Brown, 1980)
To All a Goodnight (Hess, 1980)
Absurd (D'Amato, 1981)
The Burning (Maylam, 1981)
Dark Night of the Scarecrow (De Felitta, 1981)
Final Exam (Huston, 1981)
Friday the 13th: Part 2 (Miner, 1981)
The Funhouse (Hooper, 1981)
Graduation Day (Freed, 1981)
Halloween II (Rosenthal, 1981)
Happy Birthday to Me (Thompson, 1981)
Hell Night (DeSimone, 1981)
Hospital Massacre (Davidson, 1981)
Just Before Dawn (Lieberman, 1981)
My Bloody Valentine (Mihalka, 1981)
Night School (Hughes, 1981)
The Prowler (Zito, 1981)
Terror Train (Spottiswoode, 1981)
Blood Song (Levi, 1982)

Boardinghouse (Wintergate, 1982)
Death Screams (Nelson, 1982)
The Dorm That Dripped Blood (Carpenter and Obrow, 1982)
Double Exposure (Hillman, 1982)
Fantasies (Derek, 1982)
Friday the 13th: Part III (Miner, 1982)
The Ghost Dance (Buffa, 1982)
Girls Nite Out (Deubel, 1983)
Honeymoon Horror (Preston, 1982)
Humongous (Lynch, 1982)
Murder by Phone (Anderson, 1982)
The New York Ripper (Fulci, 1982)
Pieces (Simon, 1982)
Slumber Party Massacre (Jones, 1982)
Unhinged (Gronquist, 1982)
American Nightmare (McBrearty, 1983)
Curtains (Stryker, 1983)
Deadly Lessons (Miller, 1983)
The Final Terror (Davis, 1983)
The House on Sorority Row (Rodman, 1983)
Prozzie (Lommel, 1983)
Scalps (Ray, 1983)
Silent Madness (Nuchtern, 1983)
Sledgehammer (Prior, 1983)
Sleepaway Camp (1983)
Sweet Sixteen (Sotos, 1983)
A Nightmare on Elm Street (Craven, 1984)
Don't Open Till Christmas (Purdom, 1984)
Fatal Games (Elliot, 1984)
Friday the 13th: The Final Chapter (Zito, 1984)
La Muerte del Chacal (Galindo, 1984)
Murder Rock (Fulci, 1984)
Shadows Run Black (Heard, 1984)
Silent Madness (Nuchtern, 1984)
Silent Night, Deadly Night (Sellier Jnr, 1984)
Splatter University (Haines, 1984)

A Nightmare on Elm Street 2: Freddy's Revenge (Sholder, 1985)
Bits and Pieces (Thomas, 1985)
Bloodstream (Murphy, 1985)
Friday the 13th: A New Beginning (Steinmann, 1985)
Horror House on Highway 5 (Casey, 1985)
Mask of Murder (Mattsson, 1985)
The Mutilator (Cooper, 1985)
Nail Gun Massacre (Leslie and Loften, 1985)
Too Scared to Scream (Lo Bianco, 1985)
April Fool's Day (Walton, 1986)
Body Count (Deodato, 1986)
Chopping Mall (Wynorski, 1986)
City in Panic (Bouvier, 1986)
Friday the 13th Part VI: Jason Lives (McLoughlin, 1986)
Slaughter High (Dugdale, Ezra, and Litten, 1986)
Sorority House Massacre (Frank, 1986)
Terror at Tenkiller (Meyer, 1986)
Aerobicide (Prior, 1987)
A Nightmare on Elm Street 3: Dream Warriors (Russell, 1987)
Blood Frenzy (Freeman, 1987)
Blood Lake (Boggs, 1987)
Blood Rage (Grissmer, 1987)
Blood Sisters (Findlay, 1987)
Cheerleader Camp (Quinn, 1987)
City of Blood (Roodt, 1987)
Coda (Lahiff, 1987)
The Majorettes (Hinzman, 1987)
Night Screams (Plone, 1987)
Open House (Mundrha, 1987)
Silent Night, Deadly Night: Part 2 (Harry, 1987)
Slaughterhouse (Rosesler, 1987)
Stagefright (Soavi, 1987)
Stripped to Kill (Shea Ruben, 1987)
Terror Night (Marino, 1987)
Twisted Nightmare (Hunt, 1987)
Amsterdamned (1988)

A Nightmare on Elm Street 4: The Dream Master (Harlin, 1988)
Deadly Dreams (Peterson, 1988)
Edge of the Axe (Larraz, 1988)
Friday the 13th Part VII: The New Blood (Buechler, 1988)
Halloween 4 (Little, 1988)
Hide and Go Shriek (Schoolnik, 1988)
I Still Know What You Did Last Summer (Cannon, 1988)
Iced (Kwitny, 1988)
Perfect Victims (Levy, 1988)
Too Beautiful to Die (Piana, 1988)
A Nightmare on Elm Street 5: The Dream Child (Hopkins, 1989)
Bloodmoon (Mills, 1989)
Darkroom (O'Hara and Mastorakis, 1989)
Friday the 13th Part VIII: Jason Takes Manhattan (Hedden, 1989)
Moonstalker (O'Rourke, 1989)
Nightmare Beach (Kirkpatrick, 1989)
Out of the Dark (Schroeder, 1989)
Rush Week (Bralver, 1989)
Scream (Craven, 1996)
Slash Dance (Shyman, 1989)
Deadly Manor (Larraz, 1990)
Mirage (Crain, 1990)
Pledge Night (Ziller, 1990)
The Night Brings Charlie (Logan, 1990)
Slumber Party Massacre III (Mattison, 1990)
Sorority House Massacre II (Stanton, 1990)
Freddy's Dead: The Final Nightmare (Talalay, 1991)
Zipperface (Pourmand, 1992)
The Baby Doll Murders (Leder, 1993)
Deadly Sins (Robison, 1995)
Scream (Craven, 1996)
I Know What You Did Last Summer (Gillespie, 1997)
Scream (Craven, 1997)
I Still Know What You Did Last Summer (Cannon, 1998)
Urban Legend (Blanks, 1998)

Selected Classroom Readings and Screenings (in Order as Assigned)

Week 1

1. Francis Miller and Frank J. Scherscel, 'House of Horror Stuns the Nation', *Life* 43, no. 23 (2 December 1957), 24–31.
2. Robert Bloch. *Psycho* (New York: Bantam Books, 1959).
3. *Biography*, episode 'Ed Gein' (A&E, 2004)

Week 2

4. Dolf Zillmann and Rhonda Gibson, 'Evolution of the Horror Genre', in *Horror Films: Current Research on Audience Preferences and Reactions*, ed. James B. Weaver and Ron Tamborini (Mahwah, NJ: Lawrence Erlbaum Associates, 1996), 15–32.
5. *Psycho* (Hitchcock, 1960)
6. *Peeping Tom* (Powell, 1960)

Week 3

7. Various clips/trailers of proto- and transitional Slashers, as outlined above in Section II
8. *Black Christmas* (Clark, 1974)
9. *Halloween* (Carpenter, 1978)
10. *Going to Pieces: The Rise and Fall of the Slasher Film* (McQueen, 2006)

Week 4

11. Carol Clover, 'Introduction' and 'Chapter 1: Her Body, Himself', in *Men, Women, and Chain Saws: Gender in the Modern Horror Film (Princeton Classics)* (Princeton, NJ: Princeton University Press: 2015 [1992]).
12. *Friday the 13th* (1980)
13. Clover, 'Chapter 2: Opening Up'

Week 5

14. Clover, 'Chapter 3: Getting Even'
15. *American Horror Story (AHS): 1984*, episode 1 'Camp Redwood' (Buecker, 2019)
16. Clover, 'Chapter 4: The Eye of Horror'
17. *AHS: 1984*, episode 2 'Mr. Jingles' (Gray, 2019)

Week 6

18. Isabel Cristina Pinedo, Chapter 3: '. … And Then She Killed Him: Women and Violence in the Slasher Film', in *Recreational Terror: Women and the Pleasures of Horror Film Viewing (SUNY series, INTERRUPTIONS: Border Testimony(ies) and Critical Discourse/s)* (Albany: SUNY Press, 1997).
19. *AHS: 1984*, episode 3 'Slashdance' (Wigmore, 2019)
20. Barry S. Sapolsky and Fred Molitor, 'Content Trends in Contemporary Horror Films', in *Horror Films*, ed. Weaver and Tamborini.
21. *AHS: 1984*, episode 4 'True Killers' (Lynch, 2019)

Week 7

22. Linda Williams, 'Film Bodies: Gender, Genre, and Excess', *Film Quarterly* 44, no. 4 (Summer, 1991): 2–13.
23. *AHS: 1984*, episode 5 'Red Dawn' (Horder-Payton, 2019)
24. Jack Halberstam, "Bodies that Splatter: Queers and Chainsaws," in *Skin Shows: Gothic Horror and the Technology of Monsters* (Durham, NC: Duke University Press, 1995).
25. *AHS: 1984*, episode 6 'Episode 100' (Peristere, 2019)

Week 8

26. John Edgar Browning, "Disability and Slasher Cinema's Unsung Children," in *Monstrous Children and Childish Monsters: Essays on Cinema's Holy Terrors*, ed. Markus P.J. Bohlmann and Sean Moreland (Jefferson, NC.: McFarland & Co., 2015).
27. *AHS: 1984*, episode 7 'The Lady in White' (Friedlander, 2019)
28. *AHS: 1984*, episode 8 'Rest in Pieces' (Horder-Payton, 2019)

Week 9

29. Jeremy Maron, "When the Final Girl is Not a Girl: Reconsidering the Gender Binary in the Slasher Film," *Off Screen* 19, no. 1 (January 2015): https://offscreen.comview/reconsidering-the-final-girl.
30. *AHS: 1984*, episode 9 'Final Girl' (Gray, 2019)

Concluding Remarks

Ed Gein symbolized something being off or amiss under America's surface in the 1950s, arrest by police in many ways disrupting the decade's illusion of happiness and tranquility. Three decades later, Gein's progeny, behind the visage of the Slasher villain, would come to achieve much of the same, only this time signaling something amiss in 1970s and 1980s culture through the Slasher's disruption of jovial times had by adolescents.

Arguably the cinematic monster has always been but a symptom of some greater sickness in the culture producing it. Yet, in the case of Slasher, culture seems to have displaced part of that sickness onto America's youth, a recurring thematic well at home during a conservative era like the Reagan presidency (1981–1989). With a penchant for murderously reifying the moral and behavioural imperatives audiences had been socially conditioned to accept as proper and universal, Slasher cinema offered time and time again a predictable and fulfilling experience.

So then, what, may we surmise is 'Behind the Eyes'? The answer is probably closer than we realize: perhaps it is we who don those masks, those faces not our own, and maybe it always has been. When victims die, maybe we are killing that part of ourselves we (are told to) hate most, a story Slasher would retell with exceedingly lucrativity across its many iterations. Perhaps more to the point though, Slasher's propensity for repetition makes the subgenre a kind of folktale in a way. It might be said even that Slasher films comprise the only true American folk mythology: that 'good times' can, at any moment and without warning, be rendered illusion at the hands of some dark past that emerges from the American psyche to accuse and avenge itself upon us.

Such is Slasher cinema, and it is unsurprisingly comforting.

Author's Note

I wish to thank my students at the Georgia Institute of Technology and the Savannah College of Art and Design (SCAD), as well as insightful friends like Michael Detrick and Vincent Belanger, for their indirect comments, that helped me to flesh out my own conception of Slasher.

Lauren Rosewarne

The Cyberbully: *Cyberbully* (Binamé, 2011)

The fears, insecurities, hang-ups and sources of revulsion for a culture have long been embodied in the monsters of the big screen. Monsters exist to not only terrify us but also to alert us to the bubbling concerns of a society. The cyberbully is an example of a screen archetype that both builds upon the templates of monsters of bygone eras but also exists to showcase the new things we're fretting about. This essay explores the monster of the cyberbully via its presentation in the 2011 ABC family film *Cyberbully*. The narrative centres on Taylor (Emily Osment), a high school student who becomes a victim of cyberbullying. The film's twist is that Taylor's cyberbully turns out to be her best friend, Samantha (Kay Panabaker), who herself had been tormented online by classmates.

To understand the current internet era monster, we need to understand the zeitgeist leading up to the new millennium: a time when the internet was still new enough to remain freshly frightening and where it was frequently conceived of as a place where a new breed of villains was birthed. In the years following, use of the internet has changed and mainstreamed, and constant connectivity and, notably, the rise of social media, has delivered both great familiarity and comfort with the technology but has also increased the opportunities – real or imagined – for it to be connected to bad happenings.

This essay begins with a discussion of the cyberbully as a contemporary incarnation of the screen's bogeyman. I explore some of the defining attributes of cyberbullies on screen as connected to ideas of place, psychology, and the creation of new victims and new perpetrators. Such attributes are then compared and contrasted to other kinds of monsters detectable in cinema.

The Internet Era Bogeyman

All over the world and throughout history, the bogeyman has been cast in media to provide lessons on morality. Such figures frighten people into adjusting their behaviour to preserve personal as well as social safety. While the physical appearance of the bogeyman changes depending on the culture that created it, commonly the aesthetic attributes are deliberately vague so that we can project onto the figure whichever characteristics we find most scary. The Internet era has birthed a variety of bogeymen, many of which have found a place in film: Slender Man for example, emerged from a 2009 meme and entered the mainstream when he became connected to a real-life 2014 stabbing (Jones 2014);[1] the monster was then memorialized offline through films like *Slender Man* (White, 2018) and appearances in television series like *Supernatural* (Kripke, 2005–present) and *Lost Girl* (Lovretta, 2010–16). In 2019 the creation of the Japanese character Momo was another – albeit short-lived – internet bogeyman (Dickson 2019).

The cyberbully shares similarities with bogeymen like Slender Man and Momo but there are also some notable differences. Like Slender Man and Momo, the cyberbully has led to high level moral panic (Maddox 2018): with self-harm and suicides often connected to online activity, rampant fears exist about the dangerous capacities of the technology. A key difference, however, lies in the fact that Slender Man and Momo are – as is the hallmark of the bogeyman – *mythic*. While their existence might lead to real-life consequences such as the aforementioned 2014 stabbing, these entities are monsters who were invented to scare us. In contrast, cyberbullying is not something borne from a meme or, like Momo, invented to become a viral hoax (Lorenz 2019), but rather is a real and extensively documented social problem leading to outcomes such as Taylor's suicide attempt in *Cyberbully*. Equally, while Momo, Slender Man and cyberbullies are each disembodied entities that haunt nightmares and screens, cyberbullying is conducted by a *real* person and thus there exists

---

1   Two girls, who were convicted of stabbing a classmate, alleged that they had been told to do so by the Slender Man, see <https://www.bbc.com/news/world-us-canada-42450641>.

a sharp fantasy/reality distinction between the cyberbully and Slender Man and Momo: the cyberbully appears disembodied online but is actually a real person. This distinction likens the cyberbully to other screen monsters that are human and thus perhaps more frightening in that they are not immediately identifiable as a threat. The notion of monsters like cyberbullies coming *from* the internet taps into the technology being understood as a kind of geographic place and, more specifically, as a kind of unregulated badlands.

Thinking of the internet as a physical place has been common since the inception of the technology. Terms like 'cyberspace' and 'information superhighway' were common in the earliest discussions of the internet and framed the technology as somewhere you could go – or be from. While *cyberspace* and *information superhighway* carried connotations of new and uncharted possibilities, it was also common for the internet to be construed as a kind of unregulated wild west, and a place where monsters could be from, could retreat to and generally where bad things can happen.

In the pre-internet era, bullying was something understood as associated with the schoolyard. Such attacks were characterized as (primarily) physical assaults that were time- and place-bound in that they took place at or around the schoolyard and the school day. The internet changed this enabling bullying to happen at any time and potentially – when conducted on social media – to occur in front of an infinite audience. The idea of the internet understood in geographic terms and, notably, as providing a new site for, and *type* of bullying is illustrated throughout in *Cyberbully*. In one scene, an unnamed female teen is at a group therapy session for cyberbullying victims and explains how social media increased her vulnerability:

> In elementary school it was like 'hey there goes Jelly Donut', you know, stuff like that. And it sucked, right? But at least I could go home and get some peace. Now it's like I can't even post pictures on my own profile 'cos people want to be telling me how fat or disgusting I am. This stuff follows me home.

A victim is not only more vulnerable online given how normal it is to be constantly connected, but episodes of bullying – particularly when conducted on social media – occur publicly but are not fixed in a temporal sense, meaning they can occur at anytime and any episode of bullying can potentially be revisited across time and by new audiences. In *Cyberbully*, in the aftermath of Taylor's suicide attempt, Dr Rilke (Marcel Jeannin) counsels Taylor's mother, Kris (Kelly Rowan). Key in Dr Rilke's comments is the notion of cyberbullying being constant because of the technology:

> Being bullied online, that can push a kid over the edge. It's like a group assault, very traumatic. Anyone with a computer can see it, it's always there, 24/7. Makes the victim feel even more trapped, unable to escape from it.

Dr Rilke's mention of a 'group assault' is something that makes cyberbullying a markedly different experience to a physical attack. When Taylor, for example, asks her mother 'How am I going to face going to school on Monday'? she alludes to her suspicion that her bullying would continue over the weekend and at school her humiliation would only exacerbate. The inescapability and constant presence of the cyberbully in the life of the victim likens this character to other screen monsters who can't simply be outrun rather, have the ability to effortlessly traverse standard barriers. Some kinship, for example, exists with undead monsters like ghosts and poltergeists – travelling easily through space and time – as well as shapeshifter monsters morphing into new presentations dependent on context, each possessing special abilities to target victims who can't easily evade them. Further, the idea of cyberbullying leading a victim to suicide – as transpired for Taylor and, in fact, as occurs in a range of cyberbullying films (Rosewarne 2016a; Rosewarne 2017) – also relates to narratives whereby a monster is linked to coerced suicide attempts. From *The Exorcist* (Friedkin, 1973), to the more recent *Bird Box* (Bier, 2018), the horror genre offers several examples where monsters cajole victims to take their own lives. In *Cyberbully*, Taylor's cyberbullying episode functions this way, whereby an ordinary, well-adjusted student became suicidal directly because of her interactions with a new breed of monster.

While bullying has occurred throughout history and thus is not an internet age phenomenon, *Cyberbully* nonetheless, frames the technology as the instigator in several ways. First, Taylor is given a laptop for her birthday: throughout the narrative, the laptop is positioned as the very thing that put Taylor in a position of vulnerability. Second, social media is presented as the primary means by which cyberbullying is encouraged. Here, the technology is framed as akin to monsters who find victims through completely normal activities thus turning the ordinary into the horrific: monsters, for example, target victims through their television consumption in films like *The Twonky* (Oboler, 1953), *Poltergeist* (Hooper, 1982), and *A Nightmare on Elm Street 3: Dream Warriors* (Russell, 1987). Such scenarios are extra scary precisely because the situations are so very ordinary. The same thing occurs in *Cyberbully* whereby the tool teens use for recreation and entertainment is also the means by which they are made vulnerable. Such narratives also exploit the long history of human technophobia and, more recently, *cyberphobia*, whereby modern technology is demonized and positioned as making us especially vulnerable.

A theme apparent in academic discussions about the internet is the idea of cyberspace as a world of its own: that online activity is perceived as different from other parts of life – time moves differently, people act differently, and different rules apply – and thus, anonymity or alternate identities can be considered as something separate from reality and from the real self (Rosewarne, 2016a; Rosewarne, 2016b; Rosewarne, 2016c). One theory that helps to explain these concepts is dissociative imagination whereby 'users make the mistake of assuming virtual worlds are make-believe spaces ... suggesting that their virtual life is a game where the rules don't apply to real life' (Gray 2014: 42). Such thinking is certainly visible in *Cyberbully* as apparent in a scene where Samantha attempts to explain how she managed to bully someone she loved: 'When you do it online, you don't even realise you're doing it. You can't see the other people and you can do or say anything and it doesn't seem to matter. It doesn't feel real'. This idea of the internet blurring reality and, in turn, creating news means for vulnerability has much relevance to film's long history of presenting dreams as a special space by which monsters can access victims. Films such as *The Cabinet of Dr. Caligari* (Wiene, 1920), *Wizard of Oz* (Fleming, 1939), *A Nightmare on Elm Street* (Craven, 1984) and *Dead Awake* (Guzman, 2016) each present sleep – and thus the real/fantasy blur of the subconscious – as a unique site of vulnerability. Cyberspace therefore, similarly, becomes a kind of nightmare-scape and a special site where people are made uniquely vulnerable based on the impossibility of completely avoiding falling asleep and thus ever completely avoiding vulnerability.

Just as cyberspace creates new places and ways for people to be victimized, it also changes the *who* of the victim and perpetrator. A key characteristic of cyberbullying in real life and on screen is the changed face of the bully and the bullied. In the pre-internet era, the dynamics of bullying were relatively clear cut: the larger and stronger kid preyed upon the weaker one. There was also a distinctly gendered component to this: the physical bullying scenario almost always involved a bigger boy picking on a smaller one. The internet overhauled this dynamic. Nowadays, anybody with internet access can be bullied; equally, anyone with access to such technology can become the bully.

In *Cyberbully*, Taylor and Samantha each fulfilled the roles of being cyberbullies as well as being victims of it. The film opens with the girls making snide comments on social media, thus establishing from the opening scenes that recreational bullying is normal. Both girls bully but both girls also become victims of bullying themselves. Samantha's bullying of Taylor has already been discussed; Samantha herself has been a victim of nasty remarks from classmates in a school chatroom, and at the same time she created an alternate persona online to befriend Taylor and then spread rumours about her; Samantha is both bullied and a bully. Samantha in fact, verbalizes this at one-point reflecting, 'You know, I'd always thought of bullies as people at school who pick on you'. At another point Samantha says, 'It's hard to picture myself like that'. For Samantha it was difficult to reconcile the impression she held of herself with the person she had become online: she was able to not only alter her identity online but even conceive of herself as two separate people.

The idea of new perpetrators – more specifically Taylor's discovery that her cyberbully was Samantha – and also the revelation that Samantha was, herself, a victim of cyberbullying, relates to two key ways monsters are presented on screen: one, the monster being closer than we might imagine, and two, the screen's tendency to pathologize them. First, in several films, by the conclusion of the narrative the monster is revealed to be someone known to the victim: in *Psycho* (Hitchcock, 1960) for example, the perpetrator turns out to be Norman via his dissociate personality disorder; in *Sleepaway Camp* (Hiltzik, 1983), one of the terrified girls turns out to be the killer after all. In such examples, the terror emerges from the notion that identifying a monster is not always possible – particularly when they take on human form – thus amplifying fears that *anyone* could be a monster.

Second, the idea of presenting monsters as such because of past trauma is apparent in films like *Psycho*, as well as *Carrie* (De Palma, 1976), *Silence of the Lambs* (Demme, 1991), the *A Nightmare on Elm Street* films, etc., whereby monsters are presented as having traumatic childhoods – thus a link is presented between the bad things done to them and the bad things they do to others – and are indicative of the modern horror film which attempts to *explain* evil rather than just document its existence. With every new technology, new fears are spawned and film has stepped up to offer us new representations. Whether cinema normalizes and encourages behaviour like cyberbullying or simply mirrors such monsters is a conversation for another essay, suffice to say, the internet era has delivered us a cast of new monsters and film has given us a way to give them shape and form with the opportunity to scare us over and over again.

Anthony Curtis Adler

Lady Gaga: Stefani Joanne Angelina Germanotta (1986–present)

Nothing could be said about monsters in general. There is no monster in general, no individual monsters; there can only be individuals when there are species. There is only the monster in its singularity. This suggests the affinity that binds the celebrity and the monster; that makes every monster into a kind of celebrity, and every celebrity into a kind of monster. For the celebrity is also always a singularity. The calling card of celebrity, and hence of celebrity monstrosity, is *ecce homo, ecce monstrum*. Yet if there is no celebrity in general, no monster in general, there is a celebrity of celebrities, whose career has been consecrated to the exposition of fame; a celebrity monster of celebrity monsters. Lady Gaga, of course, the 'mother monster', and hence 'mother of all monsters', 'monster of all monsters'. What does she show us? What is her warning, her monstrous monition? Lady Gaga and her entourage pass through Springfield.

Everyone there suffers low self esteem – melancholia, one could say – but Lisa Simpson most of all. After discovering she was the least popular student in her school, she attempted to salvage her reputation through a fake social media account. Her ruse was discovered, making her a complete outcast. When Lisa's suffering appears to her in an empathic vision, Lady Gaga stops the train. She treats the town of Springfield to an impromptu concert, singing 'You're all my little monsters'. Everyone swoons over her; even the town's old fogies, even Smithers and Mr. Burns, even an actual monster, have become Gaga's little monsters.

Only Lisa remains, despite a hint of a smile, unmoved. Gaga then whisks Lisa off and has a tête-à-tête in her bedroom. Lisa eventually calls out Gaga's narcissism. Lady Gaga leaves Springfield dejected; she has, for the first time,

Figure 25. Lady Gaga's train passes through Springfield. *The Simpsons*, 'Lisa Goes Gaga' (Season 23, Episode 22), directed by Matthew Schofield (20th Television, 2012).

Figure 26. An impromptu concert at the Springfield train station. *The Simpsons*, 'Lisa Goes Gaga' (Season 23, Episode 22), directed by Matthew Schofield (20th Television, 1989-present).

failed in her mission of spreading relentless positivity. Finally, though, Lisa sees that Lady Gaga, by becoming a focal point for her hatred, has in fact rescued her from it; freed her to see her own good traits and love herself. She has become a little monster after all.

When this episode aired on 20 May 2012, *The Simpsons* had reached the close of its twenty-third season. During two decades that, bridging millennia, witnessed profound changes in the shape of the world and media culture – the collapse of the Soviet Union, the transformation of China into an economic superpower, the rise of personal computing, the Internet and social media – there has been one constant thing: week-in week-out we have sat down before our TVs and watched Homer, Marge, Lisa, Bart, and baby Maggie sit down in front of theirs. We have changed, our world has changed – "and so, indeed, has their world. Their TV and ours have become flat screens. And yet they have remained the same. Eternal forms, eternal verities within the flux of historical time. This exposes the paradoxical logic of celebrity: most iconic can only be those celebrities who, no longer given over to the frailty of the flesh, transcend the element of time. Kermit the Frog, Bart Simpson, Mickey Mouse. And in just this way, moreover, the celebrity special – and Lady Gaga's is indeed the only *Simpsons* episode ('Lisa goes Gaga') to incorporate the celebrity's name – serves a special function in the phantasmagoria of mass-mediatic consciousness.

It is a magical moment: the collision of two ontological domains, unbridgeable and yet somehow correlated. The human celebrity, who always remains something that has emerged, come into existence – speaking to historical time itself as a time of becoming even while returning again and again to the familiar order of repetition – briefly enters into the world of the eternal repetition of everyday life in the estranged familiarity through which alone it can present itself – ourselves – to us. The celebrity literally enters our living room and then our bedroom.

But only insofar as we have crossed over to the other side, having abandoned actual real life to the creative-destructive dynamism of historical time, and find our salvation in celluloid or digital abstraction. In the cartoon and puppet world, by contrast, there are only monsters, and every monster is a kind of celebrity. Homer, Marge, Bart, Lisa and all the rest are celebrity-monsters becoming human. Lady Gaga is the human (Stefani Joanne Angelina

Figure 27. Lady Gaga tries to console Lisa in her bedroom. *The Simpsons*, 'Lisa Goes Gaga' (Season 23, Episode 22), directed by Matthew Schofield (20th Television, 1989–present).

Germanotta) becoming monster; reborn as monster-celebrity. As mother-monster, celebrity of celebrities, monster of monsters.

This impossible symmetry, this super-star asymmetry, is the strangeness of our situation. Before, when we spoke of monsters, the monster was a kind of singularity that, appearing as an exception to the natural order, betokened the eternal providential order hidden behind it. Now there are only monsters. Neither nature nor providence, neither the transient nor the eternal. These exist only as a constellation of fixed types or an enchainment of singularities.

'You're all my little monsters'. Everything depends on this possessive and diminutive. In a world where there are only celebrities and only monsters – where everyone, even if they are no one, has a social media presence and must function as their own PR team; where everyone has a retinue of followers, even if only their closest friends and family – then the true measure of celebrity is the measure of asymmetry. The gesture of celebrity is to bring the little celebrities, the little monsters, under its fold; to claim them for its own. Crucial to this is the act of naming, which, according to a *Vice* article, began during the concert tour of 2009, and had a double function: it not only defined the fans as an 'us' opposed to the 'them' of the rest of the world, but it also 'grouped them all together in a way that made sense online' (Hall 2017). Lady Gaga's little monsters soon became a force to be reckoned with; millennial devotees using their tech-savvy to proselytize for their lady. There is even a book, titled *Monster Loyalty*, which, devoted to Lady Gaga's marketing genius, has stressed this interactive dimension (Huba 2013). Yet despite the profound asymmetry in the relation between the mother monster and her minions, there remains at least a trace of reciprocity: sometimes Gaga will respond personally to her fan's tweets; she hugs them methodically in the airport or outside her concerts.

Lady Gaga has thus become second mother, a monster mother, to her baby monsters (See Click, Lee & Holladay 2013). If the first parents are merely custodians of social norms, of the non-monstrous appearance that will be shown to the world – conformity to the recognized and acceptable genres of social being – Lady Gaga becomes a second mother to that other child, the child that is, or rather has learned to think of itself as, 'scary', 'ugly', 'stupid', 'unlovable', 'overweight', 'hairy'. This is the child kept in the dark and in the closet; repressed in the name of a sexual and social maturity that has always been a matter of suppressing this inner child, and inner truth, in the name of convention, respectability, the values of the surface, of society.

As this second mother, Lady Gaga is the mother of becoming rather than being. The first mother, of course, starts from becoming and leads the child to being; to assuming a stable place in the world. The second mother starts with being and the suffering that it entails – the suffering of roles that do not fit; expectations that do not match; of the bullying, from children and parents, that enforces socio-sexual norms – and leads her children towards becoming. She oversees a different norm, a counter norm or anti-norm: the norm of becoming, which dictates that every 'monster' must find the deep-hidden secret of transformation into their monstrosity, literally from Jekyll (nothing if not respectable, the first mother's dream, a medical doctor!) to Hyde. The first mother starts with nature and leads to second nature, the 'virtuous' habits of moderation – and moderation, going back to Aristotle, is the very essence of the non-monstrous. The second mother starts from second nature and leads back to another first nature: becoming in its becoming. And hence she cannot help but claim to be more original than the original mother.

One is reminded of another episode, 'Bart's Inner Child' (Season 5, Episode 7). Bart, during an attempted therapeutic intervention, is 'discovered' by a self-help guru, Brad Goodman, who treats his mischievous irreverence ('I do it because I feel like it') as a model of authentic self-actualization. Children preserved in endless childhood, Bart and Lisa provide the model, respectively, for those two psychic forces, the id and the superego – these two 'inner children' who will get crushed into submission with the healthy adult ego development. Thus the *Simpsons* offers uncanny insight into the mass-psychodynamics of modern celebrity culture. The id-child, the id-monster, as superficially defiant as it is of the social order, will always find the praise of the masses, whereas the superego-monster, in its perfectionism, the infinite demands to which it holds itself, will be excoriated, banished, turned into a pariah. Perhaps not surprisingly, Trump is president, while the SJW (Social Justice Warrior) has become the new outcast.

Trump and Lady Gaga, indeed, are both consummate masters of social networking, whose fan bases, diametrically opposed, converge in feeling deplorable. Both, in turn, speak not just to one little inner monster, but to two; the id-monster and the superego-monster. Their monstrous claim derives from the rapprochement that they achieve between these. The Trump-rapprochement: the id takes the form of 'political incorrectness', hatred of what is other, while the superego, doubling the id, sets itself up as border guard. The Gaga-rapprochement: the superego-monster turns against itself, purifies itself of *all* judgement. The only law to remain is the law of infinite acceptance; the judgement of non-judgement. Both rapprochements, however, gain their force by bypassing the development of the ego, mature adulthood. They both have a regressive characteristic.

Lady Gaga's second manifesto, the 'Manifesto of the Mother Monster', the opening speech of the video 'Born this Way' (2011), presents this logic with an admirable precision. Far away in a government-owned alien territory, a magnificent, magical, infinite, eternal birth took place. A new race emerged – without prejudice, without judgement, infinitely free. But another birth also took place: the birth of evil. The eternal mother herself was split into two – two mothers – torn in agony between the two forces. And as easy as it might seem to gravitate 'instantly and unwaveringly towards good', she nevertheless asks herself: 'How can I protect something so perfect without evil'?

Like Jean-Jacques Rousseau, the exemplary celebrity of eighteenth-century reading culture, Gaga incessantly reminds us that we were 'born this way'; she recalls us to our original nature. Yet Rousseau's monstrosity confronted him only towards the end of his life, as mirror image of his naturalness; his naturalness and honesty seen through the moralizing, conventional eyes of the world. Thus, in the *Dialogues*, 'Jean-Jacques', the monstrous public-image, confronts 'Rousseau', the author of the books. No synthesis results; only madness (Rousseau 1990). Lady Gaga, in contrast, will seek a kind of ultimate solution to the primary division. This reveals itself as a political-theological cliché: evil – nothing else than judgement and prejudice, pre-judgement – will be necessary to protect the good. Yet this solution is only possible through a fateful transformation. For Rousseau, following a Cartesian trajectory, the site of division is the self. The self divides into the authentic self and its public image – into the self that belongs to itself and the self that has been consigned to others; into *amour de soi* and *amour propre*, interiority and exteriority, speech and writing (Rousseau 1990). For Gaga, it is not the self that divides, but the mother. Or rather, the becoming-mother, the mother-in-becoming, herself becomes this division – between the womb as the mythic site of primordial unity, and the placenta, the womb's wall; the intricate, ingenious biological mechanism that serves at once to nourish, facilitate metabolic exchange, and as an immunological barrier; the temporary organ that alone allows for the womb's myth of primal unity.

According to this Gaga-solution, there is only becoming; being is a mere hypostasis, a passing caesura, of becoming. Outside and inside have been folded together into a logic that, having taken upon itself a logic of exception, allows no exceptions to this logic. The state, and the violence of the state, has not only been approved by the mother, but has been taken into her essence. In the name of the myth of non-judgement, infinite acceptance and infinite freedom, the existing order, the placental organ of the state, the order of the law, posterior but actually prior to the womb's mitosis, has been granted an absolute legitimization.

Lisa Simpson's resistance to Lady Gaga, and to her message of positivity, may now be seen in the proper light. It is the resistance of the one who says no to the beguiling, seductive synthesis in which the same old law and order (the law of the father, after all) is offered in the name of the mother and the protection of her monsters – or indeed, as the law of the mother, a matri-archy rather than patri-archy. If, in the end, she herself seems to capitulate, going

Gaga, becoming another little monster, this is perhaps merely a tactical gesture. Or indeed, just as the healthy development of the child, according to psychoanalysis, demands that its unbounded, monstrous love find a proper object, so too must the germinal revolutionary find an object for her hate.

Of all monsters, celebrity monsters are certainly the most comforting. For they allow us to recognize something in ourselves that does not fit together with that clean, dependable, safe image that orients our everyday lives – the image, the face that we show to the world and to ourselves. Yet they also restore this monstrosity to a new, and even more iconic familiarity; the monster inside becomes the iconic face of the celebrity monster, which, in turn, comforts and coddles it. This suggests the specific role that the celebrity monster will play in the affective economy of contemporary capitalism. If, for the first time, we find ourselves to exist at the very limit of the natural order within which human life has been inscribed, we also find ourselves faced with a becoming that, no longer merely occurring at the periphery, calls contemporary existence into question.

Alexandra Heller-Nicholas

The Slit-Mouthed Woman: *Carved* (Shiraishi, 2007)

If ever there was a category of horror monster that seamlessly slid into the popular imagination, it is surely that spawned from the strange, dark, ubiquitous realm of the urban legend. From the *A Nightmare on Elm Street* franchise (Various, 1984–2010) to that literally called *Urban Legend* (Blanks, 1998) itself, horror films predicated around dark mythologies linked directly to the world in which their characters are diegetically situated are far from rare in the genre. As discussed here, urban legend horror films and their iconic monsters populate examples across a range of different historical moments and cultural contexts.

As Mikel Koven states in his foundational book *Film, Folklore and Urban Legends* (2008), 'Urban legends, those apocryphal stories told in university dormitories and around campfires about hook-handed psycho-killers and boyfriends discovered hanging above the parked cars, are a form of oral literature' (2008: 99). A transnational phenomenon, as Jan Harold Brunvand notes, 'urban legends seem to be truly international in their distribution' and 'are surely found in virtually every modern nation' (2001: xxiii). Likewise, despite the rise of the Internet proving to be 'a major conduit for the spread of once-strictly-oral urban legends' (Brunvand 2001: xxi), urban legends have a long history; from the urban legend of 'Spring-heeled Jack' in nineteenth-century Britain – a 'tall, dark cloaked figure who pounced on individuals, predominantly women' (Woodbridge 2012: 1) – to the more famous so-called 'demon barber of Fleet Street' Sweeney Todd in nineteenth-century London (see Mack 2007), urban legends are by no means a particularly recent phenomenon.

Despite their frequently being overlooked in critical discourse Koven makes a convincing case for why urban legends are so perfectly suited to the horror genre especially, noting: 'these orally circulated stories are copyright free, and therefore horror film producers do not have to pay any rights for the stories, and, second, urban legends are good, gross, frightening, and suspenseful stories' (2008: 11). There is an aspect of the "tried and tested" here; for urban legends themselves to endure and evolve as 'a form of oral literature' (Koven 2008: 11), they must necessarily contain something – some element or "hook" – that remains intriguing to those who maintain the intrinsic virality of the tales, accounting for their endurance.

This may superficially at least be identified in what we might think as their "potential realistic proximity" to our own lived experience; in the United States, urban legends about college life and campfires are arguably potent in part because it is an experience familiar to the very people marked by hearing them, so much so they feel the compulsion to pass the tales on. This question of verisimilitude is central to the endurance of urban legends and the impact of their legacies. Of all the urban legend horror monsters whose presence is so notable amongst the cannon of the genre's menacing forces, those whose origins can be traced – however tenuously – to the "real world" are the ones that are the most critically intriguing, and often the most enduring.

For instance, horror films including *Candyman* (Rose, 1992), *Carved: The Slit-Mouthed Woman* (Shiraishi, 2007) and *The Bye Bye Man* (Title, 2017) each in different ways are inspired by real-world factors (be they events or places), reimagined for the screen in fictional horror stories. But this question of "fiction" itself has proven to be highly elastic and fluid when it comes to the urban legend monster on film; the documentary *Cropsy* (Zeman and Brancaccio, 2009) is told by filmmakers who grew up haunted by the legend of the local boogey man of the film's title. Their investigation leads them instead to the real Andre Rand (1944–), a very much alive child kidnapper who was convicted of the disappearance of a number of children and at the time imprisoned on Rikers Island. On the flip side, the real world impact of the so-called "creepy-pasta" Internet boogeyman Slender Man was headline news in 2014 when it was cited as the inspiration behind a horrific stabbing of a young teen by two other girls in Wisconsin. While a fictional creation, the invented urban legend surrounding Slender Man was and continues to be solidified in web series like *Marble Hornets* (2009–2014) and films such as *Always Watching* (Moran, 2015) and *Slender Man* (White, 2018). And of course, one of the most famous films of the late twentieth century – *The Blair Witch Project* (Sánchez and Myrick, 1999) – was presented in a found footage documentary style to imply authenticity, the students investigating the urban legend of the eponymous monster famously meeting an unfortunate end. As has been widely documented, when the film was originally released many struggled to distinguish if the events depicted were real or not (see Heller-Nicholas 2014).

While this chapter will focus primarily on the Japanese horror film *Carved: The Slit-Mouthed Woman* to emphasize the global ubiquity of urban legend monsters and to underscore how they can be framed with specific ideological intent through the genres familiar codes and conventions, both *Candyman* and *The Bye Bye Man* are worth discussing briefly beforehand. With notably similar titles, these films evoke child-like descriptions of nightmare beings – the unsophisticated language of the titles speak of an intrinsic regression to an infantilized state of mind where monsters lurking in closets or underneath the bed are an acceptable and rational belief.

With a story about a white academic Helen (Virginia Madsen) and her black friend Bernadette (Kasi Lemmons) investigating the 'Candyman' urban legend of the title. This 'Candyman' is Daniel Robitaille (Tony Todd), an educated artist from the late seventeenth century and son of an ex-slave who is murdered for falling in love with a white woman. The site of his death is where Chicago's Cabrini-Green housing project now stands, an actual real-world location which the film emphasizes is riddled by black gang-related violence. As Helen and Bernadette research the urban legend that 'Candyman' appears if you say his name five times, they discover – after a number of iconic and extremely violent vignettes – that the legend is in fact true, as 'Candyman' effectively courts Helen to be his otherworldly lover.

As Kirsten Moana Thompson observes, Candyman 'circulates across differing boundaries of

Figure 28. Tony Todd as the Candyman. *Candyman*, directed by Bernard Rose (Propaganda Films, 1992).

class, race and gender in Chicago ... that ... links a supernatural tale to the horrors of a racist past and the poverty and urban segregation of many African Americans today' (2007: 59). Notably, the original short story *Candyman* is based on – British author Clive Barker's *The Forbidden* from 1985 – was originally set at Liverpool's Spector Street Estate, likewise a public housing development for lower-class people, the difference being that while Spector Street was effectively a white ghetto, the relocating of the story to Chicago's Cabrini-Green required a shift in focus to urban black crime and poverty (Hoeveler 2007: 102). This shift in racial focus, as Robin R. Means Coleman is quick to point out is fundamental to *Candyman* as it 'play[s] ... on fears of the big Black boogeyman coming in and taking away a white woman' (2011: 189); as such, she concludes that 'in the end, this is a movie about celebrating white womanhood'(2011: 190).

While *Candyman's* fictional urban legend and its monster is attached explicitly to a real-world place – Chicago's Cabrini-Green housing project and all the accompanying racial, social and economic implications that space brings with it – *The Bye Bye Man* purports to be based on a true story. Adapted to the screen from a chapter from Robert Damon Schneck's 2005 book *The President's Vampire: Strange-but-True Tales of the United States of America*, an anthology of 'eight different (allegedly true) campfire tales about ghosts, monsters, murderers, and hoaxes' (Squires 2017). As Schneck tells it, he heard the story from a friend who claimed to have been haunted by the monstrous presence, a supernaturally gifted blind albino serial killer active in the early mid-twentieth century whose crimes were spawned initially out of revenge for being bullied in their youth. In the film, this is reimagined in the contemporary day with less focus on the Bye Bye Man's back story, and instead more on the three teens who evoke him simply by saying his name. The film's catch-phrase – repeated

Figure 29. Doug Jones as the Bye Bye Man. *The Bye Bye Man*, directed by Stacy Title (STX Entertainment, 2017)

throughout the film – is 'don't think it, don't say it', the implication being that it is the very utterance of his name that brings him to life. While reviews of the film were broadly negative,[1] from a critical perspective what is so intriguing about the film is how explicitly it articulates what fundamentally lies at the core of the mechanics of the most enduring legends to continue: we have to believe in them. As Koven shrewdly observes, 'it is insufficient for folklorists examining popular culture to leave their discourse at the level of merely identifying folkloric motifs within film and television texts' (2008: 79), but – far more importantly – 'Like the legends themselves, filmic and televisual representations of urban legendry are a useful barometer to contemporary social norms and beliefs' (2008: 80). As I shall now explore in relation to the cult J-horror film *Carved: The Slit-Mouthed Woman*, this phenomenon is far from uniquely North American.

Western scholars such as David Schaefer have long compared the history of Japanese folktales called *setsuwa* with more contemporary urban legends, noting a number of parallels; they are short, primarily an oral tradition, and lack evidence of an original source (see Schaefer 1990). One need only look towards the popularity of the J-horror *Ringu* franchise to find a famous example of the impact of urban legends in Japanese popular culture, its successful American remakes underscoring the transnational flows that mark the phenomenon.

Cult Japanese horror director Kōji Shiraishi is a horror auteur who likes to shock, and his *modus operandi* generally (although not always) manifests at the intersection of his unflinching approach towards the viscera of body horror, and an almost signature fascination with the blurring of the fictional and non-fictional in the stories he chooses to tell. In terms of the latter, this is most overt in his consistent return to the found footage horror subgenre with films such as *Noroi: The Curse* (2005), *Occult* (*Okaruto*, 2009), and *Shirome* (2010), *Noroi* in particular – with its mountain of writhing undead aborted foetus-ghosts – perhaps typifying Shiraishi's less-than-subtle approach to body horror.

In the West, Shiraishi may be best known for his non-found footage horror films *Carved: The Slit-Mouthed Woman* (*Kuchisake-onna*) and *Grotesque*

---

1   See the film's *Rotten Tomatoes* rankings: <https://www.rottentomatoes.com/m/the_bye_bye_man>.

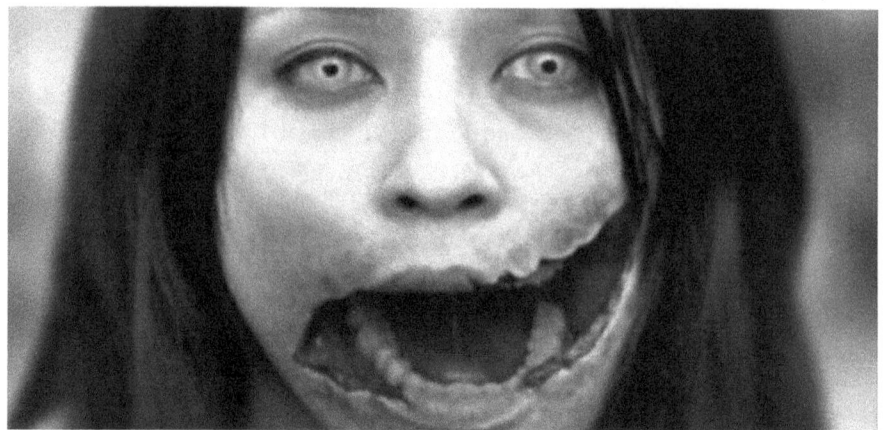

Figure 30. Miki Mizuno as the Slit-Mouthed Woman. Carved: *The Slit-Mouthed Woman*, directed by Kōji Shiraishi (Tornado Film, 2007).

(*Gurotesuku*; 2009). While *Grotesque* is a satisfyingly gory horror film for those whose tastes lie in such terrain, *Carved* importantly shares a fascination with the hazy grey area between fiction and non-fiction as Shiraishi's found footage horror films, but here through his focus on a real-world Japanese urban legend rather than on the formal and stylistic replication of documentary realism. The Japanese urban legend of *Kuchisake-onna* sparked a highly publicized moral panic in the country that reached a crescendo in 1979 when a number of unsubstantiated rumours culminated in the formation of a core narrative that – despite nuances in regional variations (Foster 2009: 185) – largely held the figure responsible for a number of tragedies. These include whispers of a never-verified coroner's report that claimed a woman who looked like the *Kuchisake-onna* was killed in an automobile accident while she pursued children, assumed to be potential victims (Leddon 2014: 43); so great was the belief in the threat of the *Kuchisake-onna* at the time that children in the Ibaraki Prefecture were told to keep away from anyone wearing a mask (Foster 2009: 185). Michael Dylan Foster has observed that the urban legend 'had a profound effect on Japanese life', concluding that the fears rose from increasing anxieties in the national psyche at the time linked to 'rapid urbanization and the breakdown of traditional village communities' (2009: 186).

Shiraishi's filmic reimaging of the urban legend that drove these events thus position the film in a fascinating relationship to the belief systems that underscore urban legends as identified by Koven. Despite the difference in cultural contexts – both *The Bye Bye Man* and *Candyman* can be correlated to real-world urban legends like Bloody Mary[2] – a 'game' of verbal utterance lies at the heart of the *Kuchisake-onna* urban legend; the monster is brought to life through the spoken word, perhaps echoing Koven's identification of urban legends themselves as a form of oral literature. For Yoki Inagi, the ritual encounter at the heart of the *Kuchisake-onna* urban legend played out generally as follows:

> A tall woman with long black hair in a trench coat wearing a large white mask would walk up and ask a person, 'Am I pretty'?... If the person replied 'Yes', the woman would take off her mask and reveal her mouth widely slit all the way up to her ears, asking, 'even with this'? And she would slit the person's mouth and/or stab the person to death with a sickle. (Inagi 2007: 176–7)

Taking the *Kuchisake-onna* and the national memory of the moral panic it caused decades earlier, in *Carved* Shiraishi powerfully incorporates the urban legend into his story about the horrors of the very real trauma experienced by victims of domestic violence. Following a group of school girls who are spooked by the urban legend, Shiraishi ultimately configures the *Kuchisake-onna* as a kind of virus that spreads between mothers, causing them to abuse their children (according to the films logic, then, this is why the mask is so crucial to her iconography; to stop the virus from spreading). As Inagi observed, this combination of the supernatural urban legend of the *Kuchisake-onna* with the very real phenomenon of family violence created a remarkable impact: perhaps the storyline suggests that just as the tale of the *Kuchisake-onna* is horrifying, 'it can be equally horrifying in real life when a person who is supposed to be a guardian turns abusive and harmful' (2007: 178).

The endurance and cultural impact of the urban legend monster thus intrinsically unites notions of belief, orality, virality and a conscious destabilizing of categories of fact and fiction. When urban legend monsters are brought

---

2   Also called Mary Worth rituals, 'Bloody Mary' is an urban legend that 'involve[s] the ritual summoning of a witch in a mirror' (De Vos, 1996: 58).

to life through the codes and conventions of the horror film, across a range of different cultures and with a striking diversity of ideological themes, these figures are granted enormous power. Their symbolic impact overtly straddles the divide between fiction and fantasy and far more earthly, familiar aspects significantly marked by their very familiarity and 'closeness' to the lived experience of their intended audience. Yet despite this, as horror films these stories can flow almost seamlessly into cultures very different to those in which they originated; there can be no denying that for non-Japanese audiences, for example, *Carved* is simply a terrifying and very powerful horror movie with a strong, undeniable message about the impact of domestic violence on both its victims and perpetrators. The stories may evolve and adapt to different historical and cultural contexts, but the symbolic and visceral force of these urban legend monsters speak to something shared by all of us, regardless of how close we are to the specificity of their origins.

W. Scott Poole

Melmoth: *Melmoth* (Perry, 2018)

The very first word of Sara Perry's 2018 novel *Melmoth* makes the aggressive demand that the reader 'Look'! The paragraph that follows, an evocation of both ancient and contemporary Prague, wilfully obscures the power this imperative acquires as we walk the novel's lengthening shadows. Perry's tale will force us to recognize the nature of horror, the horror of both looking and failing to look. She puts the demand that the reader witness the world's pain into the mouth of the peculiar monster she evokes for us.

Perry intentionally portrays Melmoth as a lurid notion, a horror flick shadow watching us, something horrible just out of our line of sight that we might catch an eerie glimpse of if we quickly look behind us, a sort of embodied jump scare. However, as we follow the bloody footprints of the damned wraith through history, the novel becomes a reflection on the pain of millions and the way in which we may, almost but not quite unwittingly, are also implicated.

The popularity of horror at the present cultural moment allows the entertainment industry to churn out monsters that range from the terrifying to the boring, monsters that are embodiments of explosive violence and monsters that force us to sympathize with their plight. Perry has done something difficult in locating the monster elsewhere in popular horror culture. She has brought to life a monster that asks us to look at the problem of evil and to recognize our own capacity for what Hannah Arendt described in 1963 as 'the banality of evil' (135), and our own complicity with inhumane, indeed lethal, systems and social structures. Seldom does this happen because we carry in our hearts the Miltonic sentiment of 'Evil, Be Thou my Good'. It's just easier to go along to get along, to simply refuse to look, or perhaps look when suffering appears at a safe distance in time or place.

The need to look perhaps has a special meaning for anyone interested in teasing out the politics of horror. In fact, it raises questions for both the casual and the deeply devoted fan of horror films, horror fiction, and horror culture more generally. Why do we look at the violence and cruelty that plays an inherent role in the genre? What do we want from sagas of vicious disembowelments that we cannot get from our newsfeed? What does it even mean to look, to watch, to play voyeur to pain?

One answer frequently given suggests a purgative effect, essentially the theory of catharsis that stretches all the way back to Aristotelian conceptions of tragedy. Horror offers a social imaginary where we can place our nightmares, close them up in books, click off our screens and resume our normal life having had a dire emotional experience that allows us to clear our heads of real-world fears. As such it is not precisely escapism, because we are actually encountering nuanced feelings of dread, terror, sympathy, and rage. We are simply diffusing our emotions in the field of fantasy and entertainment rather than having an explosive, and usually inconclusive, effusion of grief and anger at the latest mass shooting or the most recent story people murdered, maimed, and made refugees by war.

This may be one of the varied effects of viewing cruelty and murder as entertainment. Yet the discussion of horror often moves towards the suggestion that the repeated viewing of cruelty can have a numbing effect. Susan Sontag has suggested, in a short book entitled *Regarding the Pain of Others*, that one can 'become habituated to the horror of certain images' (2003: 82). Sontag insists that the flood of photography, digital material, and up-to-the-minute news of brutalities around the world – carefully curated and selected by the censorship of consensus, political atmosphere, and 'good taste' – creates 'a culture of spectatorship [that] neutralizes the moral force of photographs of atrocity' (2003: 105).

A recent article appearing in the American journal *In These Times* features a cover with a headline in all caps 'DON'T LOOK AWAY', with the caption 'The war in Yemen is our war'. The substance of the article by Alex Kane, featuring photographs of the aftermath of a bombing of a market in Sanaa, Yemen, concerns the responsibility the United States bears for arming, and advising, the Saudi military in a war on the way to becoming one of the great humanitarian disasters of the early twenty-first century. The pleading nature of the title's rhetoric assumes that the reader might be inclined to look away, or worse, see the violence as an abstract tragedy with no agency behind it, accentuated by the passive voice that speaks in our heads of victims with no real perpetrators. Sarah Perry's Melmoth comes to tortured life creating a narrative that demands a look, a gaze, both more intense and more brutal, something with more ballast than empathy.

Despite its title, Melmoth really has only slender links to Charles Marturin's 1820 Gothic novel *Melmoth the Wanderer*. Perry constructs the story around the experience of Helen Franklin, an English woman living a monkish existence in Prague. She works as a translator, trudging daily from the sad apartment she shares with a garrulous and mean-spirited elderly woman, to work at the Czech National Library. Perry seeps all the possible romanticism she can from Helen's life. She does not translate the works of great Bohemian writers like Kubin or Hrabel; instead she transcribes instruction manuals for appliances and power tools. Even worse, not only does she engage in a kind of self-immolation of her own happiness, she does so because she believes denying oneself happiness is an act of penance.

Helen forms an unlikely friendship, the only human connection she appears to have, with a scholar named Karel and his English wife Thea. Karel mysteriously disappears leaving Helen with a sheaf of documents that are essentially a small library of historical cruelty and violence, presided over by Melmoth (also called Melmotka). Melmoth is a withered, ancient, creature who wanders the world, gazing at it's terrors, choosing to come to some and offer her dubious companionship. The witness, as the novel describes her, does not lunge at her victims from out of mirrors or chase them down dark hallways. She does something that in every way seems more chilling... she watches them. Helen first experiences her as 'the pricking sensation of an implacable eye fixed on a bare neck' (Perry 2018: 55).

Cursed for being the only one of the female witnesses of Christ's resurrection to deny it, Melmoth must now play the part of godmother to human pain, to atrocity, and ultimately to the reality of evil. Her wanderings across the earth must last until the end of time and she is, in a line that becomes increasingly chilling as the novel progresses, '*so lonely*'. Those that she chooses are themselves suffering from different kinds of loneliness, generally an alienation from both themselves and humanity because of the evil they have done to others.

Critics and readers have overwhelming found pleasure in luxuriating in the Perry's delicate style. Whether describing Prague at the end of Christmastide or the inhumanity of the concentration camp Theresienstadt, there's a near universal consensus that Perry sweeps us out into an inky sea with her prose. Many of the same critics that praise Perry as a master of language also seem wilfully obtuse about her monster, or indeed the need to introduce the supernatural at all into the narrative.

Perhaps the most quibbling criticism appears in the suggestion that Perry's work links atrocities at random without explanation as to why Melmotka makes her appearance to the people and in the places of her choosing. On the one hand, this makes it seem as if some of the nation's most important book critics have never before engaged in a wilful suspension of disbelief. On the other hand, their critique, even if only by accident, guides them into the heart of the novel, the problem of looking and not looking at evil.

Helen's exploration of the documents takes up most of the novel's landscape. She's going about the recognizable Gothic task of piecing together a story out of fragments, a method that appeared in the eighteenth-century Gothic and grew in importance with the work of Shelly, Stoker, and Lovecraft. As readers, we are Helen in the book's early pages. We have got a cracking good mystery, made better by some well-wrought pathos. Perry has used this well-worn trope in a new way, one fit for a twenty-first-century reader surveying the last 100 years of history.

'What nonsense is this-primary sources! A failed opera, a folk song and a novel nobody reads'! exclaims Helen when she first sees a list that her friend has left for her to peruse (Perry 2018: 76). We learn, however, that this very attitude, a desire to find answers that the materials themselves can never sate, makes her a perfect companion to Melmotka the witness. In the dark shadow that haunts her, and the world, we experience the sheer exhaustion and frustration of staring at the world's horrors.

Critics are right that Melmotka comes out of the ether to show us very specific horrors. They are wrong when they suggest there's no rhyme or reason vouchsafed us concerning the horrors selected. There is connective tissue, all of it malignant, between these tales. Melmotka the monster from the ancient past demands her victims understand their role in a kind of viciousness peculiar to recent colonial history. Evil as apathy, evil as unintended consequences, evil as 'just following orders'. The notion of 'following orders' might mean a bureaucratic imperative directly given or the cultural instructions issued to us to keep our heads down, keep our mouth shut, don't risk your reputation ... let evil flourish.

The stories that Perry tells us are miniature narratives of historical fiction, but history with a serrated edge. Through Helen's reading, we meet an aged German who, as a young boy in 1938, sealed the fate of his Jewish neighbours in Prague. He did this in a moment of spite, born out of his envy at their seemingly happier life. Helen also reads the diary of a petty bureaucrat in the Ottoman Empire who quite literally signs the death warrants of thousands of Armenians. He does not set out to commit genocide, he simply does the paperwork on behalf of ancient hatreds weaponized by the modern state.

Melmoth watches and comes for all the perpetrators of these crimes. But she's no avenging angel. She asks that they look! and offers her companionship, the chance to become a terrible witness to history. Perry allows Hoffman, the young German who betrayed his neighbours, a strange attempt at redemption. He has collaborated in their murder, but as the tide turns against the Nazis he helps to save the policeman who actually arrested his friends from Czech partisans. Melmoth leaves him in the loneliness of his guilt. He is, she makes clear, damned to know her in her absence, to witness his own crime throughout his long life. 'What is left for you but suffering'? she asks, and it is an aged Hoffman who remembers her chilling words as he writes them down for Helen, and for us (2018: 142).

'Keep your mind in hell, and despair not' Sara Perry offers this as her story's epigram. She takes the phrase from the memoir of philosopher Gillian Rose, words written in *Love's Work* that tells a story both of speculative philosophy and suffering and dying of cancer. What does this tell us about Melmoth, novel and monster, and the horror of looking or refusing to look?

The question takes us to the political, or possibly the apolitical, implications of Perry's monster. What becomes of the victims of history while we simply bear witness? The exhortation to 'keep ones mind in hell and despair not' could easily seem a sort of sophisticated self-help slogan, a worldview only possible to the small percentage of the world's citizens defended behind border walls and by vast military power, those who do not find themselves in an actual hell but forced to despair.

Sontag's work again helps us to grasp the terror of *Melmoth*. The monster's victims can only think of looking and looking away, feeling sympathy or feeling nothing, engaging in a compassionate act or, often thoughtlessly, committing great evil. Sontag worries that compassion 'withers' and that we must make the attempt to transcend sympathy. She in fact suggests that, rather than letting images of suffering greet us on our various screens along with ads for autos and dish soaps, we 'set aside the sympathy we extend to others beset by war and murderous politics' (2002: 101–3). Instead of looking at them as objects of fear, guilt, or attenuated compassion at a distance, we also gaze at 'how our privileges are located on the same map as their suffering' (Sontag 2002: 101–3). We realize our collaboration. We set our minds in hell but not for the sake of despair.

Then what? The horror of Melmoth offers no traditional call to action. The final two pages of this novel makes a curious demand of the reader, bypasses the Gothic trappings of unsealed documents and archived pain in order to address us directly. Perry lets her monster speak. We are left with more than simply questions. History itself, the way for centuries it has ground human beings, animals, and our ecosystem to dust and bone, approaches us as the lean gaunt Melmoth: 'I was there when you lay in the dark and wondered who stood at the foot of your bed … I know what a fraud you are, what an imposter' (Perry 2018: 271).

We watch breaking news, newsfeeds, war waged in lands we cannot locate on a map, images of refugees dying on land and sea and all so sad (as long as they don't come here). We look at horror films and fiction that reiterate the cruelties of history, in fact restaging them either as subtext or something close to allegory. Melmoth asks us to forego the well-worn notion of 'empathy'. We must bear witness … our minds in hell while not despairing. We must not collaborate. Melmoth watches.

Part III

Cultural Intersections

Benjamin Baumann

Phi Krasue: *Inhuman Kiss* (Mongkolsiri, 2019)

Ghost films are one of the most popular movie genres in the history of Thai cinema and Phi Krasue is definitely the most iconic monster of the genre (Baumann 2013, 2014, 2016; Baumann and Verstappen 2018). In popular media, Phi Krasue is usually depicted as a woman's head floating a few feet above the ground with torn-out entrails dangling beneath it. During these flights, the uncanny creature emits a pulsating greenish or reddish glow that can been seen from afar. Phi Krasue is a nocturnal creature that tries to conceal its monstrous identity during the day by living like an ordinary human being. However, during the night Phi Krasue detaches the human head from the host's body and floats through the night in a search for impure food. It is an insatiable hunger for filth that drives Phi Krasue out of its human body. This uncanny being is attracted by foul smells, especially those of bodily secretions. *Phi Krasue* is feared during childbirth, defecation and in cases of severe sickness – whenever a body emits substantial quantities of 'stinking' matter. Raw meat is its other craving and the being usually feasts on feces and livestock, especially fowl and other small animals it snatches from rice fields, irrigation ditches and sewers. In order to feast on human waste, *Phi Krasue* may enter the body of sick persons through an excreting orifice, whereby the anus represents its favourite point of entry (Hanks 1963: 34). Coprophagy is not only Phi Krasue's most distinguishing feature in oral ghostlore, but also the rationalization why this being is most frequently encountered near toilets and public sewers. The importance of filth for the conceptualization of Phi Krasue is so thorough and explicit that it ultimately prompted Textor to translate Phi Krasue as 'filth ghost' (Textor 1973: 397).

Despite this scholarly classification as a 'ghost', *Phi Krasue* belongs to a distinctive class of monsters known throughout Southeast Asia that are

Figure 31. *Phi Krasue* most recent cinematic incarnation. *Inhuman Kiss*, directed by Sitisiri Mongkolsiri (Transformation Film: 2019).

characterized by attributes European folklore categorizes under the label 'witch' rather than 'ghost' or 'spirit'. As the European concept of witchcraft is largely absent in Southeast Asia, these beings tend to be labelled as 'ghosts' or 'spirits'. These globalized labels distort that these uncanny creatures are not necessarily associated with death (ghosts) or deathlessness (spirits), but rather aspects of living human beings. Other witch-like features are their explicitly female gender, their association with malevolent magical practices, their inclination to live of impure bodily substances, and finally their visible manifestation as flickering lights that fly around at night.

Despite Phi Krasue's popularity in Thailand's public sphere, it is important to emphasize that the being's existence is not limited to the fictitious and metaphorical in films, novels and comic books. YouTube videos and eyewitness accounts in social media and Thai TV shows indicate that these witch-like beings are rather common phenomena in 'real life' too. This impression was confirmed during ethnographic fieldwork in Thailand's Northeast, where the author collected various first- and second-hand narratives of actual encounters with Phi Krasue in rural communities (Baumann 2017).

The consistency of Phi Krasue's depiction in Thailand's popular media goes back to the popularity of cartoonist Thawee Witsanukorn's (1941–2019) graphic novel *Krasue Sao* (Juvenile Krasue) that was published between 1968 and 1973 on a regular basis in a Thai comic magazine and recently re-released in a 600-page two-volume limited edition (Thawee 2017).

Thawee's illustrated story of a young woman fighting her uncanny transformation into a Phi Krasue together with her loyal husband, also served as the story board for a ghost film with the same title that was released in 1973 (Naowarat, 1973). The film adopted Thawee's depiction of Phi Krasue in detail

Figure 32. Cover of the re-released limited edition of *Krasue Sao*. *Krasue Sao*, by Thawee Witsanukorn (Borisat E.P., 2017).

and became a huge success throughout Thailand. The story had a lasting impact on the imagination of Phi Krasue in popular media and also inspired the depiction of the Balinese *Leyak* in the film *Mystics in Bali* (Djalil, 1981) that is regarded a modern classic of Southeast Asian horror cinema.

Thawee is, therefore, credited for being the person who gave Phi Krasue its iconic form, especially the sagging intestines below a beautiful woman's head, for which the uncanny creature is known in Thai pop culture. The Preface to the recently released special edition of *Krasue Sao* states that Thawee heard of Phi Krasue for the first time from his father, who was a Thai soldier stationed in Cambodia. His father told Thawee about a fellow soldier, who was sentenced to death for killing his wife. During his trial the soldier explained how he saw his wife emitting an uncanny greenish glow while being asleep. Since such a nightly glow is an unmistakable sign of a person's witch-like character, the soldier said he had no choice but to kill his wife as she was obviously a Phi Krasue. Inspired by this story, Thawee drew on narrative elements from *Mae Nak Phrakhanong*, Thailand's most popular ghost story, to compile his epic novel *Krasue Sao* (2017).

It is important to emphasize that Thailand's oral ghostlore imagines Phi Krasue as a flickering light hovering over the rice fields or along forest edges. References to a floating head or torn out intestines are scarce and most written accounts of Phi Krasue published before the release of Thawee's graphic novel do not mention them. Thawee's graphic novel seems indeed to be the first graphic depiction of this uncanny being at all. However, despite the iconicity of Thawee's depiction and the myth that he invented the drawn-out intestines as Phi Krasue's most characteristic feature, he was not the first-person describing Phi Krasue as a woman's head with sagging entrails hanging beneath it. German polymath Adolf Bastian is arguably the first Western visitor to Siam to leave a detailed description of how Phi Krasue was imagined in mid-nineteenth-century Bangkok. In his account of Siamese ghostlore, Bastian mentions all features characterizing Phi Krasue in Thawee's novel except the drawn-out intestines (1867: 257, 76). A little later the French colonial officer Charles Hardouin explicitly mentions drawn-out intestines hanging beneath a woman's head that detaches itself from the body during the night as one of Phi Krasue's characteristic features (1904: 416). However, because of the film's popularity and the impact the graphic novel's artwork had on the depiction of Phi Krasue in the very popular one-baht comics (*khaton lem la baht*) that sold over 1 million copies each month during the 1970s and 1980s, Thawee contributed essentially to the imagination of this witch-like being in contemporary Thailand.

Figure 33. Two Phi Krasue fighting over a dead buffalo in the filmic adaptation of Thawee's graphic novel. *Krasue Sao*, directed by S. Naowarat (Sri-Sayam Production: 1973).

Phi Krasue is, furthermore, not the only uncanny being that seems to be depicted graphically for the first time in Thawee's comic book. Phi Krahang, which is usually imagined as the male equivalent of Phi Krasue, also appears in *Krasue Sao* for the first time. A Phi Krahang emerges when a man dabbles in black magic and breaks an associated taboo. It has the same craving for impure bodily substances as Phi Krasue, but looks totally different than its female counterpart. During its nightly transformation, Phi Krahang maintains its human shape but grows an animal tail. The being rides through the air on a mortar pestle and uses winnowing baskets as wings. This shape inspires little fear and some observers regard *Phi Krahang*, therefore, as a recent invention intended to create a male equivalent to the explicitly female gendered *Phi Krasue* (Rajadhon 1961: 120).

Figure 34. Phi Krasue and Phi Krahang as depicted in Thawee's graphic novel. *Krause Sao*, by Thawee Witsanukorn (Borisat E. P. 2017: 164). Reproduced with the permission of the artist.

Essential for the genesis of both monsters is, thus, a human's dabbling in malevolent forms of magic. This association with magic establishes the most important conceptual link to European imaginations of witches and witchcraft that is usually overlooked when these monsters are classified as 'spirits' or 'ghosts'. However, concepts known in Western folklore and mythology do not translate easily into Thai. This is also true for the word 'monster' that is usually translated as sat pralat in Thai-English dictionaries. Sat pralat means literally 'strange animal' and distorts the meaning of monster as much as 'ghost' or 'spirit' distort the meaning of the word phi that features as a prefix for these witch-like beings. Phi is a rather large and inclusive class of uncanny beings that cannot be translated unambiguously. The common tendency to equal Thailand's phi with malevolent 'ghosts' roots in Rajadhon's (1888–1969) influential writing on Thai folklore and mythology. In one of the few English texts that attempts to provide a general overview of Thailand's monsters, Rajadhon identifies phi as a colloquial term used to denote ghosts, devils or evil spirits (1954: 153). The text introduces a Western conceptual boundary to the classification of Thailand's *phi* that distinguish these beings primarily along the binary opposition of good vs evil. While such a classification seems perfectly logical or even 'natural' to readers coming from cultures dominated by monotheistic world religions and socialized in symbolic classification systems impregnated by Manichean dualism, in Thailand this conceptual boundary represents a modernist invention that reduced the fundamental ambiguity characterizing these uncanny beings associated with magic.

Tambiah retells a village theory from Northeastern Thailand, which attributes the origin of these witch-like beings 'to the transformation of spells into an evil force inside a magical expert, be it man or woman (the latter are sometimes said to dabble in love magic), who uses spells to achieve suprahuman effects' (1970: 320). What triggers this transformation is usually a breaking of taboos associated with powerful magical practices. Since most of these taboos are irreconcilable with the daily chores of women in village life, it is only a matter of time until a woman practicing magic becomes such an uncanny being. There is the shared belief that the host of a Phi Krasue cannot die, before she succeeds in spitting her saliva into the mouth of a female relative, who will then succeed her as the next host. The transmission of Phi Krasue from one host to the next has thus despite its origin in malevolent magic also hereditary and contagious dimensions.

These contagious dimensions and the role of saliva for the transmission of Phi Krasue features prominently in the film *Inhuman Kiss* (*Saeng Krasue*; Sitisiri, 2019) as one of two ghost films revolving around this witch-like being as their main narrative force released in April 2019. The film was not only a major success at the box offices, but also selected as Thailand's contribution to the international feature film category at the 2020 Oscars (Scott 2019). Although the film marks a temporary endpoint in the cinematic re-imagination of Phi Krasue, it is still deeply indebted to Thawee's ingenious artwork. Since I have traced the development of Phi Krasue's cinematic imagination elsewhere, it suffices to highlight the major alterations characterizing its depiction in *Inhuman Kiss* to develop an idea of how Phi Krasue's imagination changes over time, while remaining simultaneously relatively unchanged (Baumann 2014).

Phi Krasue's cinematic imagination was subject to various dominant trends in Thailand's popular culture and a growing harmonization with the globalized monsters of Gothic fiction was clearly discernable. Most obvious is the increasing vampirization of Phi Krasue that started with the emergence of elongated canines in the mid-1980s and reached its climax in the biting of a victim to suck its blood in the daily soap *Sap Krasue* running on Channel 8 in 2018. The craving for human blood replaces the being's original craving for human feces that is no longer appropriate in Thailand's globalized popular culture. These vampiristic features are largely absent in oral folklore and Thawee's artwork, but their elaboration in the public sphere led to various misclassifications in academic literature, where Phi Krasue is treated as a Southeast Asian vampire.

This vampirization is not the only transformations characterizing Phi Krasue's imagination in public media. The character and function of the internal organs the head drags along on its nightly journeys have also changed over the past fifty years. In Thawee's novel it was exclusively organs of the digestive tract, later heart, lungs and liver were added, while the heart became the organ emitting the pulsating glow. While the importance of the vampiristic elements is reduced in *Inhuman Kiss*, the film elaborates upon the function and form of the internal organs. *Inhuman Kiss* is the first film that turns the passively dangling intestines into tentacle-like grippers, which *Phi Krasue* uses not only to snatch its prey, but also to caress the cheek of its human lover feeding it with dead chickens.

Figure 35. The growing vampirization of Phi Krasue in the daily soap *Sap Krasue*. *Sap Krasue*, directed by Phumiphat Sangwanworakul (Channel 8, 2018).

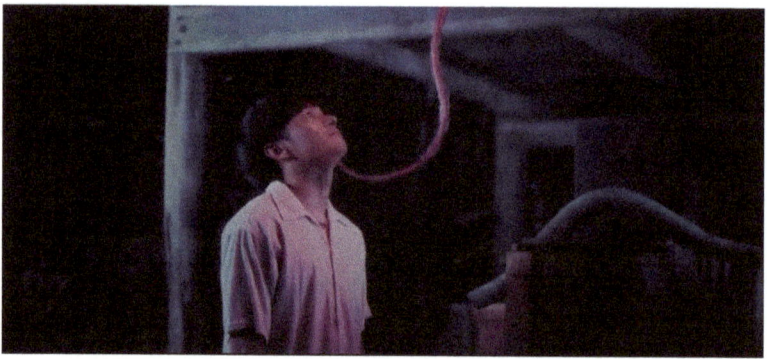

Figure 36. *Phi Krasue*'s newly emerging tentacles. *Inhuman Kiss*, directed by Sitisiri Mongkolsiri (Transformation Film, 2019).

Inhuman Kiss, thus, reverses the growing demonization of *Phi Krasue*, which manifested in national media as its vampirization, by emphasizing the phenomenon's contagious dimension. The transformation becomes, thus, not self-inflicted by the female protagonist's dabbling in black magic, but the result of an infectious kiss. The recent blockbuster's narrative is much closer to the attitude characterizing the everyday perception of Phi Krasue in rural Thailand, where the hosts are usually not feared, but rather pitied for their unfortunate destiny that forces them to live off human feces. This return to motifs from Thailand's oral tradition and Thawee's graphic novel, which reverse Phi Krasue's demonization, may explain the film's appeal for Thai audiences.

Inés Ordiz

La habitación del desahogo (2012)

The online exposition 'La habitación del desahogo/The Room of Relief' reinvents the legendary Mexican figure of La Llorona to put forward a poetic critique of the violent consequences of sexist inequality and gendered violence in Spanish-speaking countries. This chapter argues that this piece of transgressive artwork is a transcultural reinterpretation of the Mexican legend that, while maintaining some of the essential elements of the figure and addressing the relevance of the cultural community it belongs to, also exemplifies the ability of La Llorona to facilitate intercultural dialogue and to interrogate the monstrosity of transnational patriarchal structures that affect violence against women.

Because La Llorona is such a relevant figure of the Mexican cultural community on both sides of the US/Mexican border, I find it appropriate to quote Domino Renee Perez, a Chicana academic who belongs to that same community, to describe the main elements of the legend:

> Also known as the Weeping or Wailing Woman, she is a ghost said to haunt the riverbanks and lake shores. Some know La Llorona as a murderous mother who killed her children in an act of revenge or grief, and they believe she is condemned to wander the earth in search of the children she sacrificed or, as others see it, relinquished willingly. For people of Mexican ancestry, La Llorona traditionally serves as a cultural allegory, instructing people how to live and act within established social mores. At times, however, she is simply a spooky bedtime story. Her tales are told to children to induce good behaviour. (Perez 2008: x)

In many versions of the legend, Llorona is described as a native woman who becomes vengeful and murderous after being abandoned by the father of her children, a white Spanish man.

It can be argued that La Llorona's indigenous origins situates her in connection with pre-Columbian systems of belief. Prior to the Spanish conquest, a woman was heard weeping in the streets of Tenochtitlan, the capital of the Mexica/Aztec empire. This was one of the eight omens that started appearing some years before the arrival of Cortés in 1519, which were interpreted by the Natives as auguries of death and ruin (León-Portilla 1959: 11). Moctezuma believed the woman to be the goddess Cihuacoatl or the Snake Woman, an alternate aspect of Coatlicue, mother of the gods – that is, of the Sun, the Moon and the stars (Cano 2004: 72) – and Toci [Our Grandmother]. Cihuacoatl, like La Llorona, is a monstrous mother: she was referred to 'as a horror and a devourer' (Brundage 1979, quoted in Perez 2008: 136), she was believed to crave human blood and she could sometimes be heard during the night, 'crying to be fed' (Bierhorst 1984: 10). Years after the conquest, Catholicism assimilated some of the elements of the devotion to the goddess Toci who, in her form as the Virgin of Guadalupe, becomes an example of the syncretism between the religion brought by the Spanish and the original Aztec beliefs.

La Llorona is also associated with a female figure of Mexican mythical history: Malintzin or La Malinche, a Nahua woman who was given as an offering to the conquistador Hernán Cortés. Malinche has been defined by history as Cortés' lover, interpreter and counsellor. Because she is thought to have had a relevant role in helping Cortés, she is considered by many as a betrayer of her people. For instance, in *El laberinto de la soledad/The Labyrinth of Solitude* (originally published in 1950), considered a key text for the definition of the Mexican (male) identity, Octavio Paz describes Malinche as the *chingada* (violated, raped) mother of all Mexicans and states that 'as a small boy will not forgive his mother if she abandons him to search for his father, the Mexican people have not forgiven La Malinche for her betrayal. She embodies the open, the *chingado*, to our closed, stoic, impassive Indians' (2002: 25). It is due to this description of Malinche as a mother, as well as to the mistaken belief that she murdered the children she had with Cortés in order to prevent him from taking them to Spain with him, that she is sometimes conflated with La Llorona. There is, however, no historical record to support these events. This association of the figure with a La Malinche, classified by a male-defined national discourse as traitor to all Mexicans, as well as the perception of the figure as a monstrous mother, collaborate in the identification of La Llorona as a threat. This monstrosity, which is reflected in many of her representations in literature and popular culture is, as it has been made obvious, historically and culturally specific.

We can find one early example of this characterization of the figure as dangerous in the short text 'La Llorona' by Artemio de Valle-Arizpe, originally published in 1957. De Valle-Arizpe is considered one of the Mexican authors who, during the first decades of the twentieth century, attempted to recuperate the spirit of nationalism through recuperation of stories of Colonial Mexico. In the tale, the La Llorona is connected both to Coatlicue and Malinche, as well as described as a supernatural figure that evokes great fear. Horror cinema has also reproduced this version of La Llorona as monstrous; some examples of classic Mexican films are *La Llorona* (Peón, 1933), *El grito de la muerte* [*The Living Coffin*] (Méndez, 1959), *La Llorona* (Cardona, 1960), and *La maldición de La Llorona* [*The Curse of the Crying Woman*] (Baledón, 1963). Mexican director Rigoberto Castañeda adapted the legend to the twenty-first century with *KM 31*, a 2006 horror film that uses the formal parameters of Asian horror (most saliently of Takashi Shimizu's *Ju-On: The Grudge*, 2002) to modernize La Llorona lore. Castañeda's modernization of the legend mainly consists of two components. On the one hand, the cinematic elements borrowed from an easily recognizable Asian tradition makes La Llorona a 'globally appealing monster' (Byron 2011) and, therefore, situate both the film and the legend in a more transnational geography. On the other hand, the legend is updated to contemporary concerns by connecting it to gender violence and femicide. According to Gabriel Eljaiek-Rodríguez, the predilection of the ghosts in *KM 31* for attacking (mostly young) women and killing them in a systematic and grotesque way makes it impossible to overlook a connection with the constant disappearances of women in Ciudad Juárez (ongoing since 1993; 2018: 151). More recent horror films with a transnational scope that engage with the legend are *Mama* (Muschietti, 2013) and *The Curse of La Llorona* (Chaves, 2019).

Other reconfigurations of the legend move away from these depictions of La Llorona as horrific and attempt to change the social conventions that define the figure as monstrous and her fate as deserved and inescapable, therefore putting forward the type of transgressive notions that will later define 'La habitación del desahogo'. Chicana feminists are perhaps the cultural community who most insistently have fostered these repositionings of La Llorona.

In their texts, the eternal torture of the murderous mother, as opposed to the fate of the man who neglects, abandons or deceives her (depending on the version of the legend), is often interpreted as a reaffirmation of the continuation of the subordination of women under the patriarchy (Perez 2008: 73). Some examples of a type of subversive use of the figure of La Llorona that destabilizes social and cultural assumptions are Sandra Cisneros, Gloria Anzaldúa and Cherríe Moraga's work. La Llorona in Cisneros's 'Woman Hollering Creek' has been interpreted by many as a figure of resistance (Limón 1990; Perez 2008); in *Borderlands/La Frontera*, Anzaldúa theorizes La Llorona as one of the symbolic mothers of Chicanxs, along with La Malinche and La Virgen de Guadalupe, to affirm that the identity of all of them has been defined to reinforce dichotomy virgin/whore as an oppressive patriarchal tool that restricts the roles of women in society. In the theatre play *The Hungry Woman: A Mexican Medea*, Moraga situates Llorona in a dystopic future which warns us about the possible consequences that maintaining a homophobic, sexist and heteropatriarchal order will have on vulnerable communities.

Many of the meanings explored so far are directly or indirectly reproduced in the online exposition 'La habitación del desahogo', a transnational take on La Llorona that positions her as a figure with the power of extend beyond her own cultural and geographical origins. After all, and as Perez affirms, 'bridging different cultural communities has always been one of her roles' (2008: 151). The transnationality of this version of the legend lies in multiple factors. On the one hand, the text is informed and inspired by the original Mexican legend but also deals with issues affecting women worldwide. On the other hand, the visual renderings of La Llorona seem to be inspired not only by these traditional versions, but also by transnational horror. Finally, the fact that the exposition is freely available to anyone with an internet connection makes it a global cultural artefact.

The exposition was presented on 25 November 2012 by the non-profit organization Feminicidio.net. This organization defines itself as a multidisciplinary observatory of civil society which attempts to build a bridge between society, academic and public institutions, to visibilize feminicide at a global scale, and to be a portal of information and journalism created from a gender perspective. 'La habitación del desahogo' is a hybrid exposition that combines photography, journalism and creative writing. In the images, ghostly, semi-transparent images of La Llorona are positioned over different scenes representing instances of gender inequality and abuse: feminicides, sexual violence and exploitation, child abuse, human trafficking, and state legislation over female bodies. The text under the spectral images offers data on the violations of human rights represented by the images in several countries of Latin America and Spain. These are accompanied by short extracts of prose poetry.

The legend of La Llorona that 'La habitación' summarizes reproduces many of the traditional elements of the legend: her existence in pre-colonial times, her act of vengeance when abandoned by a Spanish man, her wailing. The text also points out the fact that the legend exists in many Latin American countries, moving beyond the Greater Mexican context but obviously starting there – in fact, the destabilization of patriarchal assumptions proposed by 'La habitación' owes a lot to the cultural work done by Chicana feminists.[1] The introduction concludes establishing the aim of the exposition: to link the figure of Llorona with femicide, a connection already explored by *KM31*.

The revisited figure of Llorona asks herself: what have they done to me? Why have they murdered me? I am condemned to live in the limbo of negation and that is why I return. My punishment is to remind the living that there is no justice for me. I carry and drag the deafening silence of societies that have little conscience about violence against women[2] ('La habitación').

Her physical appearance reproduces many of the usual features of a horror movie monster: she is a tall, thin figure wearing what looks like an oversized white burial shroud. Her long, dark hair covers her face, giving her a disturbing aspect that resembles Japanese *onryō* – a quintessential ghost of contemporary global horror made famous by the film *Ringu* (dir. Hideo Nakata, 1998) and its adaptations – and therefore adding to the transnationality of the depiction.

Despite La Llorona's horrific semblance, it is not her monstrosity that defines her. In reality, she is a witness, a warning sign of societal and structural violence, and a companion to the women experiencing it. The text on the first

---

1   Sandra Cisneros in *Woman Hollering Creek: And Other Stories* (1992) proposes a new name for La Llorona – La Gritona. This renaming changes the meaning from the passive 'wailing' as intimated in La Llorona to the more agentic 'shouting' in La Gritona. See Santos 2016.
2   Translated from the Spanish original. All translations are my own.

full-sized image summarizes this new role: 'La Llorona questions. La Llorona discovers. La Llorona interprets. La Llorona testifies. La Llorona knows' ('La habitación'). Instead of being a passive signifier to be interpreted and/or used by the to reinforce the patriarchal rule (to induce good behaviour, to blame women for the fall of the nation), she becomes an acting subject who defines her own story.

The extracts of prose poetry are written in the second person and directed towards an unnamed 'you' who is blamed for this violence: for not speaking up for women, for raping them while friends cheer, for paying for prostitutes regardless of whether they are being exploited. La Llorona observes and becomes a reminder of these acts, haunting the perpetrators: 'Now you try to escape yourself and La Llorona appears' ('La habitación'). Not only she becomes monstrous for the victimizers, but she also denounces the complicity (and responsibility) of the states that protect them. Thus, governments, their armed forces and the police are accused of being involved in the violation of human rights taking place during wars, of not giving enough priority in their political agendas to prevent gendered violence, of being complicit to human trafficking, of criminalizing abortion and of not doing enough to free sexual slaves from mafias.

These extracts are intertwined with data on femicides ('In El Salvador 129,430 femicides are committed by one million women'); rape ('More than two thirds of rapes reported between 1998 and 2008 in Nicaragua were committed against girls younger than 17'); the situation of migrant women worldwide ('Each year, between 60,000 and 80,000 people cross international borders as victims of sexual slavery. 80% of them are women, 50% are minors'); lack of abortion rights ('Deaths derived from illegal abortions [in Argentina] amounts to 300 women each year'); and prostitution ('90% of women being prostituted in Spain do it against their will'). The numbers highlight the appalling consequences of the power imbalances permitted by patriarchal states. These are, as suggested by the piece, the true monsters.

The horror of filicide that originally defined La Llorona and that, in some of the versions of the legend justified her punishment, stops being a crucial feature of the figure: in turn, in 'La habitación del desahogo' she becomes both a spectator and an actor, as well as a subject of her own story. Instead of representing a frightening bedtime story designed to keep people to act within established social mores, she collaborates in the destabilizing of these assumptions. In this sense, La Llorona is no longer defined from a patriarchal perspective which picture her as dangerous: she becomes a figure of transgression and a transnational defender of women worldwide.

Gail de Vos

Baba Yaga: *Hellboy* (Mignola, 1997–2004)

> A Baba Yaga is inscrutable and so powerful that she does not owe allegiance to the Devil or God or even to her storytellers.
> — Forrester (2013: viii)

A comprehensive analysis of Mike Mignola's reworkings of the legendary and ancient Baba Yaga and the roles she plays in his *Hellboy* comic book series is beyond the scope of this chapter. I will, instead, focus briefly on an assessment of his adaptation regarding her attributes, her distinctiveness as witch and monster, her hut, her iconic mode of transportation, and her timeless fascination with counting spoons. The Baba Yaga has become 'a transcultural and intermedia figure' (Rudy 2016: 1) since the first English publications in the nineteenth century.[1] Her image was furthered popularized by the ninth movement in Mussorgsky's *Pictures from an Exhibition*,[2] Ivan Bilibin's illustrations, and a continuing expanding popular culture products and productions in the West.

She is recognized as an intriguing, fascinating, ambiguous, dangerous, and memorable figure in academic scholarship as well as in popular culture (Armknecht 2017: 62). She is compelling and dreaded because she forces protagonists to test themselves without reaching for easy solutions. 'This is also why Baba Yaga transcends Russia and has become woven into the social-cultural texture of other cultures that are, to be sure, much different from the

---

1   William Ralston Sheddon-Ralston published several Baba Yaga stories in English in *Russian Fairy Tales: A Choice Collection of Muscovite Folklore* (1873), followed by George Post Wheeler's Russian *Wonder Tales* (1912).
2   'The Hut on Fowl's Legs' is a portrayal of the Baba-Yaga on the prowl for her prey.

Figure 37. Vasilisa the Beautiful in the hut of Baba Yaga. Ivan Bilibin, 1899 (In the public domain).

nineteenth century Russian tales' (Zipes 2012: 63). This is also why she is such a perfect foil for Hellboy.

The Baba Yaga and Hellboy are both monsters. Hellboy is a hulking, red-skinned demon, draped in a trench coat, with cloven hooves, a lithe tail, two cropped stumps of horns, with one hand a perilous weapon and habitually wielding a huge gun in the other. He was summoned by the Nazis near the end of the Second World War as a small and frightened demon but quickly developed into one of the foremost paranormal investigators fighting against evil (Bukatman 2014: 107). 'Mignola's visual treatment of his character preserves the 'monster' quality of Hellboy without sacrificing sympathy for his hero' (Anderson 2007: 35). Hellboy's missions for the Bureau for Paranormal Research and Defense (BPRD) brought him into continuous and interrelated contact with, along with a plethora of intertextual and folkloric references, the Baba Yaga.

Mike Mignola assumes his readers bring a body of prior knowledge to the reading of his comic (Anderson 2007: 13). He will, on occasion, identify his inspirations but:

> play[s] with mythology, taking things which are familiar to some and re-introducing them in twisted, new ways. People who don't know these mythologies are often baffled by their weirdness, their *otherness*, but by changing these legends (sometimes slightly, sometimes in grand fashion) even those who know them find themselves off balance. (Shapira 2019: 51)

His popularity also transcends borders as several panels from the comic are included in a recent academic monograph and compilation of tales: 'The old witch with a mortar and pestle, blatantly modelled on Baba Yaga, follows the Russian predecessor's example by pressing an animated skeleton into service' (Forrester 2013: 17n).

The Baba Yaga is ascribed as a witch and a horrific monster. The word witch, like the word monster, is mimetically loaded and the Baba Yaga challenges our comprehension of this ambiguous and dangerous figure (Zipes 2012: 56). Like other witches, the Baba Yaga resides on the outskirts of society, is asexual, old, ugly, and extremely powerful. She is dreaded by most of those who are in her vicinity, especially men, and feared, because as an ambiguous force; she can be either an opponent or the helper of any protagonist. She is intimidating as she contains the powers of annihilation and the life force at the same time (Estes 1992: 92). The tangible Baba Yaga a protagonist encounters 'depends on the age, gender, and status of the hero; it seems likely that different kinds of aggressive (or kind) behavior might be related to different kinds of protagonists' (Johns 2004: 85) In a survey of all Baba Yaga folktales featuring male heroes, the Baba Yaga is almost exclusively identified as a villain (Johns 2004: 110). Mignola's witch follows this pattern.

In the consideration of the positive Yaga (who gives advice, magic objects, or valuable gifts), Novikov enumerates the most typical features of Baba Yaga: her dwelling and its location, the hero's arrival, the request that the hut turn around, the way she lies inside and fills her hut, smelling the 'Russian scent', and potentially threatening to eat the hero, her questions about his goal, the hero's reproach and demand for hospitality, Baba Yaga's compliance, the frequent appearance of three Baba Yaga sisters, and the various magic objects or gifts she gives the hero (Johns 2004: 39).

Novikov identifies six categories of adverse Baba Yaga: 'warrior, avenger, possessor of magic objects, evil enchantress, crafty well-wisher or evil advisor, and abductor of children' (Johns 2004: 40). No other folktale figure embodies as many human vices as does the Baba Yaga: cunning, treachery, falsehood, envy, stinginess, cruelty, and cannibalism (Johns 2004: 40). All these categories and vices are embodied in Mignola's construct of the Baba Yaga, one of the most powerful manipulators of magic in the Hellboy universe.

Mignola takes only a few liberties with the folklore. Both Baba Yagas inhabit the realm of the *leshii*,[3] the forest spirits who have a cameo in the *Hellboy* saga, and both are associated with death, bones, and Koshchei the Deathless,[4] who has a noteworthy presence in *Hellboy*. Possessing iron teeth, penetrating eyes, a huge nose, huge drooping breasts, and a bony leg, the Baba Yaga travels in a utensil frequently used for household labour: riding in the mortar, rowing with the pestle and using a birch broom to sweep away her tracks (Zipes 2012: 61). Midori Snyder observes:

3   The *leshy (leshii)* is a sportive forest spirit who enjoys playing tricks on people, though when angered he can be treacherous. He is seldom seen, but his voice can be heard in the forest laughing, whistling, or singing. When the *leshy* is spotted, he can be easily recognized; for, though he often has the appearance of a man, his eyebrows, eyelashes, and right ear are missing, his head is somewhat pointed, and he lacks a hat and belt, <https://www.britannica.com/topic/leshy>.

4   Koschei maintained his life and immortality through the removal of his soul. Taking it from his body, it was said he hid it in a needle, inside an egg, in a duck, in a rabbit, then locked it in an iron or crystal chest, and buried it under a green oak on an island... the most prominent tale of Koschei the Deathless had nothing to do with the egg that is the source of his immortality and strength. Instead, it had to do with his womanizing ways, <https://www.ancient-origins.net/myths-legends-europe/slavic-legend-immortality-koschei-deathless-002717>.

> Baba Yaga is the most powerful of the ambiguous and transformative cooks in the fairy tale tradition. She straddles the threshold between life and death, between the promise of change and the imminent threat of destruction, between learning to cook a meal or become the meal. This is no sugar-coated, one-dimensional Gingerbread House witch. Baba Yaga is a potent mix of domestic and fantastic ... (Snyder 2005: n.p.)

Her iconic rotating hut, balanced on chicken legs, is encircled by a fence of human bones and lit by lanterns made from the skulls of her previous meals (Snyder 2005: n.p.). 'The bolts on the doors and shutters were made of human fingers and toes and the lock on the front door was a snout with many pointed teeth' (Estes 1992: 77). It is positioned on the edge of a dark forest and the descriptions of the interior always reference the symbolic life-giving and -depriving stove (Balina 2014: 13). This iconic hut is every bit as monstrous as its inhabitant but plays a lesser role in the *Hellboy* series. Here an aristocratic manor rests on a chicken leg surrounded by a fence of lit skulls providing a contrast between the familiar, fluctuating, folkloric hut on chicken legs. The ghostly lanterns made from the skulls of her victims are shown to completely fill the interior of her house. In the comic book series, the skull lanterns are one source of her power in manipulating the army of undead souls under her control.

Irrespective of how the Baba Yaga is portrayed in contemporary illustrations, 'it is her strange Russian otherness that paradoxically strikes a common chord in readers of her tales' (Forrester 2013: ix). Because of this, Mignola's Baba Yaga is immediately familiar as she travels through the series. Baba Yaga's epithet 'bony leg' has been taken to mean that one of her legs is literally made of bone – or just that she is old and skinny in a culture that valued plumpness (Forrester 2013: xxvi). Instead of the ubiquitous bony leg, Mignola portrays her with prosthetic wooden ones hinged at the knees. She is draped in a long colourful garment, offering a glimpse of her huge breasts through its gapping front, and the matching headdress suggesting her Otherness as well as her Russian heritage. She markedly persists as a cannibalistic monster and a witch.

One of Mignola's strengths is the interweaving of story arcs throughout the series, offering minute hints that are followed up and expanded several times in subsequent issues. Mignola was captivated by the Baba Yaga's bizarre habit of counting spoons. Mignola refers to his fascination with folklore, stating that 'for some reason, somebody made up a story where the Russian witch

Figure 38. Baba Yaga's Hut. *Hellboy: The Wild Hunt*, Issue 4, created by Mike Mignola, March 2009. © Dark Horse. Image presented under Fair Use legislation.

Figure 39. Baba Yaga's wooden legs. *Hellboy: The Wild Hunt*, Issue 4, created by Mike Mignola, March 2009. © Dark Horse. Image presented under Fair Use legislation.

Baba Yaga sneaks into a guy's house every night to count his silverware'. While Mignola did not understand why she did this, he did know that he wanted to incorporate the action in his story (Grannell). Based on one of the first Baba Yaga stories to be published in Russia (1820), 'Baba Yaga and the Youth', recounts the tale of the boy who hides on the stove behind the chimney pipe in the hut he shares with a tomcat and a sparrow. He is warned not to make any noise when the Baba Yaga comes to count spoons but regardless of the warnings, he is unable to keep himself from shouting out to her and putting himself in danger (Johns 2004: 86). 'The tomcat and the sparrow left, and the kid climbed up on the stove and sat behind the stovepipe. Suddenly a Baba Yaga appeared, picked up the spoons, and started counting: 'This is the tomcat's spoon, this is the sparrow's spoon, and the third one ...' (Forrester 2013: 9–13). After three attempts to count the spoons, and two rescues of the boy by the cat and the bird, the Baba Yaga takes the boy away, presumably to cook and eat him. In Mignola's short tale, 'Baba Yaga's Feast', the protagonist also cannot keep quiet and after the third repletion of the event he is taken away to the Baba Yaga's daughter's house to be prepared for the oven. 'She is a witch and a monster. Her ways are not for men to understand. But the man was told that SHOULD she come, he should hide himself and make no sound at all. And one night she DID come. 'Here's a spoon for a bird, her for a cat, and here for a ...' (Mignola 2009). Although he begins with a faithful retelling of the folktale, Mignola subsequently applies his own twist for a nourishing ending, delivering one of the few tales where Hellboy does not make an appearance.

Mignola had reworked this folktale and the motif of counting several times previously throughout the series. He casually alludes to an incident in which Hellboy shot out the Baba Yaga's eye but provides no context in *Hellboy: Wake the Devil* (1997). Ironically one of Baba Yaga's attributes is a fearsome adversary who gouges out eyes but is forced to heal her victims (Johns 2004: 43). Subsequently he published the short story 'The Baba Yaga' expanding on the shooting. Mignola states, in the tale's introduction, that he made up the business about counting the dead man's fingers but that the 'thing about Baba Yaga counting spoons is an actual folktale' (Mignola 1998). Mignola's habit of addressing his reader and putting the intertextuality in context acts as a storyteller of an oral tale, establishing a robust connection between the world of traditional folktale and his contemporary creations.

In Mignola's previous account, set in Bereznik, Russia in 1964, an old woman in the cemetery tells Hellboy that 'Each year on this night the Baba Yaga comes to call up dead sinners and count their fingers ... I knew a man once ... he lived in a house near the woods, and each night the Baba Yaga would fly into his kitchen to count his spoons ... It tells you something. She has curious habits. It's not for you and I to understand' (Mignola 1998). The Baba Yaga arrives when the old woman finishes her tale and leaves. She commences counting and when finished, Hellboy rushes out to confront her. 'Insolent Devil'! she screams, 'Cannibal'! he retorts. After shooting the Baba Yaga, the creatures of the woods are despondent thinking that it is the end of the witch. But it is not. The Baba Yaga and her missing eye remain an essential issue for Hellboy for the rest of his time on earth and beyond. The Baba Yaga's evil plans for revenge on Hellboy becomes her total motivation and, ultimately results in her loss of magical power and influence. She is extremely oppressive to all that she encounters and, unless they are useful to her plans, she kills them without hesitation if they are in her way.

There has never been a solitary and precise interpretation or understanding of the Baba Yaga in Russia or beyond. Mike Mignola is but one creator who adapts, plays, and reworks with her folkloric image and presence, engaging with the multiplicity of meanings that exists for every individual teller of tales, listener and reader (Johns 2004: 43). Because of its popularity and its continual revisiting and revitalizing the Baba Yaga and the folklore in new readers, the *Hellboy* stories play an important role offering an additional glimpse of this mystical and monstrous witch who is always contrary and contradicting. She remains one of my favourite characters regardless of the media in which she resides.

Partha Mitter

Deumo: *Indiana Jones and the Temple of Doom* (Spielberg, 1984)

In a famous scene in Stephen Spielberg's film, *Indiana Jones and the Temple of Doom*, human sacrifice takes place in front of the Hindu goddess Kali. Spielberg seeks to recreate the worship of Kali by the Thuggees, the notorious band of stranglers that terrorized northern India in the nineteenth century. The actual monster depicted is, however, closer to traditional European images of the devil with glowing eyes than to an actual Hindu deity. So, where does Spielberg receive his inspiration from? The journey is a long one which will eventually lead us back to Spielberg's icon of colonial imaginings.

From the sixteenth century onwards, the pages of European travels accounts are filled with stereotypes of monsters and devils that masquerade as Indian gods. The roots of the tradition go back to the medieval period, and to the Greco-Roman tradition it had inherited. In the Middle Ages, India had been reduced to a fabulous name, the site of the earthly paradise. But the Greeks claimed to have also discovered monsters that inhabited India. These were later compiled lovingly by the Roman historian Pliny the Younger. Stories of monopods [single-legged creatures], cynocaephali [dog-headed ones], martikhora [garbled version of tigers] formed the collective fantasy of the educated in the Middle Ages. The art historian Rudolf Wittkower comments that the Greeks 'rationalized [their instinctive] fears in another, non-religious form by the invention of monstrous races and animals which they imagined to live at a great distance in the East, above all in India' (Wittkower 1942: 159–97).

Pliny's monsters were strange but utterly harmless. The monopods, for instance, used their large flapping single leg to cover their face when they went to sleep. The situation changed drastically around 1000 CE when terrifying images of monsters and demons haunted popular imagination during the fearful days of the first millennium that foretold the end of the world. These images mixed together conceptions of hell, demonology and the Antichrist of the Apocalypse. Therefore, by the late Middle Ages, an elaborate and frightening imagery of demons and hell had grown up, consisting of elements from diverse sources. The Greco-Roman monsters and the Christian demons converged at some stage in medieval history, which was made easier by St Augustine. He asserted that pagan gods were mortal just like other creatures and subject to the same Divine Law that they were powerless to break. In short, Greco-Roman monsters and gods, Biblical demons and Indian gods were all indiscriminately lumped together with congenital malformations under the all-embracing class of monsters. In this twilight region it is difficult to say with certainty where the world of facts ends and that of imagination takes over (Mitter 1977: 7–15 and Mitter 2012). Significantly, in 1493, Hermann Schedel's *Nuremberg Chronicle*, which was illustrated with woodcuts provided by Dürer's teacher Michael Wolgemut, included among its monsters, a strange multiple-armed creature.

As I have shown elsewhere, there is no doubt this is a garbled version of a Hindu god though by no means easy to recognize (Mitter 1977: 9).

The representation of Hindu gods as monsters had an amazing persistence in the colonial imagination. When the first travellers arrived in India from the fourteenth century on, they preferred to trust what they had read in Pliny rather than the actual deities they saw with their own eyes. This preference for inherited knowledge to actual observation reflects a universal principle, explained by the art historian E. H. Gombrich in *Art and Illusion* (1960). Whenever we attempt to understand something unfamiliar, we go from the known to the unknown. The human mind can only process information by classifying it under a known category. The pre-existing schema or mindset serves as a starting point, which may then be adapted in the light of the actual experience. But when the object under observation is outside our experience, it creates stereotyped images (Gombrich 1960: 60). And nowhere is this better illustrated than in the description of Indian gods masquerading as monsters.

Our mindsets are made up of our inherited culture. Therefore, one person's god could be another person's monster, as we shall see. In the case of early European visitors, the two most important heritage were classical Greco-Roman and Christian. The first led to a clash of taste between the classical and the ancient Indian world: an image of even a god with more than two arms was against nature, therefore irrational. Even more important for the early modern period, reaction to Hindu gods demonstrates the conflict of two major faiths, Christianity and Hinduism: one a religion of the book that believed in unity, uniformity and suppression of dissent, while the other was a form of pluralism that embraced a bewildering variety of views and beliefs accumulated over millennia. From the moment early explorers set foot in India, after a long and hazardous land or sea journey, they were faced with the problem of making sense of what they identified as the vast theatre of idolatry that was India. Early reports, which contributed to the growing image of the Hindus in the West, their religion and their religious art, were at once, fragmented, and disparate, and yet so sensational that they were extensively published in a large number of European languages, widely read and endlessly discussed by the educated back home (Mitter, 1977: 3–24).

The full extent of idolatry, practised by pagans the world over, only slowly dawned on Europeans. The question posed was: how did the error of idolatry arise in view of God's gift of monotheism to mankind? So how was it that he had left such a large region of the globe in the dire abyss of idolatry? Idolatry fascinated as well as perplexed the first visitors. One popular explanation was that germs of 'monotheism' were jealously guarded by the higher orders of Hinduism, such as Brahmins but forgotten by the ignorant masses. Given this framework, European visitors to India set forth to recover the 'monotheism' concealed behind the monstrous forms of Hindu polytheism (Mitter 1977, Schmidt 1988: 13–91).

We now come to our key text in the creation of the myth of Hindu gods as monsters. One of the best-known early visitors to India was the aristocratic traveller from Bologna, Ludovico di Varthema (*c*. 1470–1517). A learned, open-minded man, Varthema was the first non-Muslim European to go on pilgrimage to Mecca. Keen to understand other religions, he reached the conclusion from his visit to South India that even though the Hindus had received the revelation they nonetheless persisted in worshipping many false gods. He provided the following explanation: Hindus acknowledged one god, who had created heaven and earth. But they also held that, as god did

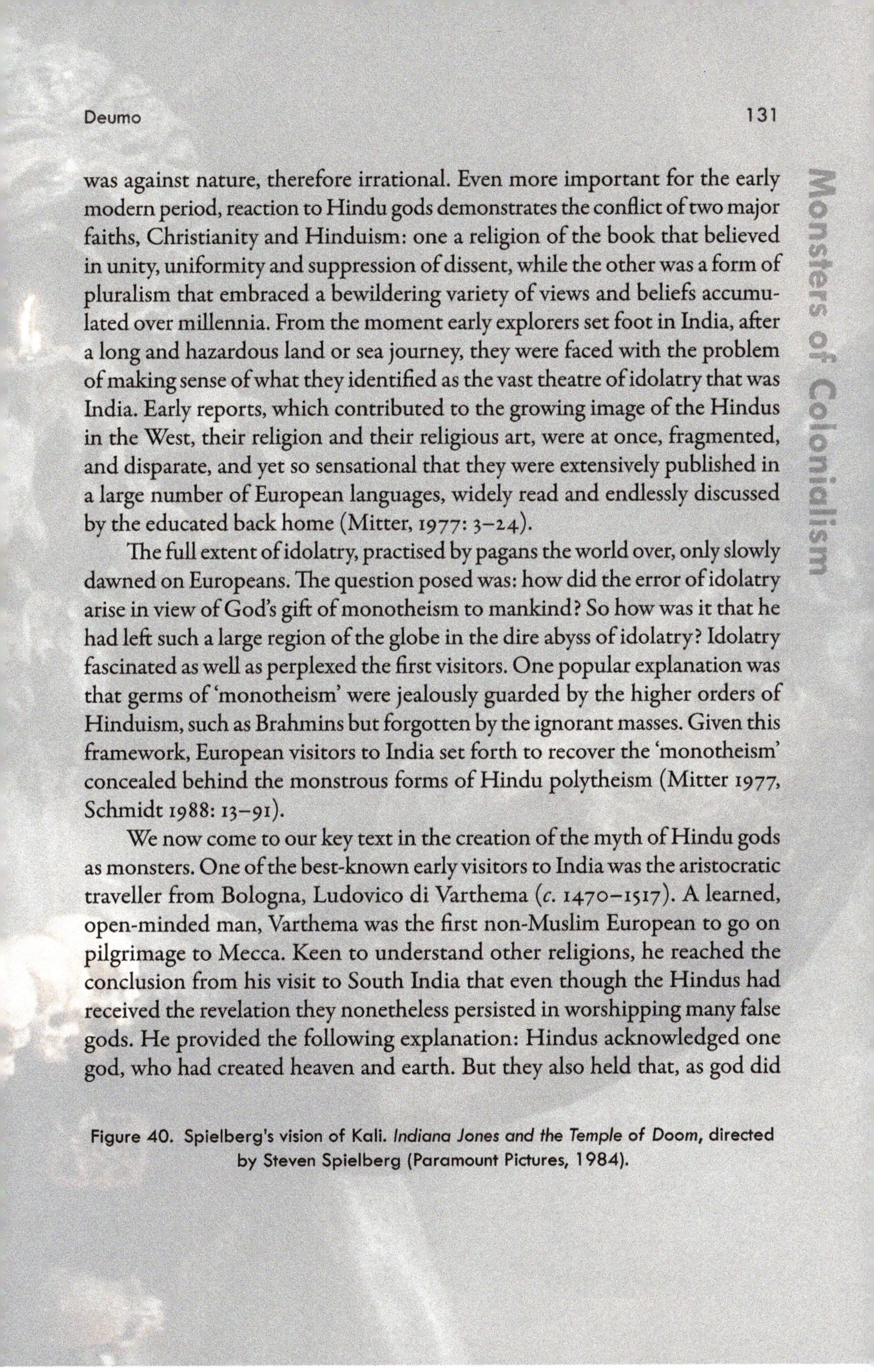

Figure 40. Spielberg's vision of Kali. *Indiana Jones and the Temple of Doom*, directed by Steven Spielberg (Paramount Pictures, 1984).

not wish to take on the task of judging, he sent his spirit, namely, the devil, to dispense justice. Having established the ultimate terms of Hindu monotheism to his satisfaction, Varthema then devoted most of his attention to the demon worship of Calicut (present Kozhikhode in Kerala), based, as he claimed, on personal observation.

The description itself is worth quoting *in extenso* to appreciate the impact it had on his contemporaries:

> the king of Calicut keeps this Deumo in his chapel … in this wise … In the midst of this chapel there is a devil made of metal, placed in a seat also made of metal. The said devil has a crown made like that of the papal kingdom, with three crowns; it has also four horns and four teeth with a very large mouth, nose and most terrible eyes. The hands are made like those of a flesh-hook and feet like those of a cock; so that he is a fearful object to behold. All the pictures around the said chapel are those of devils, and on each side of it there is a Sathanas seated in a seat, which seat is placed in a flame of fire, wherein are a great number of souls … And the said Sathanas holds a soul in his mouth with the right hand, and with the other seizes a soul by the waist. (Varthema 1863: 137)

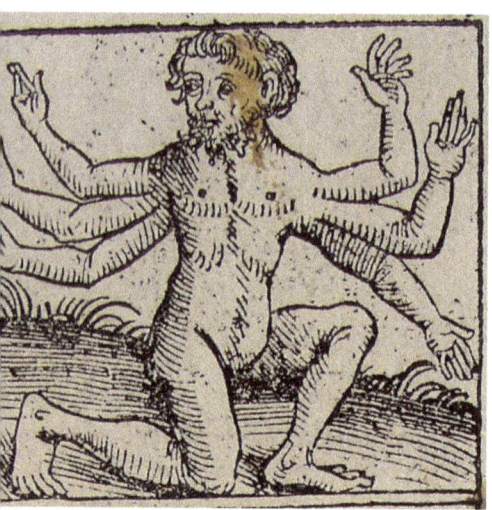

Figure 41. Six-armed man. From the *Nuremberg Chronicle*, by Hartmann Schedel (1440–1514). In the public domain.

To put it bluntly, there is no Hindu god corresponding to this image. So, where does it come from? If one examines closely, the image is a conflation of different images of Antichrist current the Middle Ages. Varthema claims that he had visited the chapel of the king of Calicut; why then did he use medieval stereotypes to describe a Hindu god? We know that he wished to translate an unfamiliar image into a language understood by his contemporaries. But at this time, knowledge about Hinduism was rudimentary. Varthema was forced to fall back upon his inherited values. And these values in turn were informed by his Christian background, which considered all non-Christian religions as inspired by the devil. The first illustration comes not from Varthema's native city Bologna but from Augsburg, the undisputed centre of print technology. Commissioned to illustrate Varthema, the renowned artist and engraver Georg Breu had a field day. He knew what Varthema was talking about and fished out some of the best-known images of the devil, thus putting flesh to the Italian Humanist's words. But he also transcribed faithfully the description of Varthema (Varthema 1515: i).

The towering figure of Satan devouring sinners, while his attendant creatures torture the damned, reminds us of the great fresco by Francesco Traini at the Campo Santo in Pisa. The triple papal crown alludes to Popes in hell; the most notable one in *The Inferno*, the first part of Dante's great poem, the *Divine Comedy*. The Pope in hell was a parodistic image in Dante well known to a Humanist like Varthema. The reference to three crowns, four teeth and four horns plays on numbers, reminding us of the dragon of the Apocalypse. Let us not forget this was a period of uncertainty and religious schism leading to the rise of the Protestant faith preached by Martin Luther (Mitter 1977: 17–18).

It is extraordinary how this one particular image (see Figure 42) captured the imagination of educated Europeans and held sway until the middle of the seventeenth century. The next elaboration of monstrous gods appears in the *Itinerario* of the Dutchman Jan van Linschoten (1563–1611) who was in Goa at the end of the sixteenth century. As the Portuguese Viceroy's secretary, Linschoten took part in the Inquisition in Goa. He accepted that the Hindus acknowledged one god, but that this knowledge was perverted by devil worship. Finally, Linschoten offered the prayer that God grant the Hindus enlightenment, because 'they are like us in all other respects, made after god's image and He will release them from Satan's bondage' (Burnell 1885: 289).

Figure 42. Idol of Calicut. Attributed to Jörg Breu the Elder, in Ludovico de Varthema, Die Ritterlich und lobwürdig Reisz. Johannes Knobloch: Strasbourg 1516, p. K4 r. Zentralbibliothek Zürich, Rara 4.256.

Linschoten wished to illustrate the buildings of non-Christian faiths in India, namely, Islam and Hinduism, and his engraver, Baptista à Doetechum duly offered a panoramic view of a mosque and a temple. Both the Muslim mosque and the Hindu temple were imagined by the engraver based on Linschoten's description. The temple in particular was inspired by the cave temple to Shiva on the island of Elephanta off the coast of Bombay, celebrated in Portuguese literature. Quite strikingly, when Linschoten wanted to convey the impression of Hindu gods, he turned to Varthema's Deumo of Calicut. Baptista à Doetechum duly placed this monster in the actual setting of Elephanta temple (Mitter 1977: 21–2).

Eventually this image of Shiva became a shorthand for explaining Hindu idolatry. Sir Thomas Herbert (1606–82), diarist, historian and a gentleman of the bedchamber of Charles I, visited Surat in the early seventeenth century. His description of the religion of the Hindu merchants, reproduces verbatim Varthema's description with some embellishments. Accordingly, his illustration, 'Picture of an Indian Merchant or Bannyan with his idol', shows a variant of the Georg Breu image of Deumo with added pendulous breasts. A Christian, Herbert of course accepted Hindu gods as horrible misshapen monsters but he preferred to cite previous authorities than to trust his own experience in India (Mitter 1977: 23).

Figure 43. Shiva on Elephanta. Jan Huyghen van Linschoten in *The Voyage of John Huyghen van Linschoten to the East Indies: From the Old English Translation of 1598; The First Book Containing his Description of the East*. Edited by Arthur Coke Burrell and P. A. Tiele, 2 Vols, 1885 (New York: Burt Franklin, n.d.).

Although Hindu gods had been identified with the demons as early as the fourteenth century, from the fifteenth to the seventeenth centuries, Varthema's stereotype of the Hindu gods dominated. Not only was he translated in major European languages, but also the major compilers of travels and cosmographers did not fail to include Varthema in their compendia. One of last cosmographies,

Sebastian Münster's classic, *Cosmographia Universalis* (1544), reproduced Varthema's 'Idol of Calicut' in its description of the famous entrepôt (Mitter 1977: 22–7).

The seventeenth century marks a turning point that paved the way towards a more objective study of Hinduism. In 1651, we encounter an event that was to have a profound effect on the western worldview of other cultures. That year the Dutch pastor Abraham Rogerius's posthumous work, *The Open Door to the Mysteries of Hinduism* (1651), was published. Rogerius had painstakingly studied Hindu religion with the help of translators and offered a more objective view of the religion. Correspondingly, the frontispiece to *The Open Door* sought to provide more authentic images of Hindu gods (Rogerius 1917).

This was followed by a number of other works of a similar nature with constant improvements in knowledge of the original sources.

In 1757, the East India Company laid the foundations of the British Empire. The Company officials began documenting systematically Indian antiquities as well as translating ancient Sanskrit texts, which offered the West a new insight into Hindu religion and art, leading to an Oriental Renaissance in the nineteenth century (Schwab, 1950). At last the monsters stereotypes of Hindu gods began to fade away in the light of a more objective knowledge of Hinduism. Ironically, even such impressive accumulation of knowledge did not necessarily lead to a better appreciation Hindu religious architecture and sculpture. The many-armed Hindu gods remained an object of puzzle and distaste and assigned an inferior status in art history in comparison with the

Figure 44. Deumo of Calicut. Sebastian Münster from *Cosmographia Universalis*, Book V (Basel: Sebastian Heinrich-Petri, 1552).

Figure 45. Shiva in Trimurti Elephanta Caves. In the public domain.

classical Apollo or Aphrodite. The great essayist John Ruskin admired Indian decorative art such as carpets, metalwork and textiles, which he considered superior to European machine-made counterparts. Yet he could not but lament the absence of nature in Indian art, 'It is quite true that the art of India is delicate and refined. But it has one curious character distinguishing it from all other art of equal merit in design – *it never represents a natural fact* ... if it represents any living creature, it represents that creature under some distorted and monstrous form ... it will not draw a man, but an eight-armed monster' (Ruskin 1905: 265).

In short, Spielberg was following a time-honoured tradition of Indian monster deities, subliminally if not consciously, a tradition that continues to spring up in unexpected circumstances.

Yasmine Musharbash

The Hairies: *Cleverman* (Griffen, 2016–2017)

First Nations' ontologies across Australia arise out of and are nestled in 'country' – lifeworlds that extend from far below the ground up to the stars, that are arid, coastal, temperate, whatever the case may be, and home to distinct flora, fauna, wind and weather, language and people, as well as monsters. Considering the size of Australia and the distinctiveness of each 'country', it is astonishing that there is one monster that seems to haunt across Indigenous Australian time and space. First Nations across Australia possess countless origin stories, songs, myths, legends, and encounter narratives about this monster.

In Warlpiri country in central Australia (where I work as an anthropologist), it is called *Pangkarlangu*. In a book on monsters produced by the local literacy centre, it is succinctly and evocatively described as 'like a person but very large with huge feet, long claws, very big eyes and a big head. The belly, back, arms and legs are covered with hair' (Poulson et al. 1990: 18). Other First Nation have different vernacular names for it, and *Hairy People* is a term often used in Aboriginal English – pinpointing the monster's hirsuteness as a key characteristic. Other traits, such as its size (always either distinctly larger or smaller than humans) or its intentions (cannibalistic, wild, scary or mischievous but helpful), vary from one country to the next but enough family resemblance remains between variations to legitimately think of it as pan-Australian.

Since the early days of colonization, over the past 200 years, the sightings of it by non-Indigenous people have been regularly reported in the mainstream Australian media, where it is known as *Yowie* or *Yahoo*.[1] And, recently, it made

---

1   Here, it is sometimes linked to similar monsters elsewhere, such as the Sasquatch or the Yeti (see <https://www.yowiehunters.com.au/historical-articles> for listings).

its TV debut in the two-season series *Cleverman* (2016–17) created by Ryan Griffen and directed by Wayne Blair and Leah Purcell.

Set in a heavily surveilled dystopian near future, *Cleverman*'s primary plotline revolves around the (mythical) rivalry between two Aboriginal brothers – the younger of which inherits the superpowers of cleverman at the death of the former cleverman (to his and everybody else's surprise) while the older one tries to steal what he believes is rightfully his. A secondary plot revolves around *Hairy People*. Much like the Pangkarlangu of central Australia, they are characterized through their hirsuteness, exceedingly tough and sharp nails, extensive lifespans (some were born before colonization), and by possessing superhuman strength. In an indigenized twist on *True Blood*'s vampires 'coming out of the coffin', some *Hairy People* came out of hiding during what the show calls 'Emergence Day' (roughly half a year before the present of *Cleverman*) and now live in a derelict industrial inner city area called The Zone.

The authorities view them with paranoid suspicion and treat them in ways reminiscent not only of Australian frontier and colonial violence but also paralleling current Australian maltreatments of refugees. Poignantly, the beginning of Season 1, Episode 1 includes a press conference with a government minister who declares that 'these creatures are not human. We do not share the same DNA. We don't exactly know what they are' and throughout the series their 'official' designation is *Subhumans* (or *Subbies*). Sympathetic humans, for the most part Aboriginal but including some noteworthy non-Aboriginal protagonists, call them *Hairies*.

The *Hairies* in *Cleverman*, can be read well along the lines of the 'Indigenous Uncanny' as proposed by Faye Ginsburg (2018). She contrasts it with the Freudian uncanny in the following way:

> Rather than the sense of overwhelming generalized fear that Freud associates with the uncanny provoked by proximity to the dead untied to any particular historical circumstance the [Indigenous uncanny is] characterized by a different register ... shaped by a kind of curiosity about and intimacy with the other side. (Ginsburg 2018: 68)

Cleverman is an Indigenous project; many of its cast and crew, including its creator, directors, and writers are Indigenous, as are the protocols that were followed in its writing, 'one of the reasons the four-year development process was so long, because it was essential that they consult with communities and gain permission to tell Dreaming stories' (Bizzaca 2016). For example, *Cleverman*'s creator Ryan Griffen 'travelled to the Northern Territory ... and spent four hours sitting in a riverbed discussing [the *Namorrodor*, another monster that appears in the series] with an elder. He [Griffen] says it was a privilege to hear the story there and get permission to tell it for the screen' (Bizzaca 2016).

We must assume that it is no coincidence, but intentional and deeply poignant, that the *Hairies* in *Cleverman* look and act much more human than they generally do in non-Indigenous depictions. Two examples of the latter, above and beyond the recurrent newspaper reports of something large, blurry and hairy, are the charming but distinctly non-human and more ape-like illustrations by Tohby Riddle (2019) in *Yahoo Creek*, and designer Trent Jansen's 'Pankalangu Collection', which features fine art furniture inspired by fictitious traits such as scales and real traits such as hair.² Griffen detailed some of the issues around incorporating pan-Aboriginal *Hairy People*: 'There are different hairy stories throughout Australia, and they differ in each country. You have some who are a tall, some are short, some are aggressive, some are friendly. We got to sort of pick which ones will fit for us and create the Hairies for our show' (Bizzaca 2016).

The show's creature designer for the *Hairies* was Jacob Nash, who is the Head of Design at the Bangarra Dance Company, Australia's premiere Indigenous Dance Company. In the featurette *Cleverman/'Creating the Hairies' Behind the scenes* (Sundance, TV 2016) many of the intricate details of their design are outlined: choices underlying colour, length and type of hair, where on the body it is, how it curls, and so forth.

All *Hairies* are played by Aboriginal actors, with a number of visual signifiers that set them apart as other-than-human:

- Most of their bodies are covered in hair, with their body hair being much thicker and longer than that of humans, their hairline being much lower, starting just above the eyebrows. Their sideburns (for women) lead into chin beards and the men have full beards covering most of their faces, grown long and thick.

2   See <https://trentjansen.com/projects/> for images of the collection and for discussion, see Nicholls 2020.

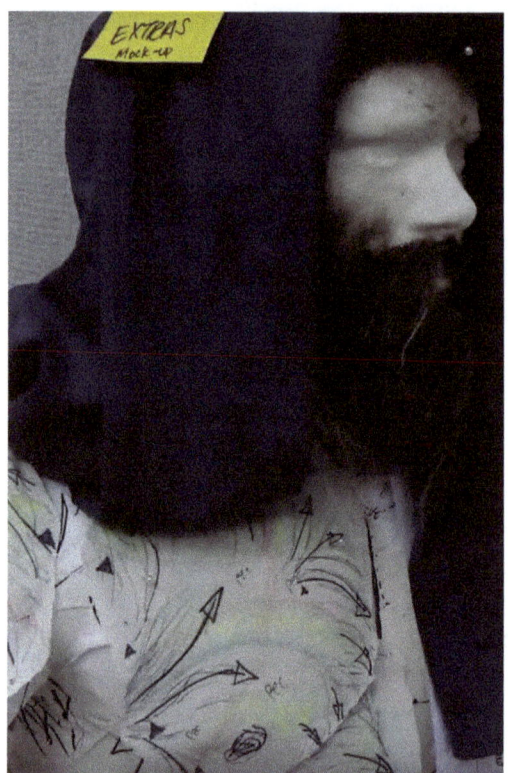

Figure 46. Designing a monster. *Cleverman*/'Creating the Hairies' Behind the scenes, directed by Wayne Blair and Leah Purcell (Sundance Studios, 2016).

- Their fingernails are exceedingly thick and sharp.
- They move faster, more fluently and effortlessly than humans, visualized by *Hairies* parkouring, especially when being pursued.
- Many *Hairies* have strikingly blue eyes; a metaphor *Cleverman* uses for connection to the Dreaming in this vein, when Koen, the younger brother, inherits the position of cleverman, one of his eyes changes colour from brown to blue).

Ryan Griffen made the political choice not to have a made-up language for the *Hairies* but to have their lines translated into Gumbaynggirr, an

Aboriginal language from northern New South Wales and the actors coached in it. Season 1, Episode 103, 'Cleverman Extra: The Language' begins with a note that says: 'There were over 300 different aboriginal languages spoken throughout Australia, the majority of these are now endangered. The Cleverman team worked with Uncle Gary Williams form the Muurrbay Language Centre on the languages that our characters speak'. Griffen is filmed saying:

> I wanted to really differentiate Hairies to the Aboriginal culture ... I didn't wanna make a story that was just Aboriginal versus, you know, colonisation. And giving them [the *Hairies*] a different language to our Cleverman differentiates them as a different species.

Rrarriwuy Hicks, the actress playing a *Hairy* called Latani adds that as the actors learned the language and how it is pronounced, they began pronouncing their *Hairy* names differently as well and how that was incorporated into the show. A theme that emerges again and again in featurettes and interviews is how bringing the *Hairies* to life on set through make up, language, and plot made many of the Aboriginal crew relate *Hairy People* stories from their respective regions. Even if not necessarily in the ways intended, this pairs well with Halberstam's (1995: 163) pronouncement that 'monsters are on us and in us'. Furthermore, it brings into focus the relationship between *Hairy People* and Aboriginal people in exactly the terms described by Ginsburg (2018). Put differently, *Hairies* are not 'just' monsters in the most general sense of the term (see Cohen 1996 and Musharbash 2014) as expressed by the authorities' nomenclature of *subhumans* and the plotline of detention and worse. Rather, they are – for First Nations people – *relatable* others.

This relationality (or intimacy in Ginsburg's sense) is tenderly suggested in the dialogue (Season 2, Episode 4) between Koen (Hunter Page-Lochard) and his Aunty Linda (Deborah Mailman), who is wiping the blood of the corpse of a young *Hairy*, who was just attacked and killed by three non-Indigenous people:

> KOEN: How can you kick a kid in the face?
> AUNTY LINDA: You can if you think he is a monster.
>
> (*Cleverman*, Griffen, 2016–17, Season 2, Episode 3)

In fact, there is a twinning in that scene of hostile non-Indigenous/*Hairy* relations and respectful Indigenous/*Hairy* relations, as the dialogue begins by Koen suggesting to Aunty Linda that for her to wash the dead *Hairy* teenager might not be culturally appropriate: 'They [the other *Hairies*] might wanna wash him. I am not sure how they do it or what they do, but you, know'.

This twinning can be further contoured by drawing on Ken Gelder's (2012) definition of the Australian (meaning, mainstream) Gothic. He emphasizes how the Australian Gothic is undergirded by early 'explorers' pervasive sense of the Australian landscape as empty, defined through absence, loss, and melancholia. He defines the Australian Gothic through perceiving the land as 'void', which stands in direct opposition First Nation peoples' embodied emplacement in sentient 'country': where Aboriginal people treat *Hairies* as equal, familiar, and relatable, non-Indigenous people recoil in horror and fail to see what is there.

A further angle is to read the interaction between Indigenous people and *Hairies* in *Cleverman* as decolonizing mainstream television. As Kate Warner (2017, n.p.) points out, this can be seen to be an interaction between Aboriginal people and Aboriginal mythology or between Indigenous past and present. It demonstrates Aboriginal identities being created in relation to other Aboriginal identities and not in relation to white people, where in this narrative, Aboriginal people have an identity other than that allowed for in colonialist terms.

Conclusion: On the Liveliness of *Hairy People* across Time and Space

Halberstam observed that monsters are 'constantly being rewritten by historically and culturally conditioned fears generated by a shared sense of otherness and difference' (Halberstam 1995). Fear is but one aspect; Indigenous people have understandings of monsters that encompass but are not limited to fear. And yet, their monsters are 'constantly being rewritten', or, for that matter, may actively rewrite themselves.

Consider the abundance *Hairy People* across the Australian continent, and the similarities and differences between them as seen in the *Pangkarlangu* haunting Warlpiri people and the *Cleverman's Hairies*: the monstrosity of Central Australian Pangkarlangu is highlighted in myths, songs, and Dreaming stories which all in one way or another tell of their ignorance of the rules that make humans human. Pangkarlangu are cannibals hunting and eating both monsters and humans; they are ignorant of social and ritual rules and obligations, including stealing children and growing them up without initiation, stealing women without reciprocity and care of affinal relationships, and failing to bury their own dead. The monstrosity of all these infringements, in Pangkarlangu as much as in *Hairies* is signified through hair itself. Anthropology has a long tradition of understanding hair as a distinct and universal marker of 'civilisation' (see, amongst many others, Hallpike 1969, Leach 1958, Synnott 1987), contrasting shaved, hidden, combed, and cut hair from long and matted (and wild!) hair. In fact, the *Hairies* of *Cleverman* are distinguished into three kinds:

- 'shavers', those who live in the city and try to blend into human society by shaving much of their facial hair and that on their hands and wearing human clothing (see Figure 47);
- 'non-shavers', who are covered in hair from head to toe and live traditional lives out in the bush, far away from both Indigenous and non-Indigenous people (see Figure 48); and
- those who accept the authority's anti-serum, which makes them loose all their hair as well as their powers (see Figure 49).

While in *Cleverman* the state of their hair indicates respective *Hairies*' closeness to or distance from human society, in Warlpiri country, Pangkarlangu exhibit proximity and difference as well, if in different ways. Christine Nicholls, for example, reports the following:

> Warlpiri friends from Lajamanu ring me every now and again to relate recent sightings of Pangkarlangu. I was told recently about a group of Warlpiri people almost stumbling upon (then rapidly taking off in another direction) an entire family of Pangkarlangu sitting in a circle on the ground having a picnic. (Nicholls 2020: 103)

Five hundred kilometers to the southeast, where I work, Pangkarlangu were until recently understood to be male, exclusively – until there was a sighting

Figure 47. Latani, a shaver.

Figure 48. Non-shavers at home.

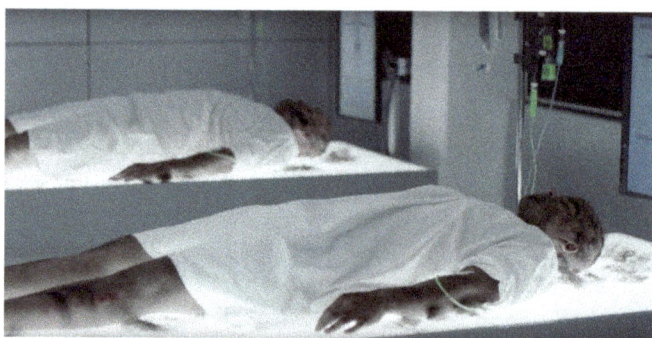

Figure 49. Hairies undergoing the procedure. *Cleverman*, Trailer for Season 2 (Sundance Studios, 2017).

Figure 50. Non-shavers gazing at the city. *Cleverman*, trailer for Season 2 (Sundance Studios, 2017).

of a nuclear family (Musharbash 2020). How better to capture this monstrous rewriting than by a family of non-shavers gazing at the city from the distance?

Part IV
Gender

Eddie Falvey

Satan: *The Witch* (Eggers, 2015)

Screen Satans

Has there ever been a more iconic, enduring, and mythic monster than Satan himself? Satan, the biggest of big bads, the great horned adversary, chief villain in various theistic constructions of the world, has been a source of inspiration for artists working in a range of mediums since antiquity. In the realm of Western art, and most recently film, Satan has long maintained an iconographic and allegorical function as a concentrated vessel of evil and his image on screen has been informed by an amorphous and culturally inflected range of representations that convey shifting ideas about faith, morality, and, of course, the monster.

Satan's monstrosity has been long debated by theologians and biblical scholars, and has been scrutinized in defining works of art taken from various mediums, including but not limited to Raphael's oil on canvas *St. Michael Vanquishing Satan* (1518), John Milton's epic poem *Paradise Lost* (1667), the works of William Blake (1757–1827), Mikhail Bulgakov's magic realism novel *The Master and Margarita* (1967), and even The Rolling Stones' pop-rock anthem 'Sympathy for the Devil' (1968). It is far from the objective of this work to try to simplify the dialogues generated by such a complex touchstone for negotiating humanity's constructed moral universe. Rather, this piece will offer a short survey of screen Satans in order to place into context the ongoing, yet adaptive currency that the figure has fostered as a transcultural icon of film.

No doubt due to the contentious matter of the figure's origins, images of Satan did occur during the period of early film, though with significantly less frequency than they do today.[1] As Peter Malone notes, 'Most serious films with Satan themes date from the late 1960s to the present [where] the focus is on Satan in our world' (Malone 2016: 337). During this period came a significant benchmark for film impressions of Satan, *Rosemary's Baby* (Polanski, 1968), which finds Mia Farrow's Rosemary raped by Satan and impregnated with the Antichrist ('He has his father's eyes', she is famously told towards the film's end). After the critical and commercial success of *Rosemary's Baby*, other thematically aligned prestige studio horrors followed, including *The Exorcist* (dir. William Friedkin, 1973), in which a demon possesses a young girl, and *The Omen* (dir. Richard Donner, 1976), in which a young couple finds themselves unknowingly raising the Antichrist, inadvertently positioning the film as an appropriate companion to *Rosemary's Baby*.

All three films, *Rosemary's Baby*, *The Exorcist*, and *The Omen*, mount their horrors upon the graphic rendering of Christian iconography, especially satanic or devilish imagery. Despite the fact that all three were considerable sources of controversy upon release – especially *The Exorcist*, which prompted reactionary campaigns from audiences around the world – they collectively represent a watershed for the depiction of religious horrors on-screen. Rosemary's rape in *Rosemary's Baby* stands as an act of violent embodiment that injects evil into the conspicuously sexed framework of the (violated) female body. Indeed, Tony Williams, writing on Rosemary's rape, observes this violation: 'Rosemary undergoes submersion into the dark forces behind Western civilisation. Society and satanism wish to use her body' (Williams 1996: 104). Adjacently, in *The Exorcist*, Barbara Creed observes young Regan's possession as an embodied 'struggle between the subject and the abject [...] slime, bile, pus, vomit, urine, blood – all of these abject forms of excrement are part of Regan's weaponry' (Creed 2007: 40). In *The Exorcist*, sinfulness and its expression directly correspond with and are conveyed through Regan's abominated body. Regan's embodied abjection, or her monstrosity, makes literal the fight for her soul that is taking place within her, with the violent erosion of what Julia Kristeva identifies as the body's 'inside/outside boundary' (Kristeva 1982: 114) being employed to allegorically express the fight between good and evil for which Regan's body serves as battleground.

---

1   For examples of earlier Satans, see *Häxan* (Christensen, 1922) and *Faust* (Murnau, 1926).

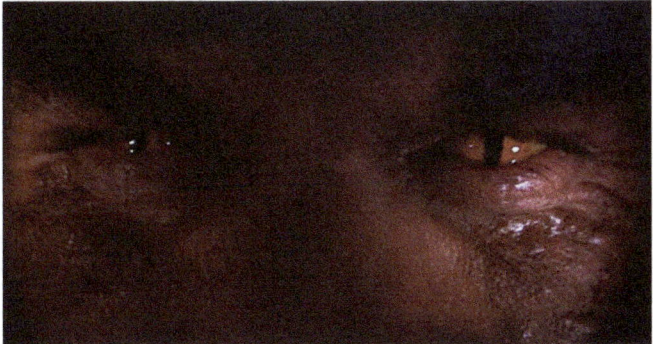

Figure 51. 'His father's eyes'. *Rosemary's Baby*, directed by Roman Polanski (Paramount Pictures, 1968).

During a period between the late-1980s and 1990s there was a motif to frame satanic figures as businessman-types, as seen in films such as *Angel Heart* (Parker, 1987), *Jesus of Montreal* (Arcand, 1989), *Needful Things* (Heston, 1993), *The Devil's Advocate* (Hackford, 1997), and *End of Days* (Hyam, 1999), with the latter following *Rosemary's Baby*'s precedent by presenting satanic monstrosity as sexual violence.[2] Indeed, *End of Days* places emphasis on the selection and capture of a young female carrier for Satan's progeny. So much so, in fact, that much of the film's plot centres on his attempts to track down the woman who has been marked for the task; therefore, the spectre of her rape lingers heavily above his actions and is fundamental to the execution of his *raison d'être*, to bring about the Antichrist. The recurrence of the sexual violence motif reflects linkages that have been established in theological debate since Augustine on the relationship between sin, sex, and Satan as the serpent of Eden (see Mann 2014). For Augustine, sex, even in its reproductive capacity, functioned as the *modus operandi* for consigning sin onto the child. After their literal or figurative rape, female protagonists such as Rosemary, Reagan in *The Exorcist*, and Christine in *End*

---

2 For an example of satanic monstrosity as sexual violence in literature, see Andrea Dworkin's analysis of Isaac Bashevis Singer's 1933 novel *Satan in Goray* (1987: 85–100).

of Days, become embodiments of the sin they have been forced to carry. It is striking that, in their utilization of the female body as the site of satanic monstrosity, of sin, these films correspond with ancient theological discourse while offering evidence of the acuity of Creed's view that 'the womb [in horror] is horrifying [...] and within patriarchal discourse [...] has been used to represent the woman's body as marked, impure and a part of the natural/animal world' (Creed 2007: 49). Characterized by a propensity for sexual violence, satanic monstrosity is markedly masculine; by tricking men but raping women, screen Satans convey sustained notions about sex and power both past and present.

For Douglas E. Cowan, the growing taste for graphic horror films such as these marked 'horror movies as one more indication that "real" religion no longer occupies pride of place in society, that the appeal of horror implies the ongoing Edenic appeal of evil' (Cowan 2009: 404). While this view does not entirely reflect on the intention to horrify, not undermine, that is fundamental to these iterations of Satan, such concerns can be mapped onto other screen Satans, not least the series of decidedly less monstrous comic Satans that feature in films such as *The Devil and Max Devlin* (Stern, 1981), *Legend* (Scott, 1985), *The Witches of Eastwick* (Miller, 1987), *Bill & Ted's Bogus Journey* (Hewitt, 1991), *South Park: Bigger, Longer & Uncut* (Parker, 1999), *Bedazzaled* (Ramis, 2000), *Little Nicky* (Brill, 2000), *Tenacious D in the Pick of Destiny* (Lynch, 2006), and *This is the End* (Rogan and Goldberg, 2013). Such playful Satans might seem blasphemous to some, yet have been defended by others, with Peter Malone noting that 'it has been remarked by spiritual sages that one of the best ways of coping with the devil and bringing him down to size is to laugh at him' (Malone 2016: 333). Indeed, Noël Carrol, exploring the relation between horror and humour, observes that 'comic amusement is bound up with transgressive play with our categories, concepts, norms, and commonplace expectations' (Carrol 1999: 154). It is more likely that such depictions are less illustrative of a religiously motivated rejection of Satan and, therefore, of evil, per Malone's suggestion, and that they are in fact just capitalizing on familiar iconography that has been adopted for mockery in the format of 'transgressive play', per Carroll.

Satan's Soiree: Goats and other Religious Horrors in *The Witch*[3]

THOMASIN: The Adversary oft comes in the shape of a he-goat. And whispers. Aye, whispers. (Eggers, 2015)

There has, past and present, been significant correspondence between witch narratives and various deployments of satanic monstrosity. While illustrative, once again, of the misogynistic associations that have been constructed between women and evil, witch-hunter films – such as *Black Sunday* (Bava, 1960), *Witchfinder General* (Reeves, 1968), and *Mark of the Devil* (Armstrong, 1970) – are underscored by a fear of Satan's influence, if not by his actual presence. Witch-hunter narratives such as *Witchfinder General* evoke evil not from the witches themselves but from the religious zealots who are eager to offer up women's bodies as front lines for their religious crusading, before going on to reveal such practices to be nothing more than misogynistic oppression cloaked as noble Christian campaigns against evil. As well as witch-hunter films there are the more supernaturally spirited witch films, such as *Suspiria* (Argento, 1977/Guadagnino, 2019) in which Satan's monstrosity spectrally looms in the periphery as an evocation of absolute evil.[4] Witch horror films such as *Suspiria* evince satanic monstrosity by proxy, finding currency once again in the monstrous-feminine that codes women as primary sites of sin.

Unlike *Suspiria*, Robert Eggers' debut feature *The Witch: A New England Folk Tale* (*The Witch* hereafter) makes literal the thematic co-dependence between witchery and satanic horror. *The Witch* takes place in early seventeenth-century New England, and follows a family of Puritans headed by William, an embittered, scripture-quoting patriarch whose pride and Christian dogmatism

---

3   I would be remiss if I did not acknowledge the tremendous help kindly offered to me by Dr Jon Morgan as I prepared this piece; his knowledge and advice was fundamental to its preparation.
4   Consider also that, while not directly stated, Minnie, the unsuspecting but slyly vindictive neighbour in *Rosemary's Baby*, plays a witch's role in that film.

has led to his family's banishment from the Puritan colony to which they belonged. The family relocates to a remote farm at the edge of a large and supernatural forest and soon begin to unravel, following the abduction and murder of the youngest child by a local witch. Suspicions quickly rise against Thomasin, the eldest daughter who has been marked as the most likely villain by her increasingly hysterical family. The family disintegrates thereafter, falling one by one to murder, possession, or madness. Thomasin, the lone survivor, finally discovers that the devil himself has been lurking in the family's midst in the form of a goat;[5] with nothing left, she accepts his invitation to 'live deliciously', and follows him naked into the forest where she joins a witches' coven as they begin to conduct a satanic sabbath. The film ends on Thomasin levitating over a bonfire surrounded by the coven of naked witches.

Figure 52. The family prays together. *The Witch*, directed by Robert Eggers (A24, 2015).

The entire film is ambiguous enough that it might even be read as a fever dream wherein their madness has been brought about by hallucinations caused by corn fungus. The film constructs a markedly unstable diegetic world. Indeed, its hallucinatory qualities have been observed by critics, with Dom Sinacola noting the film's peripheral elements, a wilderness 'in which primeval forces – lust, defiance, hunger, greed – simmer at the edges of experience, avoided but never quite conquered' (Sinacola 2019: n.p.). Others have taken the film more literally. In a chapter

---

5   Associations between Satan and goats developed mostly in medieval iconography yet has some biblical basis. In Leviticus 16, for instance, links are established that present Azazel as a goat demon. Early European historian Malcolm Gaskill has identified goats recurring in witch imagery also, stating that 'in European engravings and painting[s] that depict the witches' sabbath – that is, the remote meetings where witches were supposed to gather to pay homage to Satan – the devil is often depicted as a goat or a goat-like man' (qtd in Bloomer 2016: n.p.). In popular culture, the linkage has been given further weight, as seen in a variety of instances up to and including Netflix's recent series *The Chilling Adventures of Sabrina* (2018–), and the CBS series *Evil* (King & King, 2019–).

on the theme of isolationism in *The Witch*, Brandon Grafius writes that the film reflects a mounting political tendency towards fortress mentalities and border control, identifying links between the film and nationalistic rhetoric deployed by the Trump administration (Grafius 2018: 119–28). Sadly, this reflectionist approach fails under close scrutiny, mostly due to the fact that *The Witch* premiered at Sundance film festival some six months before Trump formally announced that he was running for president.

And yet, the question of the film's allegorical function remains pressing, especially given Eggers' wishes to ground the film with historiographic feeling.⁶ Certainly, the film is preoccupied with notions of fanaticism and the pervading theme of women's oppression, a persistent motif for presentations of satanic monstrosity. It is telling that Thomasin only succumbs to the powers of witchcraft after her first menstrual cycle and after her family has already begun to tear itself apart with religiously motivated hysteria. Andrea Dworkin has written on the thematic coalescence between women, witchcraft, and Satan, stating that:

> In many cultures and tribes, men can be similarly possessed; and the key to the possession – the dreams, the sex, the physical reality of desire, the obsession – is that the woman herself is magical and evil; through wickedness and magic she exerts illegitimate (therefore magical; therefore wicked; therefore originating in Satan) power over men. (Dworkin 1987: 82)

Figure 53. Black Philip/Satan leads Thomasin into the woods. *The Witch*, directed by Robert Eggers (A24, 2015).

Bad faith misogyny, such as that which Dworkin observes, has the potential to present a very real problem for a film like *The Witch*, which makes literal the demonic forces that led to the oppression and murder of many thousand women in the seventeenth century (see Demos 1982). However, any temptation to condemn the film for legitimating

---

6   The filmmaker makes clear the fact that he drew much of the dialogue from historical sources relating to the New England witch trials.

real-world murder will be at the cost of stripping it from the historical context on which it is trying to offer comment. Theological anxieties were instrumental to the construction of society at that time; in other words, in the context of seventeenth-century New England puritanism, the existence of demonic forces was held to be true, and with conviction. While this acknowledgement does not vindicate the actions of powerful men historically responsible for the oppression and murder of women, it does illustrate how the film works as both a parable for the dangers of fanaticism and for the ongoing systemic abuse of women, a recurring theme in the representation of Satan on-screen. Black Philip's, or Satan's, invitation to Thomasin to come with him and 'live deliciously' might equally be read as an enticement to live *freely*, away from the society quick to condemn her. Evil (and therefore Satan) must, as Hegel observes, offer some form of a reward to be worthy of pursuit, 'for the purely negative is in itself dull and flat and therefore either leaves us empty or else repels us' (Hegel 1975: 222). As Thomasin sheds her clothes, she symbolically untethers herself from the archaic, patriarchal order that has wantonly abused her. In her newfound sisterhood with the witches, Thomasin steps into a new order free from the shackles of a system that has marked her womanly body as a site of sin.

Emily Brick

Warlocks: *AHS Apocalypse* (Murphy and Falchuk, 2011–present)

Apocalypse (2018), in the eighth season of *American Horror Story*, produces a series of male monsters which reflect contemporary discourses on masculinity. The narrative jumps back and forward through time and converges existing story arcs from *Murder House* (Season 1, 2011) and *Coven* (Season 4, 2014) to bring about the apocalypse via a nuclear holocaust and then goes back in time to reverse it. The first three episodes deal with the lead-up to a nuclear explosion and the assembly of the cast of survivors heading for a nuclear bunker. The post-apocalyptic time frame is fragmented by the arrival of the witches from *Coven*. The narrative (with a few exceptions) delineates the opposing forces as good/female/witches vs bad/male/warlocks trying to destroy humanity. 'Toxic masculinity' is a term originating in feminist analysis that entered popular discourse as the framework through which men are currently read as 'bad'. Toxic masculinity is the 'wrong' type of masculinity, grounded in 'anti-femininity, achievement, eschewal of the appearance of weakness, and adventure, risk, and violence' (American Psychological Association, 2019). *Apocalypse* locates its male monsters within frameworks of religion, magic and capitalism denoting masculinity as monstrous in a number of different ways, through both individuals and systems of power. There are three narrative strands that generate three types of male monster: the coming of Michael Langdon (Cody Fern), the Antichrist; the battle between the witches and warlocks; and the backstory of how the nuclear explosions were engineered by a group known as the Co-operative.

The Monstrous-Masculine

The Monstrous-Feminine (Creed 1993a) is an influential text in understanding the relationship between gender and monstrosity. Barbara Creed's work provides a framework within which to understand the historical, cultural, political and physical conditions which position women as monsters on screen. She uses 'monstrous-feminine' as the term 'female monster' implies a simple reversal of 'male monster' and 'the reasons why the monstrous feminine horrifies her audience are quite different from the reasons why the male monster horrifies his audience' (1993a: 3). In 'Dark Desires', she argues that for male monsters 'the process of being constructed as monstrous, the male is "feminized"… it stems from the very nature of horror as being an encounter with the feminine' (Creed 1993b: 121). In *Phallic Panic*, she categorizes male monsters into a series of tropes: 'vampire, wolf-man, mad scientist, ghost, ripper' (Creed 2005: viii) aligned to what she terms 'the primal uncanny' – that is, 'woman, the animal and death' (Creed 2005: vii) and 'the male symbolic order designates these areas as "other" as being outside the realm of what constitutes proper phallic masculinity' (Creed 2005: viii). Creed's work reads gendered monstrosity as being produced by frameworks of abjection and castration (female) and, femininity, masochism and the uncanny (male). Kirk Combe and Brenda Boyle identify a series of male monsters that are generated by the socio-political rather than symbolic or psychoanalytic constructions of masculinity. Each of their case studies looks at power relations between men and 'involves the formulation of a dominant masculinity and a suppressed monstrosity' (Combe and Boyle 2013: 24), the 'concepts of monstrosity and masculinity are two essential ingredients in any recipe of power relations formulating a predominating world view' (Combe and Boyle 2013: 6). Here, the male monster is an inversion of male hero and becomes monstrous through his association with disability, warfare, cultural hegemony and capitalism, primarily by their oppositional relationship to other men. Within these approaches – the psychical and the political, both male and female monsters are products of the male imaginary and are symptomatic of specifically male fears about women and other men.

The heroes of *Apocalypse* are women, which frames the male monsters in a different way. It continues the story of the witches from *Coven*, led by Cordelia (Sarah Paulson) and reunited as the only force powerful enough to save the world. *Coven* comes close to producing a model of what the monstrous masculine might look like. The male monsters are a specific threat to women rather than other men. *Coven* sets up specifically male tropes of monstrosity as predatory individuals in the form of the rapist, paedophile, serial killer and domestic abuser and as institution through Delphi, the corporate face of a group of witch hunters. All demonstrate what I would term specifically 'male pattern monstrosity' – typified by sexual abuse, domestic violence and institutional, capitalist patriarchy, directed at women and lacking reverse female tropes. The only counterpoint to male monstrosity in both *Coven* and

Figure 54. 'I never wished so hard that Alyssa Milano was a real witch'. Meredith B. Kile [Twitter], 27 September 2018 [15 December 2019]. Available from: <https://twitter.com/em_bee_kay/status/1045432500296634368?lang=en>.

Apocalypse is witchcraft, which also links into contemporary perceptions of toxic masculinity. Witchcraft as feminist protest has become prominent in popular discourse as a reaction to Trump's presidency and linked to #MeToo. A group known as Magical Resistance have placed a binding spell on Donald Trump each crescent moon (Ellis, 2019), a recent spell book called *Hexing the Patriarchy* proposes witchcraft as a tool of political resistance (Gore, 2019) and the viral tweet above of Alyssa Milano from *Charmed* at Brett Kavanaugh's hearing all clearly draw parallels between witches and feminists. The male monsters in *Apocalypse* are not positioned as sexual predators but they are propelled by rage against women/witches and positioned against female heroes. The violence has a purpose and a common political goal and is enacted via various social, religious and political contexts.

Michael Langdon is a complex monster. He is framed within the traditional Antichrist narrative and iconography of the Book of Revelations – he has 666 on the back of his neck, is the Son of Satan and is destined to bring about the End of Days. Michael was born in *Murder House*, his mother died in childbirth and he was raised by his grandmother. His powers and malevolence became apparent in childhood: he kills animals; then people; ages ten years overnight; and he influences those around him to commit evil. His grandmother covers up his violence until he tries to kill her and she throws him out stating: 'I thought I was raising a garden variety serial killer' before it becomes clear that Michael was 'far outside the natural realm' (Season 8, Episode 6). He displays various monstrous tropes beyond the satanic – seductive vampire, serial killer, cannibal and witch hunter. Michael's innate powers are greater than those of the witches or warlocks. When Cordelia executes Miriam Mead (Kathy Bates), the only person he loves and trusts, he directs his fury at the witches and he is driven to end the world in order to kill them all. He is beautiful, powerful and seductive, his interrogation of the survivors to decide who he will save is punctuated by moments of intense erotic tension with men and women. Michael is a contradictory and

Figure 55. 'Hail, Satan' – Michael Langdon ascends. *AHS Apocalypse*, created by Ryan Murphy and Brad Falchuk (20th Television, 2018).

fluid character, simultaneously monstrous and highly desirable, all powerful and vulnerable, prophesied and directionless, seductive and suggestable, born with extreme privilege and lacking in agency. Michael's monstrosity is not explicitly coded in relation to gender, he is neither hyper-masculine excess nor feminized lack. Cody Fern, who plays Michael, explained that:

> in this female-dominated world, it didn't feel like I was playing in the gender dynamic because Michael moves so seamlessly between them. To me, Michael doesn't have a gender. He's very fluid in how he presents himself, his emotions, his sexuality and how he's able to entice men and women. (Strause, 2 November 2018)

Although Michael is the chosen one in a traditional male story, his monstrosity is not explicitly coded as masculine.

Warlocks are unusual in that they are a male version of a female archetype. Men with magical powers are represented very differently to witches. Woman as witch is an archetype produced by a series of religious, ideological, cultural and political frameworks, influences that are absent or different for men. From the late Middle Ages onwards, fear of the demonic became entwined with the persecution of perceived witchcraft. Beliefs about magical practice could be structured into maleficia – beneficial or healing folk magic and diabolic witchcraft which involved making a pact with the devil. *Apocalypse* centres Satanism but divorces it from diabolic witchcraft. Although the cultural history of witchcraft and its depiction on screen is associated with women, men accounted for around 20–25 per cent of those accused of witchcraft in Europe (Rowlands 2009) and seven out of the twenty executions at Salem (Hill, 2000: xv). Male witches are sometimes referred to as warlocks, wizards and sorcerers, all terms which specifically apply to men. Although they are essentially the same, a wizard, a warlock and a witch are conceptually very different things and inhabit generic different spaces. In general, wizards are found most commonly in fantasy universes such as *The Lord of the Rings*, *Harry Potter*, and *Merlin*. In *Harry Potter*, witches and wizards are simply male and female versions of the same thing. Like witches, wizards can be good or bad but do not connote monstrosity and historical persecution in the same way as witches. Warlocks are different. The term itself implies violence and dominance and is derived from the Old English *wǣrloga* meaning 'oathbreaker' or 'deceiver' (*OED*), it has implications of monstrosity beyond simply possessing magical power.

Figure 56. The Warlocks. *AHS Apocalypse*, created by Ryan Murphy and Brad Falchuk (20th Television, 2018).

The Warlocks in *Apocalypse* practise magic in the same way as the witches – through spell craft, they form a Coven, run a school and are governed by the same Council and (female) Supreme. They are more hierarchical and unlike the witches, are assigned levels according to their magical ability. Their motto reflects macho values of 'Wisdom, Perseverance, Strength and Courage'. They do not appear to typically practise diabolic magic and are aligned with Satanism only through their belief that Michael is a powerful (level 4) Warlock, the mythical 'Alpha' (male) who can end the witches' domination of warlocks. As well as their desire for greater power, they also desire a strong male leader 'I would never have fought for Michael to be Supreme if I had known who he truly is. We just needed a leader' (Season 8, Episode 6). In *Apocalypse*, they are primarily motivated by their need to dominate (female) witches. The warlocks have natural magic powers, but they are less powerful than witches: 'no man has ever reached the level of Supreme; men are simply not equal to women when it comes to magical ability. Testosterone is a known inhibitor, it impedes access to the ethereal realm' (Season 8, Episode 4). They continually articulate their bitterness about their comparative lack of power: 'Warlocks have always been second class citizens', 'The Alpha will allow us to take our place at the top of the hierarchy' (Season 8, Episode 4). Their inner thoughts, revealed by a mindreading witch, also reveal their innate hatred of witches: 'I can't wait until they are dead, every last stinking witch', 'I can't wait to see those bitches squirm with a man in charge. Back on top where we belong' (Season 8, Episode 7). They see their exclusion from power as 'bigotry': 'You're just a scared bigot ... of a man rising to the level of supreme, of the end of female dominance', 'Those bitches love to go on about how a warlock will never become one of them' (Season 8, Episode 4). In desperation, they try to kill the witches by making a magic powder that kills only women. Cordelia burns them at the stake according to witch law, for betraying one of their own. Their desire for leadership, obsession with male hierarchy and rage against female power in any form has parallels with contemporary Red-pilled Men's Rights Activists. Their specific hatred and targeting of women here frames them as a form of monstrous-masculine rather than simply a male version of a typically female trope of monster

The final type of male monster is drawn from the socio-political rather than the supernatural realm. Pre-apocalypse, a new world order is run by 'The Co-operative' (the Illuminati rebranded), a master organization that 'controls the money, the arts, the armies, everything: they run the fucking world ... And everyone in the Co-operative has sold their soul to the Devil' (Season 8, Episode 8). The nuclear holocaust allows for the creation of a new social order and the survivors have been chosen for their superior genetics, expertise and wealth. Overall, their plan to destroy and reconstruct humanity is eugenic as well as satanic. The new world order adopts a Calvinist mode of thinking, appointing itself to choose the elite and reprobates to be saved or damned by giving them access to the nuclear bunkers. Most of the Co-operative are nameless vessels of power – 'world leaders, tech giants, media moguls and cultural influencers' (Season 8, Episode 9). The plan is explained by Jeff and Mutt, a pair of computer nerds who are introduced snorting cocaine, posting faeces to Mark Zuckerberg and working on their robotic sex doll. They are politically nihilistic – 'The world is run by prep school fails, Russian oligarchs, everyone else just slaves away to make these assholes richer'. So they make a deal with Satan, 'Sold our souls, did the whole black mass thing, now we own a robotics company worth billions' (Season 8, Episode 9). They exemplify the online Manosphere-Redpill-gamergate-incel-PUA-4Chan culture that Angela

Nagle describes in *Kill All Normies* as a 'strange vangard of teenage gamers, pseudonomous swastika-posting anime lovers, ironic *South Park* conservatives, anti-feminist pranksters, nerdish harassers and meme-making trolls' motivated by a 'love of transgression for its own sake' (Nagle 2017: 2).

Figure 57. Mutt and Jeff. *AHS Apocalypse*, created by Ryan Murphy and Brad Falchuk (20th Television, 2018).

Mutt and Jeff on one level represent non-hegemonic masculinity; they are Other to traditional dominant 'normie' forms. However, they hold power in a new world order formed through virtual capitalism, dominance over technology and online space. They persuade Michael to make the Co-operative destroy the world with nuclear weapons instead of Hellfire, as 'all you need for Armageddon is three people in the right places pushing the right buttons' (Season 8, Episode 9). It is ultimately Mutt and Jeff who cause the nuclear apocalypse because of their hatred of humanity.

Monstrosity in *Apocalypse* is not exclusively male. There are bad, sadistic and monstrous women – Miss Venable, a rogue witch who sells her soul in a diabolic pact, key Satanists, and Michael's surrogate mothers – but overall, it is male monstrosity that is posited as the primary threat. Female power is healing and world-saving, male power is destructive and diabolic. *Apocalypse* uses a series of causal frameworks in its formation of monstrous men – patriarchy, magic, religion, capitalism, and produces a range of male monstrosity from the social, political and supernatural realms. The monsters produced here map on to contemporary perceptions of toxic masculinity – a charismatic and destructive leader, a group of men's rights activists angry they are not in charge, incels, corporate capitalism and the machinery of war. The construction of male monstrosity has a diverse range of origins and forms. The 'monstrous-masculine' present in *Apocalypse* is not quite a cogent inverse male version of the 'monstrous-feminine'; however, the monsters it produces can be read as having specifically male pattern monstrosity.

Craig Ian Mann

She-Wolves: *When Animals Dream* (Arnby, 2014)

In 2014, *Fangoria* published an article titled 'Where Are the Wolves?' in which Craig Anderson bemoans a lack of werewolf films in the twenty-first century and suggests that the monster has grown metaphorically stale. He asks: 'are werewolves, as central characters ... simply too limiting, the Dr. Jekyll and Mr. Hyde conflicting nature overplayed and now infertile as subject matter'? (2014: 74). There are a number of problems with this question. The first is that the author ignores that the twenty-first century has actually seen the release of an enormous amount of werewolf films. In fact, eight films featuring werewolves were released in 2014 alone. The second is that the author assumes that contemporary werewolf films can only be understood as a unified articulation of a 'conflicting nature' – more commonly referred to in scholarly work on werewolf media as the 'beast within' (see Bourgault du Coudray 2006) – that has been typically associated with wolf-men as symbols of unchecked masculine aggression. He is certainly not alone in this view; Carys Crossen argues that the 'cinematic werewolf is still trapped in the classic representation of the werewolf as a (male) monster continually at war with itself, unable to find a socially acceptable form of masculinity' (2019: 49).

We need only to look at *Late Phases* (Bogliano, 2014) for evidence that this claim is inaccurate. The story of a Vietnam veteran who is forced to do battle with a werewolf hiding inside a pious man of faith, it is a film concerned with indicting not only aggressive masculinity but fervent militarism, social conservatism and religious fundamentalism in the contemporary United States; far more than just a comment on the 'beast within'. But even if we were to accept the spurious notion that werewolf films have always been and continue to be in the business of exploring male aggression, the third problem with Anderson's rhetorical question (and, by extension, Crossen's statement) is that he overlooks those films in which the monster is a woman. After all, she-wolves have been at the centre of several werewolf narratives in the twenty-first century alone, including *Ginger Snaps* (Fawcett, 2000), *Ginger Snaps 2: Unleashed* (Sullivan, 2004), *Ginger Snaps Back: The Beginning* (Harvey, 2004), *Cursed* (Craven, 2005), *Blood and Chocolate* (Garnier, 2007), *Trick 'r Treat* (Doherty, 2007), *When Animals Dream* (Arnby, 2014), *Female Werewolf* (Alexander, 2015), *Wildling* (Böhm, 2018) and *Among the Shadows* (Mesquita, 2019). The she-wolf narrative, then, is perhaps the best defence against the assumption that the werewolf film is, in Anne Billson's words, 'basically just the beast within' (2010: 7).

This chapter will culminate in a discussion of *When Animals Dream*, perhaps the most interesting contemporary werewolf movie to focus on a she-wolf. However, it is first necessary to outline the long history of female werewolves in the horror film; after all, cinema's first werewolf was a woman. *The Werewolf* (MacRae, 1913) was sadly lost to a fire in 1924, but a detailed plot synopsis survives in *Universal Weekly*. The film concentrated on European settlers to the United States being hounded by a Native American she-wolf, Watuma (Phyllis Gordon), who has been 'raised to hate all white men'. She attacks a group of prospectors, who flee to the safety of a Christian friary; there, a man of God repels Watuma with a cross, causing her to 'dissolve into a slinking wolf' and retreat. A 100 years later, the she-wolf tracks down the descendant of one of the prospectors, Jack Ford (William Clifford), and 'kills his sweetheart' (Anon. 1913: 16). It was, then, a film that demonized its she-wolf on the grounds of both race and gender. A Native American woman powered by tribal magic, Watuma is depicted as the bane of white men at a time when both America's women and its indigenous peoples were fighting for equal rights.

This trend of othering werewolf women on dual fronts would continue when the she-wolf narrative resurged in the 1940s, following the success of *The Wolf Man* (Waggner, 1941). *Cat People* (Tourneur, 1942) set the template: it concentrates on a Serbian immigrant, Irena (Simone Simon), who marries an American man, Oliver (Kent Smith), because she deeply wants to be 'a nurturing wife and domestic goddess' (Snelson 2015, 22). But she has a terrible secret: she is descended from a line of 'cat people' who turn into feline creatures as soon as they experience sexual arousal. A sexless marriage ultimately drives Oliver towards his co-worker, Alice (Jane Randolph), before Irena inevitably transforms into a panther. In *Cry of the Werewolf* (Levin, 1944), a Romany princess named Celeste (Nina Foch) has the power – like her female ancestors – to shapeshift into a wolf. While attempting to hide her true nature, she lures the all-American Bob (Stephen Crane) away from his fiancée Elsa (Osa Massen), a hard-working Romanian immigrant.

Both of these films essentially figure the she-wolf as a kind of femme fatale. And like the vampish women of the film noir cycle, their negative depiction is heavily linked to America's entry into the Second World War; it is no coincidence that both Irena and Celeste hail from nations either allied to or occupied by the Axis powers, and they both adhere to the conception of the femme fatale as a character who seeks 'to advance themselves by manipulating their sexual allure' (Krutnik 1991: 63). But these films challenge the common conception that such characters were produced by anxieties surrounding the entrance of women into the workplace during wartime (Fay & Nieland 2010: 148). Neither Irena nor Celeste possesses stable employment, and in each narrative there is a working woman that is depicted positively in direct contrast to the she-wolf. These were films, then, that figured both women and immigrants as monsters – if they refused to contribute to the war effort. As Mark Jancovich suggests, they are examples of the 'kept woman', who 'had come to signify decadence and corruption in the war years' (2010: 176). This attack on 'kept women' is also apparent in *She-Wolf of London* (Yarbrough, 1946), in which the aristocratic Phyllis Allenby (June Lockhart) is manipulated into believing she is suffering from werewolfism by her aunt, Martha Winthrop (Sara Haden), who wants to use Phyllis' considerable fortune to finance a life of leisure.

Such negative conceptions of the she-wolf would resurge in the American werewolf films of the 1980s, released during the presidency of Ronald Reagan. A social conservative, Reagan represented the New Right, a political movement staunchly opposed to (amongst many other symbols of progressiveness) feminism, abortion, pornography and extra-marital sex, all things it believed 'fostered a destructive "permissiveness" that undermined the value of family, church and state' (Schaller 1992: 93). Meanwhile, Western culture became increasingly aware of the dangers posed by sexually transmitted infections, particularly in the mid-1980s as the AIDS crisis began. It was in this context that *Howling II: Your Sister is a Werewolf* (Mora, 1985) was released: perhaps the film to most blatantly use a shapeshifting woman to preach the apparent dangers of sexual freedom. The film's antagonist, Stirba (Sybil Danning), is the hyper-sexualized leader of a werewolf cult.

The castle where she and her followers reside is depicted as a hive of sexual deviancy. For example, a new member of the cult is inducted into the fold via group sex; she writhes on an ornate bed with Stirba and one of her male followers as all three transform. Ultimately, Stirba is destroyed by Stefan Crosscoe (Christopher Lee), a self-righteous man of faith representative of Reagan's traditional values.

But the previous decade had witnessed the release of a film that sought to depict she-wolves more positively. Italy's *Werewolf Woman* (Silvestro, 1976) focuses on a rape victim, Daniella (Annik Borel), who has been traumatized since she was attacked as a teenager. She begins to believe she has inherited a family curse after reading about her ancestor, who was burned at the stake for apparent werewolfery. Released at the height of both the sexual revolution and the women's rights movement, *Werewolf Woman* depicts werewolfism as a symbol of power and freedom from patriarchal control: it allows Daniella to enact revenge against men who would objectify and abuse her. Similarly, *My Mom's a Werewolf* (Fischa, 1989) spoofs the typical depiction of the she-wolf as a sexually aggressive monster: it sees its protagonist, Leslie (Susan Blakely), turned into a she-wolf after she has an affair to escape her uncaring husband. Unbeknownst to Leslie, her new lover (John Saxon) is a werewolf, who passes his curse to her when he bites her during foreplay. Her budding werewolfism thus represents her resurgent sexuality, which has been repressed over years trapped in a mundane marriage. *My Mom's a Werewolf* echoes *Werewolf Woman*, then, in using werewolfery as a symbol of emancipation; it attacks and satirizes the Reganite conception of the nuclear family, which rigidly positioned the 'husband as breadwinner' and the 'wife as mother and homemaker' (Schaller 1992: 92).

It is these more progressive narratives that have had the most influence on twenty-first-century she-wolf films. The most famous and widely studied contemporary example is *Ginger Snaps*, which has been the subject of a number of feminist readings since its release at the turn of the millennium (see Barker, Mathijs & Mendik 2009; Cherry 2009; Mathijs 2013). But, of course, there are

Figure 58. Sybil Danning's Stirba, the hyper-sexualized leader of a werewolf cult. *Howling II: Your Sister is a Werewolf*, directed by Phillipe Mora (Metro-Goldwyn-Meyer, 1985).

many other examples: *Blood and Chocolate* sees its she-wolf protagonist overthrow the patriarchal regime that rules over her werewolf pack, while *Trick 'r Treat* has a group of she-wolves pose as helpless would-be victims in order to lure lascivious young men into the woods, where they kill them as punishment for their sexual aggression. In the 2010s, three more films –Denmark's *When Animals Dream*, Canada's *Female Werewolf* and America's *Wilding* – saw release following the global rise of fourth-wave feminism. All three take their lead from *Werewolf Woman* in depicting their she-wolves as young women determined to slip the bonds of patriarchy and express their sexuality in deeply conservative communities.

When Animals Dream is perhaps the most interesting of these films. It follows Marie (Sonia Suhl), a 16-year-old who lives with her father, Thor (Lars Mikkelsen), and catatonic mother (Sonja Richter) in a rural village on the coast of Northern Jutland, an area of Denmark that has long been associated with religious repression due to the prevalence of the Church Association for the Inner Mission in Denmark (or simply the Inner Mission), a Lutheran revival movement. Marie soon comes to discover that her mother is unresponsive because she is under the influence of drugs, administered to her by Thor and the village doctor (Stig Hoffmeyer), in order to stunt her hereditary werewolfism – and that she, too, will soon turn into a monster as her own werewolfery begins to come to the fore. As she transforms into a lupine creature, she discovers that her regressive and male-dominated society will do anything to stop her from embracing her true nature.

The oppressive atmosphere of Marie's community is revealed throughout *When Animals Dream*, as the young she-wolf finds herself objectified and subjugated both in her workplace and her own home. At her job – as a worker in a fish-packing plant – she is subjected to a number of humiliating hazing pranks by her male colleagues, which culminate in her co-worker, Esben (Gustav Giese), cornering her in a locker room, stripping her to her underwear and threatening her with rape. In her own home, she is expected – just like her mother – to submit to her father's will; when Thor discovers that his daughter is now transforming, he seeks to medicate her with the same devastating substance that has rendered his wife catatonic. Marie's sorrow at being trapped in this situation is captured in the film's international poster: an image of the young woman's face, covered in blood, as her lupine eyes stare into the distance as if hoping for a better future.

She-Wolves 173

Figure 59. The sorrowful face of Sonia Suhl's young she-wolf, Marie. *When Animals Dream*, directed by Jonas Alexander Arnby (Alphaville Pictures Copenhagen, 2014).

Marie's mother eventually commits suicide as an escape from patriarchal control, while Marie herself finds another way out: she embraces her werewolfism with aplomb. As her transformation advances, she uses her werewolfery to lash out against the community that would force her to repress her animal instincts, which function as a metaphor for her freedom of expression and her budding sexuality. For example, she initiates a sexual encounter with the meek Daniel (Jakob Oftebro) by telling him she needs to 'get laid' before she turns into a monster. She then partially transforms as she has sex with him, the film linking her apparent 'monstrosity' with her developing sexual desires – desires which, importantly, it depicts as perfectly natural, but which Marie's conservative community condemns. By refusing to hide or suppress her 'curse', Marie is clearly refusing to allow herself to be brutalized, controlled or subordinated.

Director Jonas Alexander Arnby suggests that it was his intention 'to show Marie's quiet rebellion, how she stands outside the community, while she is forced to go on a journey where she learns who she is' (Arnby in Carlsen 2014). Marie's werewolfism certainly does represent rebellion, but it is not a particularly quiet one: following her mother's death, Marie begins to wear her 'monstrosity' as a badge of pride. As her fingernails fall out to be replaced by lupine claws, she displays her bleeding fingers to the mourners at her mother's wake, before chewing glass in front of her father as a symbol of her defiance. At the narrative's end, when her community's elders seek to capture and destroy her, she takes revenge against the men who have oppressed her, starting with Esben. With her oppressors dead, the film ends on a note of hope as she is reunited with Daniel, the only man in the film who encourages her to be her true self.

The she-wolf narrative, then, has evolved a great deal in the century since the werewolf's first howl in 1913; where werewolfism was once used as a metaphor through which to demonize and other women, in the wake of *Werewolf Woman* it is now more often used as a symbol of emancipation, which grants the she-wolf the power and strength she needs to resist and rebel against male dominance and control. Importantly, it is also a clear indicator that the dominant discourse surrounding the werewolf film – which suggests that this is a monster incapable of articulating anything other than a fear of acute masculine aggression – is short-sighted and reductive; horror cinema's werewolf women are proof enough that werewolfery is a far more versatile metaphor than the 'beast within' can account for.

Daniel Sheppard

Serial Killers: *Bates Motel* (Ehrin, 2013–2017)

While the queer monster takes many forms, this chapter characterizes the queer monster as the crossdressing or transfeminine individual who, despite their narrativized gender identity, often presents male. Popularized by Anthony Perkins' Norman Bates in Alfred Hitchcock's *Psycho* (1960), Harry M. Benshoff and Sean Griffin read this particular monster in a reactionary way, writing that it 'has become such an overused stereotype, it is now something of a cliché' (Benshoff and Griffin 2004: 322). This notion certainly applies to the horror genre in the late twentieth century, epitomized by *The Silence of the Lambs* (Demme, 1991) winning the Academy Award for Best Picture in 1992. However, following genre developments at the turn of the new millennium, Sam J. Miller argues that 'there are no more queer monsters' (Miller 2011: 221). Accordingly, when *Psycho* was reinvented for television in 2013, audiences avidly awaited the return of the queer monster. That was until *Bates Motel* (2013–2017) reimagined *Psycho*'s shower scene in its final season. Here, Norman Bates (Freddie Highmore) defies how he is remembered in the popular imaginary, stabbing his helpless victim while presenting male ('Marion', Season 5, Episode 6).

After the episode was broadcast in the United States, audiences were left shocked. This reaction was clearly anticipated by *Bates Motel*'s executive team because, directly following the episode's transmission, *IndieWire* published an interview by Ben Travers with executive producer Kerry Ehrin (2017). Here, Travers attempts to justify the creative decision made, suggesting that *Psycho* might be problematized because it 'propagates fear of trans individuals and supports a heteronormative viewpoint'. He identifies how, through a heteronormative viewpoint, Ehrin was 'very conscious not to reinforce a transphobic narrative'. In Ehrin's own words, *Bates Motel* is 'about a kid who very specifically thinks he's his mother, as opposed to anything else. It really became about protecting that and not letting it slip or slide into anything transphobic'.

Although the interview does not consider alternative viewpoints, it carefully explains the artistic decision made and deserves to be respected. However, a matter of weeks later, extracts from Travers' interview were claimed by the British tabloids who exploited Ehrin's words. 'It's political correctness gone *Psycho*! Remake won't show the killer cross-dressing in a shower scene in order to avoid "transphobia"', reported Chris Hastings' headline for the *Daily Mail* (2017). The following day, Charlie Parker reported for *The Sun* (2017) with a headline similarly reading 'PC GONE PSYCHO: Remake of Hitchcock classic *Psycho* axes cross-dressing killer in shower scene over "transphobia" fears'. Even *The Times* (2017) began appropriating Ehrin's words, reporting '*Psycho* revamp changes "transphobic" shower scene'. Citing the words of Frank Furedi, who is described as *the* emeritus professor of Sociology at the University of Kent, each of these articles stress the same supposed concern: 'It is the subordination of art to political dogma'.

It is important to note that Travers' *IndieWire* interview never considers the views of actual audiences and, in turn, neither do the articles by the British press. That is, the transphobia that *Psycho* is accused of eliciting is strictly hypothetical. As the series distances itself from *Psycho*'s hypothesized transphobia, the press dismiss *Bates Motel* as 'politically correct' and imply that Ehrin's concern constitutes that of the show's queer viewership. Consequently, the press mock the political integrity of this viewership, depoliticizing the ideology that underpins their hypothetical concern. Simply put, *Psycho* is weaponized against queer audiences. While scholars argue that the queer monster is an emancipatory figure, then, by drawing on *Bates Motel*'s reimagining of the queer monster, this chapter interrogates how the show reconfigures our essentialist understanding of the subject.

Writing through a psychoanalytic lens, Robin Wood set the foundation for an emancipatory perception of monstrosity. According to Wood, the return of the repressed is an inexorable feature of the 1970s American horror film, arguing that the monstrous represents the repressed other within heteropatriarchal bourgeois capitalism: female sexuality, the proletariat, other cultures, ethnic groups, alternative ideologies, homosexuality and bisexuality, and children (Wood 2003: 68–9). He suggests that, through identification with these monsters, audiences might find their freedom. 'Central to the effect and fascination of horror films is their fulfilment of our nightmare wish to smash the norms that oppress us and which our moral conditioning teaches us to revere', Wood concludes (Wood 2003: 72).

Benshoff adapts Wood's thesis to move beyond a psychoanalytic framework, conceptualizing LGBTQ+ audiences in light of their personal and cultural experience and thus 'linking the queer corpus with the figure of the other as it has been theorised by Wood' (Benshoff 1997: 5). According to Benshoff, who situates these audiences outside normative heteropatriarchal relations, 'the cinematic monster's subjective position is more readily acceded to by a queer viewer' which invites them 'to experience the monster's plight in more personal, individualised terms' (Benshoff 1997: 12–13). While the queer monster has the potential to reinforce heteropatriarchal narratives, Benshoff is keen to assert that identification with the queer monster 'can mean many different things to many different people and is not necessarily always a negative thing for the individual spectators in question' (Benshoff 1997: 13). However, Benshoff only theorizes identification on a subjective basis. Indeed, he does not consider how individual film and television texts characterize the queer monster differently, each informed by their own ideological project.

Benshoff's essentialist focus on identification, not characterization, reflects the critical discourse on Wood's theory: that all contemporary horror texts with a monstrous other are susceptible to reappropriation. Yet, as Wood addresses elsewhere, this is not his argument:

> Its thesis applies to only one branch of the genre (though it still seems to me the most important), and it fails to discriminate sufficiently in terms of value, lumping together major works and the relatively trivial simply because they reveal the same generic tropes – a common failing of 'theoretical' criticism. (Wood 2003: xxxviii)

While Miller argued in 2011 that there are no more queer monsters, the following year saw the release of *House at the End of the Street* (Tonderai, 2012) and, the year after that, *Insidious: Chapter 2* (Wan, 2013). In mind of Wood's critical reflexivity, then, when considering the queer monster's revival in more recent years, it becomes necessary to theorize how individual film and television texts use the generic trope, not to theorize the generic trope itself.

Although *House at the End of the Street* and *Insidious: Chapter 2* are significantly different films, their phobic ideological dictates remain much the same, unlike *Bates Motel*.

Representations of the queer monster are often pathological, born out of the castrating mother and misogynistic cultural mythology (see Creed 1993). While *Psycho* popularized this trope and films carried it throughout the late twentieth century – *Sleepaway Camp* (Hiltzik, 1983) being the most notable example – *Cherry Falls* (Wright, 2000) would try to undermine the trope by situating heteropatriarchal authority, the Law of the Father, at the site of pathology. Here, schoolteacher Leonard Marliston (Jay Mohr) is revealed to be the queer monster, admitting that his mother became an abusive 'psycho' after she was raped by the titular town's sheriff, Brent Marken (Michael Biehn). Marliston kills Marken who, it is implied, is his biological father. *Cherry Falls'* attempt at progress falls short, however, as the film was released at the turn of the millennium.

Considering the potentially subversive nature of *Cherry Falls*, the minor spate of films to be released in the 2010s are regressive. For example, a year before Max Thieriot played Dylan Massett in *Bates Motel*, he played Ryan in *House at the End of the Street*. The film's conclusion reveals that, following the tragic death of his sister, Ryan was abused by his mother who forced him to repress his identity and perform his sister's illusion. Not only does the queer monster revert back to a pathological relationship with his mother, however. *House at the End of the Street* focuses on the terrorization of Jennifer Lawrence's character, Elissa. While audiences might not perceive Elissa's peril to be inherently misogynistic, *House at the End of the Street*'s ideological message is timely and mimics the rhetoric of trans-exclusionary radical feminists (TERFs). Typically, TERFs prefigure the transfeminine individual as masculinized and predatory, using their claimed gender identity to access women's spaces. *House at the End of the Street* does not draw a distinction between Ryan's delusional crossdressing and transness so, by situating Ryan and Elissa in a heterosexual romance, the queer monster is presented as an undeniably male threat to the cisgender female.

While *House at the End of the Street* is problematic, the ideological implications of *Insidious: Chapter 2* taint not only the film itself but what came before it – *Insidious* (Wan, 2010). *Chapter 2* is a direct narrative continuation in which the anonymous 'old woman' that haunts *Insidious* (played then by Philip Friedman) is named Parker Crane or, rather, the Bride in Black (played here by Tom Fitzpatrick). Again, reverting back to misogynistic cultural mythology, Crane's mother is a castrating presence who, in childhood, abuses him into presenting female. This forces Crane into a pathological state of gender dysphoria and, developing into adulthood, he begins kidnapping and murdering young women while dressed as a woman himself. Mimicking the regressive ideological message of *House at the End of the Street*, the queer monster is a violently threatening man who preys upon cisgender women, depicted so vile that even trans journalists have created online spaces to critique the film (see Rude 2013). More damning, however, *Insidious: Chapter 2* bespeaks heteropatriarchy's abject fascination with the transgender individual and their genitalia, eliciting *Dressed to Kill* (De Palma, 1980) and its focus on sex reassignment surgery (see Phillips 2006). Here, Crane is admitted to hospital for attempting to castrate himself, jumping out of a window and plummeting to his death a matter of days later. Speaking in hegemonic terms, what this suggests is that an individual's gender identity is validated only by their genitals – this being the precise reason as to why the term 'transsexual' is now typically disavowed.

While films such as *Insidious: Chapter 2* and *House at the End of the Street* mimic *Psycho* to varying degrees, *Bates Motel* situates the queer monster in its source material and rewrites the script. Originally broadcast six months before the theatrical release of *Insidious: Chapter 2* in the US, the beginnings of *Bates Motel* are suggestive of the usual ideological implications, abound in misogynistic cultural mythology. Here, the show opens with Norman discovering his dead father, to which his mother Norma (Vera Farmiga) is characterized as the *femme fatale*. She proceeds to move and buy the Bates Motel, forcing Norman against his will. It is here that discomforting undertones of Oedipal abuse become apparent, as audiences of *Psycho* would anticipate ('First You Dream, Then You Die', Season 1, Episode 1).

Indeed, on initial viewing, *Psycho*'s Oedipus complex runs deep through the veins of *Bates Motel* and influences how audiences perceive the narrative. This intertextual knowledge of *Psycho* characterizes both Norma and Norman before *Bates Motel* itself, encouraging audiences to recognize Norma as the castrating mother who pathologizes her son. Midway through the first season, however, exposition requires audiences to be reflexive of their subject position and confront their unconscious reproduction of misogynistic cultural mythology. Here, Norma reveals to her other son, Dylan, that Norman's father was domestically violent. In a flashback, Norman defends Norma after a particularly traumatic attack, killing his father before blacking out and having no recollection ('The Truth', Season 1, Episode 6). Audiences come to realize that their understanding of *Bates Motel* has been manipulated through Norman's unreliable, pre-existing pathological perspective. *Bates Motel*'s Oedipus complex is a fiction of Norman's condition, suggesting that Norma is the show's real protagonist, although this becomes more apparent as the series progresses. This is epitomized when Norman starts having visions of Mother, who he actually perceives to be Norma herself, creating a Freudian double who only deepens Norman's pathological state.

Although audiences, like Norman, might be manipulated into seeing otherwise, *Bates Motel* situates the Law of the Father at the site of pathology. Here, the series fully realizes the subversive potential of *Cherry Falls*, rendering both Norma and Norman an immediate victim of paternal authority. If *Psycho*'s Norman Bates is a gay stereotype that resonates with a gay sensibility, 'complete with a harsh overbearing mother and absent father' (Benshoff 1997: 143), *Bates Motel* holds Norman's father accountable and politicizes his absence. Having witnessed the horrors of domestic violence, Norman protects Norma by murdering his father. Norman's visions of Mother are better understood as displaced visions of Father, then. Midway through the series, Mother instructs Norman to submerge himself underwater. In doing so, Norman witnesses a false memory, subjected to Norma murdering his father ('Persuasion', Season 3, Episode 3). Here, if Norman's visions of Mother are displaced visions of Father, Norman is manipulated into believing that the Law of the Father is not responsible for his trauma, implicating an innocent maternal authority in its place.

Norman's trauma is crucial to understanding *Bates Motel*'s reimagining of *Psycho*'s shower scene. Although the British press feigned outrage when Norman did not crossdress, subordinating art to political dogma, journalists who actually watched *Bates Motel* would realize that Norman does, in fact, dress as Norma in the final season ('The Convergence of the Twain', Season 5, Episode 2; 'Bad Blood', Season 5, Episode 3). *Bates Motel* chooses, instead, not to associate Norman's crossdressing with pathological violence, but this is only incidental. 'Marion' is the second episode in a two-part story arc, with the previous episode having followed Marion Crane (Rihanna) as she tries to navigate through an emotionally abusive relationship with her cheating partner, Sam Loomis (Austin Nicholas; 'Dreams Die First', Season 5, Episode 5). Here, Marion arrives at Bates Motel and befriends Norman, doubled in their psychological torment. As she proceeds to shower, a shot-for-shot mimicking of *Psycho* occurs, until Marion herself pulls the curtains back. 'Screw this shit'. She steps out of the shower, leaving to confront Sam. Norman supports Marion after she returns from Sam's family home, offering the advice she needs to escape and rebuild her life. Marion is not Norman's victim. Rather, Norman is Marion's confidant in the face of heteropatriarchal oppression – a detail that goes unremarked by the British press.

'He reminds me of your father', Mother tells Norman on Sam's arrival, searching for Marion. 'Stop talking like you're her – we both know you're not', Norman replies. Here, it is no coincidence that Sam Loomis shares the same name as Norman's father, Sam Bates. As Sam proceeds to shower in Marion's vacant room, *Bates Motel*'s shower scene becomes a restaging of Norman's trauma, explaining why Norman resumes his own gender identity. This traumatic re-enactment does little to alleviate Norman's pathological state, however. Instead, it empowers Mother to possess Norman's psyche. Although Norman kills the bearer of Marion's heteropatriarchal oppression, he is simultaneously held captive to his own. Marion might not be the victim, nor Norman inherently queer, but the Law of the Father is now, more than ever, a pathological threat.

Murray Leeder

The Skeleton: *Game of Thrones* (Benioff, 2011–2019)

Having fled the destruction of Winterfell and made their way north of the Wall in search of the Three-Eyed Raven (Struan Rodger/Max von Sydow), Bran Stark (Isaac Hempstead Wright) and his companions have, after two seasons worth of trekking, arrived at a giant weirwood. But a trap is waiting for them: from the snow emerges a force of deadly undead guardians. In the ensuing battle, Jojen Reed (Thomas Brodie-Sangster) is killed and Bran's party is rescued by magical fireballs tossed by Leaf (Octavia Alexandru), one of the few surviving members of the diminutive race called the Children of the Forest.

These events occur in the fourth season finale of *Game of Thrones* (2011–19), 'The Children' (Season 4, Episode 10). From its very first scene, *Game of Thrones* has involved zombie-like reanimated dead, raised by the villainous White Walkers; George R. R. Martin's novels call them 'wights', a term descending from Tolkien's use of 'barrow-wights', though the show does not use that term (homophonous with 'whites'). They change substantially over the series' run, interestingly rehearsing the broad trend in cinematic zombies: they start slow and shambling, and by the end of the series they are *fast*, practically able to outrun horses. But the presentation of the wights in this scene is different: they are walking, fighting skeletons.

Popular culture is rife with skeletons; that much is demonstrated by stepping into most any mall in the month of October.

Yet the skeleton, understood as a monster (Wikipedia has separate entries for 'Skeleton [undead]' and simply 'Skeleton'), has received little scholarship (Westfahl 2005 and Wang 2014 represent rare exceptions). And it is nothing new; since the *danse macabre* imagery emerged in the late Middle Ages, the skeleton has served as an allegorical figures of death and its inexorability; it

Figure 60. A skeleton wight on *Game of Thrones*. *Game of Thrones*, created by David Benioff (Warner Brothers Television, 2011–19).

plays the same role in the Death card in the tarot deck and in many paintings, including Brueghel the Elder's *The Triumph of Death* (1562). I have written about how their presence in early cinema's trick films including those of Georges Méliès is shaped simultaneously by *danse macabre* tradition and modern scientific novelty (the recent sensation of the X-ray; Leeder 2017: esp. 108–24, 135–64). Skeletons proved to have a particularly strong presence in film animation, at least as far back as the Lumière brothers' *La Squelette joyeux* (1898). *The Skeleton Dance* is only the most famous example of Disney's playful and protean skeletons, also featuring in *The Haunted House* (Disney, 1929) and *The Mad Doctor* (Hand, 1933); the imagery would filter all the way through to *The Nightmare Before Christmas* (Burton, 1993), *The Corpse Bride* (Burton, 2005) and *Coco* (Unkrich, 2017), not to mention *Pirates of the Caribbean* (Verbinski, 2003). In this light-hearted mode, skeletons often dance, contort themselves, or lose and regain limbs, maybe remove their skulls and tip them like hats; they may even turn their bones into musical instruments, especially xylophones, the instrument of choice for rattling bones at least since Saint-Saëns' *Danse macabre* (1874).

The skeleton's prominence in children's media contribute to understanding that it is a whimsical, silly, unserious monster, suited to lightly

Figure 61. Unstill life with *The Skeleton Dance* (Stalling, 1929) screen on continuous loop in The Winnipeg Disney Store. Photograph reproduced with the permission of the author.

'spooky' entertainment aimed largely at children. A trenchcoat-clad journalist named 'Dirk Bones' stars in a series of introductory 'I Can Read'! books by Doug Cushman. 'Skelly Bob,' an animate skeleton, guides readers into the Halloween-themed board book *Spooky House* (2015), also populated by vampires, ghosts, Frankensteinian monsters, robots, gremlins and the like. An especially interesting example is Vida Calavera (Gigi Saul Guerrero) in the Netflix series *Super Monsters* (Brown, 2017–), a *Día de Muertos*-styled animated skeleton whose power is the ability to make plants grow instantly ... a reflection, perhaps, of how *danse macabre* imagery is ultimately about remembering the importance of appreciating life in the face of death's inexorability.

This is not to say that horror is free of monstrous skeletons. They figure especially strongly in pre-code horror comics (Trombetta 2010) and are a recurring image in William Castle's gimmick films, especially *House on Haunted Hill* (1959); they perfectly match Castle's balance of childlike spookiness and adult perversity. Some real skeletons make a memorable appearance late in *Poltergeist* (Hooper, 1982). Mater Tenebrarum in Dario Argento's *Inferno* (1980) appears as a robed skeleton, Freddy Krueger's skeleton pops up fighting in *A Nightmare on Elm Street 3: Dream Warriors* (Russell, 1987), and the undead Templars in Amando de Ossorio's *Blind Dead* series (1972–5) combine aspects of zombies, skeleton and vampires. Yet probably the most memorable skeleton in horror cinema is a conventional inanimate one: that of Mrs Bates in *Psycho* (Hitchcock, 1960).

Threatening skeletons are found much more often in the fantasy genre than horror, and even then, they are generally a minor – in the case of *Dungeons & Dragons*, literally low-level – foe, albeit one who 'always attack until totally wiped out (Arneson and Gygax 1974: 54). In R. A. Salvatore's novel *Canticle* (1991), taking place in the Forgotten Realms campaign setting of *D&D*, the neophyte cleric Cadderly is attacked by a skeleton:

> He got his own hand up to block but found himself helplessly pinned with the bony fingers digging deeper into his flesh. He tried desperately to hook the skeleton's army under his own, to twist it around and break the monster's grasp, but Cadderly's attack was designed to twist muscles and tendons and inflict such pain on an attacker as to disable him. Skeletons had no muscles and felt no pain. (248)

It is much the same on *Game of Thrones*; though skeletons may be rather spindly and fragile foes, they are implacable ones because they are not encumbered by fear or pain and are hard to destroy entirely (one stabs Jojen fatally after it appears defeated). But skeletons rarely anchor a whole narrative since they are generally mindless and controlled, more tools of major villains (in the case of *Game of Thrones*, the White Walkers) rather than villains themselves ... unless we expand the frame to include the 'skeletal', thus allowing nemeses like Captain America's Red Skull and He-Man's Skeletor, or even Gaston Leroux's *The Phantom of the Opera* (1910). Indeed, though the *D&D* monster literally called the 'skeleton' is weak and mindless, much more powerful, intelligent undead often have skeletal appearances. This is notably true of liches, brilliant and formidable undead wizards described as 'gaunt and skeletal humanoid[s] with withered flesh stretched across horribly visible bones' (Williams 2003: 166). There are also non-human skeletal monsters, with the undead dragons called dracoliches being a fan favourite.

It will be unsurprising for fans of fantasy cinema to learn the scene in 'The Children' was an homage to stop motion maestro Ray Harryhausen and in particular the climactic skeleton scene in *Jason and the Argonauts* (1963; Calautti 2014).

In the *Argonautica* of Apollonius Rhodius, Jason sows the teeth of a dragon, which grow into a field of men he needs to fight. In the film's version, it is the Hydra's teeth, which grow into seven skeletons for Jason (Todd Armstrong) and his men to fight. Considered a high point of stop motion special effects and of effects in general, this sequence has been cited many places (e.g. *Army of Darkness* (Raimi, 1992), *The Mummy* (Sommers, 1999), *Spy Kids 2* (Rodriguez, 2002), *Ready Player One* (Spielberg, 2018)). Like Harryhausen's skeletons, the ones in *Game of Thrones* emerge from below (snow rather than soil) bearing swords. But while the skeletons in *Jason and the Argonauts* march soldierly to battle, those in *Game of Thrones* ambush their targets and attack with feral ferocity.

Skeletons seem like one of the more embodied monsters, a sort of reverse ghost with too little spirit instead of too much. Throughout a lot of its cultural history, however, the skeleton has been a curiously spectral figure.

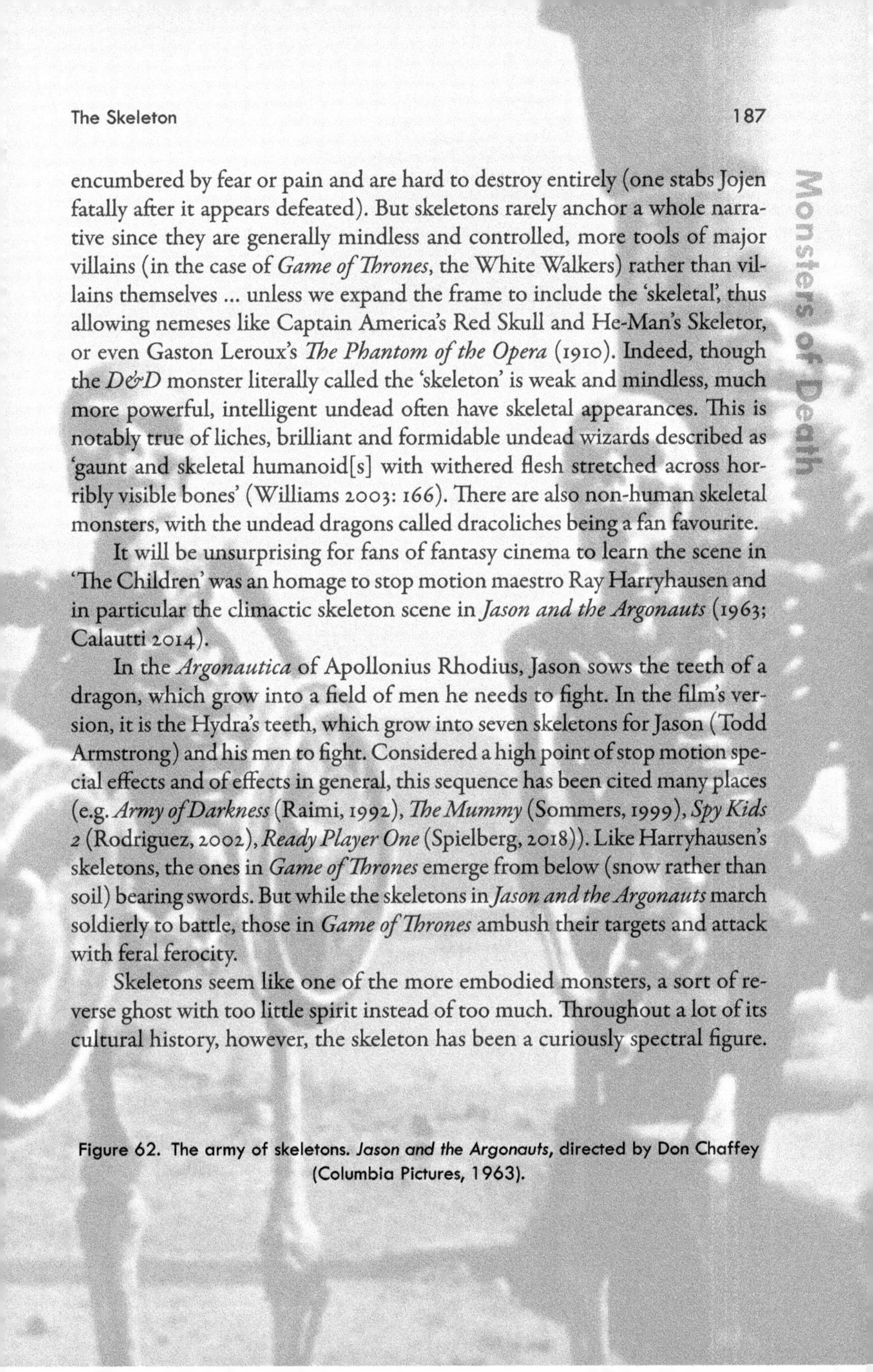

Figure 62. The army of skeletons. *Jason and the Argonauts*, directed by Don Chaffey (Columbia Pictures, 1963).

In the 1790s, they were commonly projected in the gloomy lantern shows of the Phantasmagoria, sometimes alongside the words 'the fate that awaits us all' (Barnouw 1981: 19). Before the twentieth century, skeletons were often wraithlike, ghostly beings who appeared and disappeared in a vapour. The X-ray made the living skeleton more thinkable (McGrath 2002: 111) and more embodied fictional skeletons follow. Haunting Perceval Landon's 'Thurnley Abbey' (1908) is the spectre of an immured nun, yet she appears as a robed skeleton that is violently dispatched: 'I broke the skull against the floor and stamped upon its dry bones. I flung the head away under the bed and rent the brittle bones of the trunk in pieces. I snapped the thin thighbones across my knee and flung them in different directions' (2003: 42). Shortly thereafter, however, those bones all vanish. Corporeality and disembodiment have often had a curious allegiance in the skeleton.

But do skeletons have eyes? How do they see? Or are they, like de Ossario's dead, blind? This seems like a more pressing question than 'how can a ghost see?' because of the skeleton's sense of embodiment. When asked if he can see, a skull-faced version of the D. C. Comics ghostly hero Deadman answers, 'Even though I got no eyes! Pretty wild, huh'? (Waid and Ross 1997: n.p.). A *D&D* manual specifies, 'Skeletons have no eyes' (Cook et al. 1989: 126), yet the image directly above shows glowing lights in a skeleton's eye sockets. Cartoon skeletons are often supplied with floating eyes because without them, they'd look as vacant and sinister as the *Jason and the Argonauts* skeletons. In *Game of Thrones*, the skeletal wights have vacant eye sockets and thus lack the distinct blue eyes of most wights. Yet they rush Bran with razor precision – clearly, they can 'see' somehow. In fact, the presentation of the skeleton wights fails to align neatly with the show's own logic for its undead monsters (why are they faster than the zombie wights if they are more decomposed?), but that tension speaks to the anomalous status of the skeleton within the gallery of monsters.

The classic work for representing interplay between 'skeleton as anatomy' and 'skeleton as emblem of death' is Ray Bradbury's short story 'Skeleton' (1945). Mr Harris has become acutely, morbidly aware of his own skeleton:

> Inside me now, he grasped his stomach, his head, inside my head is a – skull . . . With grottoes and caverns of bone, its rivetments and placements for my flesh, my smelling, my seeing, my hearing, my thinking! ... BUT A SKELETON! Screamed his subconscious.

The Skeleton

> I won't stand for it. It's vulgar, it's terrible, it's frightening. Skeletons are horrors, they cling and tinkle and rattle in old castles, hung from oaken beams, making long, indolently pendulums on the wind. (34)

Yet this existential dread of the skeleton is relatively uncommon even in horror fiction ... mostly the skeleton is something 'out there', whether it is a clattering mass of bone or a more allegorical, disembodied force. The skeleton is the ultimate monster within, yet we generally only seem to be able to tell stories about them if they are without.

All skeletons are magically animated undead monsters, created as guardians or warriors by powerful evil wizards and priests.
Skeletons appear to have no ligaments or musculature which would allow movement. Instead, the bones are magically joined together during the casting of an *animate dead* spell. Skeletons have no eyes or internal organs.

Figure 63. From the 'Skeleton' entry in *Dungeons & Dragons Monstrous Compendium Volume One* (Cook, David 'Zeb', et al., Lake Geneva, WI: TSR, 1989).

There is probably no monster that is as so ubiquitously 'minor' as the skeleton; skeletons are everywhere, yet rarely emphasized, just an element of the mise-en-scène of spookiness. When made central, they seem suitable only for parody, as in the 1950s B-movie spoof *The Lost Skeleton of Cadavra* (Blamire, 2001); appropriately, the webcomic *Badly Drawn Lines* depicts a skeleton with an inferiority complex, provoking only an 'EWW' from a human onlooker. So, the final point to emphasize about the skeletons on *Game of Thrones* is that they are a rarity even on the show. Through its run, it slipped generically away from realistic quasi-medieval fantasy with some supernatural elements into the generic grammar of high fantasy (notably where the dragons are concerned), yet the White Walkers and wights moved more in the direction of horror. The skeletons in 'The Children', more evocative of pulpy heroic fantasy, confused casual viewers (Sastry 2014) and earned the ire of fans (*History of Westeros*), so they seldom appeared again. Only partially skeletonized examples appear in wight-heavy episodes like 'Hardhome' and 'Beyond the Wall', in the climactic 'The Long Night', they are briefly seen bursting out of the Winterfell crypts. It makes sense: the skeleton is today a hard sell as a 'serious' monster, unless perhaps, as in the *Terminator* (1984–) films, it is encased in metal, and thus science fiction trappings.

Part V

Futures

Leah Richards

Clones: *Orphan Black* (Manson and Fawcett, 2013–2017)

If a necessary feature of being human is that of origin – that is, when a man and a woman love each other very much, they make a baby – then human-adjacent beings, created by unnatural means, have been a staple of monster lore since Pallas Athena burst fully formed from her father's head, armed for battle, in *The Iliad*. When Victor Frankenstein brought science into the mix, gathering body parts and animating his Creature through glossed-over but scientific methods, the lab-made monstrous near-human was born. In the twentieth century, real-world reproductive science became a topic of both conversation and contention, culminating, for the purpose of this discussion, in the cloning of Dolly the Sheep in 1996.

In 2013, Sarah Manning (Tatiana Maslany) walked onto a train platform in 'Natural Selection', Season 1, Episode 1 of the Canadian science fiction television series *Orphan Black* and watched her double jump to her death in front of a train. Assuming her Doppelgänger's identity, Manning soon meets several other doubles, each a fully developed individual shaped by their upbringing; it is quickly revealed that the women are clones, not of one another but of a woman, Kendall Malone (Alison Steadman), who is a biological *chimera*, a genetic anomaly with both male and female DNA and named for the mythological monster.

The word *clone* was first used in the nineteenth century to describe plants reproduced by sprouting new plants from a cutting of an existing plant; in the mid-twentieth century, the term was applied to the theoretical asexual reproduction of humans. Originally conceived of as a means of replicating talented humans with highly desirable traits, the eugenics-like potential of cloning was illustrated in *The Boys from Brazil* (1978), wherein Dr Josef Mengele (Gregory Peck) has cloned Adolph Hitler. Although it was the source material rather than the process that made the Hitler clones monstrous, that science could enable the reproduction of a human monster ensured that clones would be seen as inherently monstrous. That fiction never tells us of a single clone – there are ninety-four adolescent Hitlers, for example, and we eventually learn that there are at least 274 first-generation clones of Kendall Malone – makes them all the more uncanny.

Reproductive science more generally has historically been a contentious issue; *in vitro* fertilization is seen by many as playing God, and the term 'test tube babies' applied to the products of IVF further removes them from nature, suggesting not a normal gestation after implantation of the zygote but something more in line with Aldous Huxley's *Brave New World* (1932). Genetic testing in foetuses, intended to identify significant birth defects, is often represented as a gateway to eugenics, with the spectre of the monstrous parent collaborating with doctors to produce a made-to-order infant looming. Ultimately, attacks on the above and other procedures are about control of women's bodies, and this manifests in *Orphan Black*'s most successful clones, Sarah and her *sestra* (as one of the clones, Helena, calls them). Known by their creators as the Leda clones, a name that aligns them not only with unnatural reproduction but also with the violation of women's bodies, the women have been engineered to be infertile, that is, representing the end of natural reproduction and the genesis of a world of lab-made humans like Charlotte (Cynthia Galant), the next-generation clone of Rachel Duncan, a Leda who was raised fully aware of her origins.

In *Orphan Black*, the Leda clones and their 'brothers', the Castor clones, are the product of research into cloning that is well in advance of real-world research timelines. In the 1970s, the series establishes, Ethan and Susan Duncan headed up the research into cloning at the Dyad Institute; their first success was the Leda clones, 274 of whom were born to surrogate mothers in 1984. By the time Dolly the Sheep was cloned in our world, the Ledas would have been about 12 years old. It is eventually revealed that Dyad and the Duncans were working with an organisation practising and known as Neolution.

Neolution, identified as 'the science of self-directed evolution' within the show and the goal of which is genetic modification, ultimately to extend human life, is presented as the brainchild of P. T. Westmoreland, who claims to have been born in the mid-nineteenth century and whose early work was in eugenics; these origins align him with mad scientists like Victor Frankenstein and Dr Moreau, as well as with Charles Darwin's work on evolution, but his preoccupation with something like immortality also aligns him with the alchemists and sorcerers who predated the Age of Enlightenment. While their stated goal is an enhancement of the human, their project is at odds with this; because they were engineered, the clones that the collaboration between Dyad and Neolution produces are seen as property, non- or sub-human, despite their biological humanness. This contradiction within the show is an embodiment of the monstrous potential projected onto clones.

Neolution and Dyad are not the only shadowy organisations interested in the Leda clones; a group of religious extremists, the Proletheans, has been pursuing and executing them, using the brainwashed clone Helena as their assassin under the belief that the clones are abominations. However, Henrik, who founds a splinter group, harvests Helena's eggs (she and her biological twin Sarah are not infertile like the rest of the clones) and, using his own sperm to fertilise them, implants them in both Helena and his own daughter, convincing himself and his followers that playing God is fine as long as it is done in His name.

Obviously, the monsters in *Orphan Black* are not the clones but those who pursue them; Dyad, the Neolutionists, and the 'Old' and 'New World' Proletheans manifest the various ways that clones are conceived of as monstrous even as the audience meets, loves, and roots for more of the clones. To Dyad and the Neolutionists, who embed a tag number and list of relevant patents in each clone's DNA, they are intellectual property; to the Proletheans, they are monsters to be destroyed, although they don't hesitate to use one of the clones as their weapon, and to Henrik's sect, they are another type of property, mere vessels. That the clones are the series' protagonists challenges these more common perceptions.

While the clones' identical appearance is uncanny, and many characters recoil when first seeing two or more together, the fact that they are unique individuals shaped by their experiences challenges the narratives that their opponents would love to see perpetuated. The purpose of the series itself is to challenge audiences' notions of what is human and what is monstrous; reworking the overused trope of 'but what if the humans were the real monsters?' that has become a staple of twenty-first-century media, *Orphan Black* not only humanises the 'monsters' but embraces the monstrous as a new stage of human and, significantly, provides scientific evidence as well as the living examples of the Leda clones to support the series' view of the posthuman as not a replacement for the human but an enhancement of the human. While most of the Leda clones have a congenital respiratory disease that is ultimately fatal, Sarah and Helena appear to be immune in addition to having functioning reproductive systems and accelerated healing abilities, and these traits make them the most interesting to their creators.

And these differences, most strikingly but not exclusively Sarah and Helena's genetic anomalies, are what is most significant about the clones of *Orphan Black*, whom I will, for the remainder of this discussion, refer to by their chosen name, the 'sestra', rather than by the more clinical and dehumanising 'clone'. The sestra are distinct, they are flawed, and they are *human*. They have families and partners and careers; they have dance parties when they are happy and stab pencils into people's eyes when they're threatened. They embody a biological truth about clones: they are not identical any more than identical twins are, and their distinctions are not exclusively a product of their upbringing. Scientifically enhanced reproduction and genetic manipulation, like more widely accepted scientific advances, have the potential to improve on the human, the show argues, and to treat the products of experiments like those performed at Dyad as anything less than human is itself monstrous.

Figure 64. Sestra, Sarah and Helena. *Orphan Black*, created by Graeme Manson and John Fawcett (BBC America, 2013–17).

The show certainly plays into mad scientist tropes, with corporate biologists working without the oversight of an ethics committee or Institutional Review Board. However, where novels like *Frankenstein* cloak the scientific processes by which life is created in a lab, and films like *Jurassic Park* (Spielberg, 1993) misrepresent scientific possibility in the service of plot and theme – that is, Ian Malcolm's (Jeff Goldblum) statement that 'your scientists were so preoccupied with whether or not they could, they didn't stop to think if they should' – to 'prove' that the posthuman is monstrous, *Orphan Black* brought in scientific consultants to argue otherwise.

Orphan Black strives to be as scientifically accurate as any science fiction can be, and the differences between the sestra are scientifically plausible, albeit frequently theoretical, explorations of the multiple layers of 'choice' that influence identity—some choices are made consciously by a subject; some unconsciously, as in reaction to social conditioning; while still others are made long before a conscious subject exists, by, for instance, mitochondria, themselves influenced by their environment. The notion of genetically 'identical' means, in the case of clones like the sestra, something like 99.9815 per cent identical. The genes within the mitochondria of the eggs in which the genetically 'identical' embryos – themselves slightly different at a molecular level – were implanted would have what seems to be a numerically negligible impact, but that's not the case. And then the surrogate mother and the conditions of her pregnancy would have additional impact on the individual's foetal development. While the clones are identical enough to, for example, fool even intimate partners or make organ transplant essentially risk-free, complex biological beings like human clones will almost certainly not be 'identical' at a molecular level (see Pence, 2016 and Griffin & Nesseth, 2017). It is plausible that, just like traditionally begotten siblings or even identical twins, some clones would be more vulnerable to addiction than others or that, particularly given the fluidity of human sexuality, the clones could range from assertively heterosexual – albeit with a few power kinks and exhibitionist tendencies (Helena, Allison) – through incidentally practising bisexual (Sarah) to Kinsey-six-gay (Cosima). In presenting these layered pictures, the show departs from and complicates political arguments based on biological determinism, contributing to larger discussions about socialisation and social conditions while providing positive and, indeed, matter-of-fact and unremarkable representations of queerness – one in six clones is queer, we can extrapolate, roughly equal to society at large.

The differences between the sestra, each raised by a different family (or institution) around the world, are a textbook illustration of how we are shaped by our social milieus. From a storytelling perspective, these differences can be explained as a way to differentiate multiple characters played by a single actor, but the depth to which the characters are developed suggests that the complexity of a 'self' is what makes a human, regardless of origins. The sestra may be uncanny – identical twins certainly can be, and when identical twins exhibit distinct behaviours, that can create a second level of cognitive dissonance – but the philosophical questions that surround androids, replicants, and other near-human analogues are irrelevant to clones. The sestra demonstrate not the replacement of the traditionally human but a move towards the posthuman, more specifically the transhuman.

While the transhuman is typically perceived as the practice of making technological enhancements to the human body, and as with Bethany in 2019's *Years and Years* (Davies 2019–present), often with disastrous results, the Transhumanist Declaration, collectively authored in 1998 and revised in the intervening twenty plus years to account for scientific and technological advances, argues that the problems facing transhumanism lie within the humans who engineer it, a philosophy that *Orphan Black* enacts through the inhuman brutality of Dyad's Neolutionists, whose practises the authors of the Transhumanist Declaration would reject outright. The Transhumanist Declaration (which is certainly not the only treatise on the subject but is a simple, forthright consideration of the tenets of and objections to transhumanism and seems to align with other advocacy documents) demonstrates both the potentials and the pitfalls of transhumanism. Beginning with the statement that 'Humanity stands to be profoundly affected by science and technology in the future' and 'envision[ing] the possibility of broadening human potential by overcoming' limits to 'humanity's potential', the Declaration immediately acknowledges 'that humanity faces serious risks, especially from the misuse of new technologies' and states the ubiquitous transhumanist mantra, 'Although all progress is change, not all change is progress'. This is certainly true of *Orphan Black*, where scientific boundaries are overcome with an ease and speed matching that with which traditional morality is abandoned. The abuses of power that drive the plot of the show are at direct odds with the Transhumanist Declaration, which argues for extensive research, the only area in which Dyad excels, coupled with risk reduction, strong legislation rooted in morality rather than the drive to advance, and advocacy for all sentient beings, present and future, to be treated with respect and dignity. Clones are just one of the categories of posthuman the interests of which the Declaration seeks to protect, and the sestra and their allies are living embodiments of the potential good of post- and transhumanism.

Over five seasons, *Orphan Black* moved the conversation about cloning beyond those of copies and their value in relationship to a distinct original to engage with larger issues. Traditionally perceived as inhuman, a perception rooted in portrayals of monstrous scientists creating monsters (as with Victor Frankenstein and Drs Moreau and Mengele), clones are certainly uncanny initially, both in their similarities to and differences from one another, but as *Orphan Black* demonstrates, they are completely human, constructed from biological materials and shaped by their social milieu. If a clone becomes a monster, that is on society, not on biology.

Dahlia Schweitzer

The Master: *The Strain* (del Toro and Hogan, 2014–2017)

Monsters of Contagion

What seemed at first to be a campy show about vampires – with a zombie twist and themes of contagion – quickly evolved into a chilling portrayal of dystopian fears. *The Strain* proved itself to be utterly unique television programming, while also repurposing tropes both classic and familiar.

In the mid-1990s, a certain kind of narrative emerged. This narrative featured a large-scale viral infection, followed by various attempts to contain or cure it. There was usually some kind of resolution, but a large body count was even more likely. Modern life and air travel were usually to blame for accelerating the spread of the aforementioned viral infection, and a dramatic moment over the autopsy table and/or a microscope would yield the shocking discovery that nothing like this had ever been seen before. Generally referred to as an outbreak narrative, this specific type of story did not emerge out of nowhere – and, at least at first, the stories came out too close together to have possibly influenced each other. There were also several real-life events that correlated enough to cause a real fear of contagion.

Following the Second World War, there was a general attitude in the medical community that antibiotics had basically eradicated contagious diseases such as tuberculosis and syphilis. In fact, during the 1960s, infectious disease was seen as such a declining specialty that medical students were told to concentrate instead on 'real problems' like cancer and heart disease (Lemonick 1994). However, the AIDS epidemic of the 1980s changed that. Suddenly, viruses were in the zeitgeist, as well as an awareness of the infallibility of immune systems and the dangers of globalization. The concept of 'emerging viruses' as a coherent concept is generally credited to Stephen S. Morse, who also coined the phrase 'instant-distant infections', referencing the idea that we are only 'a plane ride away' from a 'chain of lethal transmission' (Preston 1994: D-17). Morse further established links between the largest and smallest scalar extremes. For example, he drew attention to the ways large-scale events like urbanization, globalization, environmental destruction, and war would have direct impact on the microbial level (King 2004: 64, 65). This meant that altering local behaviour could have global repercussions. For instance, an outbreak in a small African or Asian village could have a global impact.

Despite the realization that air travel could make a viral outbreak spread virtually anywhere in the world, in 1992, Americans would be even more terrified to read of an Ebola outbreak on their own soil. Richard Preston's article 'Crisis in the Hot Zone' detailed what transpired when a strain of Ebola broke out at a primate quarantine facility in Reston, Virginia, not far from Washington, DC. The strain was an airborne version of Ebola, which, if it had been susceptible to humans, could have been extremely dangerous. Even though the physical impact of the Reston outbreak was minimal, the psychological impact was anything but. In his article, Preston mentioned that both emerging viruses and mutant bacteria 'have become major and growing threats to the American population' but saved the most terrifying part of the article for the end, a quote from the same Stephen Morse who said an aerosolized form of HIV 'would circle the globe in a flash', conceivably killing 'one in three people on earth' (Preston 1992: 80, 81). The article proved such a success that Preston would be offered both book and movie deals, and the American public was confronted (realistically or not) with the notion that a deadly virus could be just around the corner, if not already here.

Hollywood quickly got on board with the first big-budget outbreak narrative, appropriately enough, *Outbreak* (Petersen, 1995), starring Dustin Hoffman and Rene Russo, which grossed $67,659,560 domestically and almost $200 million worldwide. In its tale of a virus travelling from rural Africa to America via monkey, spreading via boat and plane and ordinary physical proximity, and with a bit of military/government conspiracy thrown in for flavour, *Outbreak* established the basic format for the outbreak narrative that would be replicated for years to come. However, where certain outbreak narratives become truly fascinating is at those places where they diverge from tradition, where the original formula, laid out first by Preston and then by Petersen, would be so thoroughly reinvented that the changes speak volumes for how our understanding of the world has evolved, as well as for how Hollywood must keep updating the narrative to keep us entertained.

The Strain TV series (del Toro and Hogan, 2014–17) revolves around the villainy of 'the Master', an ancient vampire (Robin Atkins Downes) who arrives in New York City in a coffin packed with special soil. The Master takes control of New York City residents via infection, turning them into bloodsucking creatures, strigoi,[1] with no agency of their own. These strigoi are little more than his minions, acting as The Master's eyes and ears, while also assisting in his plan to take over the world. When a human is infected by strigoi, this is usually depicted by the sight of parasitic worms wriggling under the victim's skin or into their mouth or eyes. Once this happens, transformation is inevitable. The victim loses fingernails and body hair, skin grows paler, ears and nose crumble away, until he or she resembles Max Schreck as the vampire Count Orlok in the German Expressionist classic, *Nosferatu* (F. W. Murnau, 1922), itself an unauthorized adaptation of Bram Stoker's *Dracula*.

Figure 65. The Master (Robin Atkins Downes). *The Strain*, created by Guillermo del Toro and Chuck Hogan (FX, 2014–17).

1   Strigoi is the name in Romanian folklore given to vampires.

Already, we have something entirely new with this premise: we have the mind control of the original zombie, combined with the fear of infection that initially proliferated during the mid-1990s, while also integrating the very contemporary fascination we have with what the world would look with social order, as we know it, gone.

The first three seasons of *The Strain* detail the Master's efforts to take over New York City, supported by the efforts of his henchman, Thomas Eichhorst (Richard Sammel), who is literally an officer of the Third Reich who has been granted eternal life. What begins as a viral outbreak among passengers on a plane from Germany soon spreads throughout Manhattan, the few survivors of the flight turning into strigoi who then turn others. Attempts at quarantine are laughable. Barely even halfway through Season 1, strigoi swarm through the Manhattan sewer system. They are taking over. The show quickly divides into two groups: a small band of survivors determined to fight the strigoi, conquer the Master, and win back New York, versus the rapidly increasing number of strigoi, spreading their viral vampirism throughout the city.

Interestingly, in several outbreak narratives, including *Outbreak*, a nuclear bomb is briefly suggested as a solution. When the virus is localized, such a weapon is considered a viable option. In these narratives, a nuclear bomb is no longer the ultimate threat but the lesser of two evils. However, due to the unconventional vampiric nature of the villains in *The Strain*, the nuclear blast that occurs at the end of Season 3 has the opposite effect. It does not sanitize. To the contrary, it allows the strigoi – who, like many popular vampires, cannot be exposed to daylight – to take over completely once the nuclear blast has obstructed the sun.

While the implication is that the damage is far-reaching, if not worldwide, the focus of Season 4 is on the specific damage done to New York. However, we do see enough of the wreckage throughout the United States to know that the world as we know it is gone. All humanity has been enslaved by the strigoi, acting under the Master and Eichhorst, who have established a fascist dictatorship called 'The Partnership'. Everyone who is not already imprisoned or working for The Partnership is forced to survive on strict curfews, limited rations, and no available health care.

At this point, the series shifts from a combination of outbreak narrative – where scientists and doctors are frantically working to stop the spread of the strigoi infection – into a dystopian nightmare. The way the Master controls his minions echoes the first wave of zombie narratives which were heavily inspired by Haitian voodoo and almost always featured a voodoo master who controlled his zombie slaves. The strigoi also echo the cannibalistic zombie that travels in packs, as first seen in George Romero's *Night of the Living Dead* (1968). However, *The Strain* also makes reference to the most recent zombie incarnation, that which integrates infection. In the *Resident Evil* series (Various, 2002–16), for example, the zombies are a result of the Umbrella Corporation's T-Virus.

In fact, the idea of infection and contagion underpins the majority of vampire and zombie texts; in *28 Days Later*, it is the Rage Virus – a manufactured virus similar to rabies, somehow caused or triggered by televised images of violence that monkeys are forced to watch – that causes the zombie outbreak. In *Resident Evil: Extinction* (Mulcahy, 2007), Dr Sam Isaacs (Iain Glenn), the head of Umbrella Corporation's Science Division, creates the zombie in his laboratory, defying regulations and accidentally turning himself into a monster in the process. In *I Am Legend* (Lawrence, 2007), the Krippen virus – a manufactured virus based on measles – produces the zombies. In the novel *World War Z* (Brooks 2006), the vaccine for the rabies virus is pushed to market too soon. Robert Rodriguez's *Planet Terror* (2007) also ascribes a scientific cause to the zombie outbreak. Even *The Walking Dead* (AMC, 2010-present) relies on the trope of infection.

However, unlike shows such as *The Walking Dead* where zombies show up when the world ends, *The Strain* turns that future into a fascist dictatorship nightmare. For example, women are held captive in a breeding facility, where the purpose is to make as many B+ babies as possible, since infant B+ blood is especially delicious for the strigoi to drink. Women who are unable to breed are kicked out of the facility, while the women who remain are somehow expected to produce two babies per year, as a result of cleverly timed caesarean sections. Humans not suitable for making B+ babies are held captive in 'drainage facilities', kept just alive enough to produce blood for strigoi consumption. Remaining humans – those who are not making babies or being drained – are targeted via advertisements promoting farming communities called 'New Horizons'. These communities are depicted as lush and green sanctuaries from the wreckage of the cities, where residents can return to the earth, growing and preparing their own food. Volunteers line up to board the trains to these farming communities, seduced by the enticing public relations campaign. However, as we discover halfway through season four, 'New Horizons' is a lie, and a lie that looks uncomfortably like concentration camps. Staring at the camp barracks, Dr Ephraim Goodweather (Corey Stoll), formerly of the Centers for Disease Control, says: 'This is the Master's Final Solution. We're not the farmers. We're the livestock'.

Figure 66. 'We're not the farmers. We're the livestock'. *The Strain*, created by Guillermo del Toro and Chuck Hogan (FX, 2014–17).

In her book *Legacies of Plague in Literature, Theory, and Film*, Professor Jennifer Cooke describes contagious disease – and specifically the bubonic plague, also known as the Black Death – as a 'virulent metaphor', a 'powerful and historically lethal way of labeling enemies and outsiders' (Cooke 2009: 183). Of course, this is not to say that contagious disease only attacks on a metaphorical level. Rather, the outbreak narrative, narratives about how contagious disease spreads and kills, literalizes fears that may otherwise be subconscious, thus becoming a powerful tool of shaping public opinion, of dictating who is an enemy and who is a victim. A lack of scientific knowledge allowed the original spread of the plague to be blamed interchangeably on divine wrath, sinfulness, planetary alignment, refugees, or poison in the air. The plague was also used to justify anti-Semitic views, despite the fact that many Jews also died from the plague or that Edward I had already expelled Jews from England in 1290. Nonetheless, Jews were often blamed for spreading the disease, even of poisoning Christians directly, and this led directly to the persecution and murder of Jewish communities.

Similarly, following the loosely justified belief that the spread of AIDS was directly linked to African ways of life, outbreak narratives during the early to mid-1990s repeatedly placed the origin of the virus in Africa, the virus in question most likely a variation on Ebola (also linked to Africa), and the spread of the virus always moving from east to west, from 'primitive Africa' to 'vulnerable America'. After the attacks of 11 September 2001, the virus in question would not only be linked to the Middle East but would also be linked to terrorists spreading the virus intentionally to forward their own nefarious agendas. Steven Soderbergh's *Contagion* (2011), on the other hand, reflects the threat of poor hygiene standards in Asia, along with the growing awareness of how easily modern transportation can only the ramifications of that poor hygiene to travel westward.[2]

By tracing disease vectors, it becomes possible to understand not only how outbreak narratives can be shaped by real-life events, but also how they can reflect latent and/or hyperbolic anxieties triggered by changes in how the world now works (Schweitzer 2018: 2). With this perspective, *The Strain* becomes all the more fascinating for the ways in which the Master encompasses generations of fear. On the one hand, going back to ancient Biblical traditions, the Master can be seen as a representation of the Angel of Death, and therefore also linked to spirituality and religious belief, traditional causes and explanations for fear. Moving forward, the parallels between the Master, his strigoi, and actual rats – which are literally displaced, forced out of their underground tunnels as the strigoi spread throughout Manhattan – echo the threat of the Black Plague, which rats carried across Asia and Europe, the infectious fleas along for the ride. On the other hand, the Master launches us into present day ideological fears, depicting our anxious awareness of our

---

2   As seen in recent viral outbreaks such as SARS (Severe Acute Respiratory Syndrome) in 2003 and the Coronavirus (COVID-19) in 2019.

proximity to apocalypse, the fragility of modern life and the basic networks on which everything depends. One of the Master's first targets is the Internet because he knows just how much society relies upon it. With a few quick moves, one of the most populated cities on earth is overtaken and destroyed, and those not turned are taken. The outbreak narrative is a parable for our fears, evolving to depict our horrors of contagion, of the world, of monsters, and of becoming monsters. It is a template that adapts with changing cultural and social anxieties, as well as a guidepost that tells us where we are going and where we have been.

Carl H. Sederholm

The Ecomonster: *Megalohydrothalassophobia* (Abhorrence, 2018)

Ecomonsters are supposed to rise and fall with a familiar rhythm. A film like *Deep Blue Sea* (Harlin, 1999), for instance, updates the *Frankenstein* plot by showing what else can happen when human behaviour exceeds the bounds of scientific research, medical ethics, and moral expectations. Even if one's motives are generally altruistic – the film's protagonist Dr Susan McAlester (Saffron Burrows) is trying to cure Alzheimer's disease, after all – her unethical actions create monsters out of Mako sharks that ultimately devour Susan and most of her colleagues. Similarly, in Bong Joon-ho's *The Host* (2006), a monster takes shape shortly after an American military figure orders his assistant to illegally dump 200 bottles of formaldehyde into the Han River, one of the most significant bodies of water in Korea. Like the sharks in *Deep Blue Sea*, the creature in *The Host* is smart, hostile, and adaptive, defying all common-sense expectations. In one memorable sequence, the Han river monster comes ashore in broad daylight and preys openly on any human being unfortunate enough to fall in its path. Although the creatures in *Deep Blue Sea* and *The Host* are ultimately defeated, both films strongly imply that the creatures would never have behaved in those ways (or even existed) were it not for specific human deeds.

Understanding these familiar patterns requires seeing monsters as signs of imminent trouble. As Timothy K. Beal writes, 'the ecomonster represents a divine message or portent, a *monstrum* in the most literal sense, warning us to retreat into the established order of things' (Beal 2002: 161). Unfortunately, however, even the most ideologically comforting notions of order and culture have ways of shifting into even deadlier scenarios that portend further destruction. Put another way, ecomonsters represent not only localized warnings against hubris, but also suggest broader concerns over global decay. Ecomonsters may thus be understood, Beal argues, as 'personifications of an ecological chaos that is and always has been in the world, however latent' (Beal 2002: 161). To overcome the possibility that such chaos will ultimately be unleashed – and impossible to contain – the world must be recreated. As Beal suggests, the predictable patterns of ecohorror films may thus be interpreted as variations on the need for a 'cosmogonic religious event which recreates and resacralizes world order against the monstrous threat of primordial chaos' (Beal 2002: 162). Humans never simply defeat ecomonsters; they must also recreate the world that witnessed their birth.

Defeating the monster and recreating a damaged world are clearly major aspects of keeping things stable, but what if the world has already been destroyed and is no longer subject to positive renewal? That is one of the questions Abhorrence raises on their 2018 EP entitled *Megalohydrothalassophobic*, an album that assumes that, as one song title attests, 'The End Has Already Happened'. And yet, the album is not simply interested in pointing to an ultimate end. Instead, it addresses the ways monsters transform from localized warnings into realities that cannot be eradicated. In this scenario, even if the end has already come, things can still get worse. The band captures this idea, in part, by choosing an album title that names the fear of very large objects, living and non-living, that dwell beneath the waves. The peculiar thing about this fear is that it is not necessarily directed towards any singular object, such as a Mako shark or even a new species of river monster. Instead, the fear at the heart of this album refers to things that appear to lurk just outside the boundaries of sense and perception. Fear of these monsters implies a deep vulnerability, one most likely attached to larger fears of being consumed or overwhelmed by forces much larger than one can imagine.

To underscore this fear, the album frequently alludes to H. P. Lovecraft's Cthulhu, a creature that would definitely count as a large object lurking beneath the sea. But *Megalohydrothalassophobic* is not a retelling of 'The Call of Cthulhu', nor is it even a loose adaptation. Instead, it repurposes the idea of Cthulhu from a creature that suggests weird realities beyond human ken into a synecdoche of Timothy Morton's equally overwhelming concepts 'the mesh' and of 'hyperobjects'. In that sense, this album attempts to warn audiences about the likely ecological crises tied to human behaviour. Unlike the more familiar ecohorrors, however, this album avoids telling a story in which a monster simply rises and falls. Instead, it suggests that the monster cannot be defeated because the end has already come.

A Monster Reborn: Abhorrence

It is commonly understood that monsters are never truly defeated and that they always come back. What is not as well known, however, is that when they do return, they come with 'not just a fuller knowledge of our place in history and the history of knowing our place' but also 'self-knowledge, *human* knowledge – and a discourse all the more sacred as it arises from the Outside' (Cohen 1996: 20). This implies that monsters necessarily adapt to their circumstances and that they always return with even greater discursive burdens than they had the first time. These greater burdens portend new – and likely even more complex – problems that humans must confront if they want to avoid destruction. To understand the larger monstrous import of *Megalohydrothalassophobia*, we must first consider the band as a type of monster, newly returned after an initial defeat and a rather long absence.

Abhorrence formed in 1989 and broke up in 1990. Within that short time span, the band released two recordings, a demo entitled *Vulgar Necrolatry* and a self-titled 7" EP. In the ensuing years, both recordings acquired a cult status, particularly with fans of old-school Scandinavian death metal and Amorphis, a band that included some of Abhorrence's original members. On both the demo and the 7", the band tackled themes related to death and decay, pain and suffering, and darkness and collapse. Such themes are not uncommon in death metal, but Abhorrence handles them in ways that suggest something more than just a fixation for blood and gore. Abhorrence was never invested simply in shocking their listeners; instead, the band reflects on death and in social decay in ways that invite listeners to imagine the impossible. On the first demo, for example, 'Vulgar Necrolatry' focuses on reverencing decaying bodies over living bodies and imagining a world populated exclusively by newly animated corpses; similarly, 'Devourer of Souls' attempts to describe the chaos of a nasty creature awakening from a long sleep and terrorizing a shocked and unbelieving world. Neither scenario favours human protagonists or even hints at the rise of a triumphant hero. On the band's self-titled 7", Abhorrence continues in the same vein with tracks like 'Pestilential Mists' in which they follow the spread of the Black Death through the air in an undetermined time and place. Similarly, on 'Disintegration of Flesh', the lyrics predict the complete annihilation of all organic life.

Abhorrence's music generally evokes the twin challenges of a non-human world, one in which the monster cannot be defeated, and a larger mood that Eugene Thacker calls 'Cosmic Pessimism' (Thacker 2011: 17). Although Thacker's discussion mostly concerns black metal bands, the granular differences between metal subgenres are less important than is the broader musical interest in a world-without-us (Thacker 2011: 17). When Thacker describes Cosmic Pessimism as 'a strange mysticism of the world-without-us, a hermeticism of the abyss, [and] a noumenal occultism', he could be describing the bulk of Abhorrence's music (Thacker 2011: 17). Further, Thacker's insight that black metal focuses on 'the difficult thought of the world as absolutely unhuman, and indifferent to the hopes, desires, and struggles of human individuals and groups' also applies to Abhorrence's larger creative project, even more so with the release of *Megalohydrothalassophobia*, the album that marked the return of the band as monster (Thacker 2011: 17).

Abhorrence began showing renewed signs of life in 2012, the same year that Svart Records released *Completely Vulgar* (2012), a compilation of the band's available recordings. The band also began playing live shows and writing new music. By the time they released *Megalohydrothalassophobia* (2018), the band had completely returned from the grave, this time armed with an even more frightening message about global collapse and the world-without-us. Whereas Abhorrence's earlier releases evoked unnamed monsters and catastrophic events, this album delivers its new warning with help from two acknowledged sources: the fiction of H. P. Lovecraft (specifically through explicit allusions to 'The Call of Cthulhu') and the environmental writings of Timothy Morton (specifically by way of his concepts of 'hyperobjects' and the 'mesh'). Though Lovecraft and Morton wrote with different purposes in mind, they nevertheless share an interest not only in the gaps between language and experience, but also with the ways human beings essentially fail to reckon with overwhelming objects that will likely outlast all human life.¹

By joining Lovecraft and Morton with their own blistering style of death metal, Abhorrence transformed their initial monstrous themes into explicit portents of complete global and environmental collapse, a collapse brought on not only by current human action but also on the accumulated consequences of human actions across generations. Unlike other bands that have invoked Cthulhu as a rather simple metaphor for environmental destruction, Abhorrence expands him into a synecdoche of the hyperobject, thus blurring any possible distinction between the fictional Cthulhu and the accumulation of every all-too-real object that will certainly outlast the human species.²

Megalohydrothalassophobia, or the Fear of Large (Hyper)Objects in the Water

Morton defines hyperobjects as 'things that are massively distributed in time and space relative to humans' (Morton 2013: 1). Examples of hyperobjects include everyday plastics, Styrofoam products, or nonbiodegradable food packaging, all things a person might throw away without a second thought. Outside of this already unwieldy number of earthly objects, hyperobjects also include things like black holes, exoplanets, even the Solar System itself. Simultaneously a thing in general and a thing in particular, 'A hyperobject could be the sum total of all the nuclear materials on Earth; or just the plutonium, or the uranium' (Morton 2013: 1). Even if it seems strange to write about everyday plastics, planets, and nuclear materials in the same sentence,

---

1   For this part of the discussion, I have in mind Graham Harman's discussions of both Lovecraft and Morton within the context of Object-Oriented Ontology. See Harman (2012: 2–10) and (2018: 231–40).
2   For a much more detailed discussion of the ways extreme metal turns to Lovecraft and the weird generally, see especially Norman (2019) and (2013). My previous discussions of the topic may be found in Sederholm (2016) and Sederholm and Weinstock (2016).

the point is to think outside of quotidian notions of time and space and to consider, instead, the impact of objects that decay at much slower rates than the entirety of the human family. As Molly Wallace explains, because 'plastics do not biodegrade, all of the plastic produced is, conceivably, still with us – and the ever-growing, never-diminishing mass of it contributes to the sense of horror that plastic waste represents' (Wallace 2016: 127). With that specific example in mind, Morton's claim that hyperobjects transform from things taken for granted into things that will 'invoke a terror beyond the sublime, cutting deeper than conventional religious fear' seems less hyperbolic and much more frightening (Morton 2010: 131). Even if everyday plastic items do not necessarily evoke terror on their own, they are much more threatening in the aggregate, especially as one contemplates how they accumulate in the seas and in the bodies of birds, fish, and, perhaps, human beings. Like Lovecraft's monsters, hyperobjects threaten one's sanity precisely because they outlast human life to such an extent that they transform from quotidian objects into permanent fixtures, things that will surely 'outlast us all' (Morton 2010: 130). Because hyperobjects are essentially everywhere, they accumulate in ways that prevent them from being contained or defeated. A hyperobject is a monster that always wins. As Morton puts it, 'Hyperobjects don't just burn a hole in the world; they burn a hole in your mind' (Morton 2010: 130).

Abhorrence develops the thematic intersection between Lovecraft and Morton at several points throughout the album, including 'The Four Billion Year Dream' and 'Hyperobject Beneath the Waves'. In both cases, the lyrics make enough oblique references to Cthulhu to suggest that he is close by, lurking beneath the deep, waiting for the stars to be right. Rather than simply rehearse the building blocks of 'The Call of Cthulhu', however, Abhorrence transforms the creature into a sign of hyperobjects generally, a sign that reorients the world from a safe and stable sense of the everyday into something no longer stable and, potentially, no longer comprehensible. Once people develop a sense of what hyperobjects mean, their minds can never be the same.

In this light, we may also interpret the album's title, *Megalohydrothalassophobic*, as naming not only a generalized fear of large objects lurking beneath the sea, but also the aggregated fears represented by an awareness of hyperobjects. In the Anthropocene, the most frightening objects in the sea are not likely flesh-eating monsters, but the sum total of everyday objects – plastic bottles, Styrofoam cups, and trash of every sort – that are ever-present in the deep.³ Now that such objects populate the seas in overwhelmingly large amounts, they represent a new kind of monster, one that replaces the horrors Cthulhu implies with an all-too-real problem that cannot be fixed. Through the clever borrowing from Morton's environmental writings, Abhorrence transforms a vague fear of large objects into a very real fear of material hyperobjects.

The Monster Mesh?

If hyperobjects suggest conditions in which time and space extend beyond commonsense notions, the mesh names a circumstance in which reality comes all at once. Put differently, the mesh describes a dynamic and ever-changing awareness that every possible sense of the world, habitual or actual, has shifted into something so full of meaning that easy distinctions are no longer possible. Morton explains this change as a loss of background and foreground, a condition that renders all habitual knowing useless. In the mesh, everything blurs together – life and death, past and present, background and foreground – in extremely frightening ways. As Morton explains it, 'All life forms are the mesh, and so are all dead ones, as are their habitats, which are also made up of living and nonliving beings' (Morton 2010: 29). When human beings can no longer clearly sort out the range of their perceptions and experience, what could possibly make sense? Given this new, and highly unstable, sense of things, the mesh may be read as a monstrous troubling of convention and expectation.

Abhorrence introduces the most troubling aspects of the mesh on a track simply called 'Intro: The Mesh'. This track is comprised solely of ominous ambient noise that includes a dark droning tone, an unnervingly irregular sound of rippling water, and a handful of other intermittent effects that suggest otherworldly tapping, throbbing, or shimmering. After about sixty seconds, a deep

3   See Weisman (2007: 112–28) and Wallace (2016: 123–53).

and distorted voice intones several lines that refute any idealized notion of a balanced world in which human beings work with everything else towards establishing a common goal. Instead, we are now living in the Anthropocene, a 'new dark age' in which we not only forever lose the capacity to understand the world clearly but also to recognize that the world has already been lost (2018).[4] As happens so often on this album, human beings become aware of their awful circumstances precisely in the moment when they realize just what they have lost (Morton 2010: 30).

Even if it remains true that certain ecomonsters will continue to rise and fall with a predictable rhythm, there is no guarantee that the cycle will last forever. After all, monsters are supposed to mark moments of cultural crisis, moments in which humans have the opportunity to transform, perhaps even to think about the future. And yet, when the monsters are defeated, it is all too easy to celebrate victory without wondering what the monster's arrival signified in the first place. As Abhorrence's *Megalohydrothalassophobic* suggests, there will likely come a point when the monsters will shift from offering portents of destruction to revealing that the world has already been destroyed. In that circumstance, the monster is arguably indistinguishable from global circumstances. If Morton and Abhorrence are right to suggest that the world has already ended, maybe all we can do is make sense of how we got here and to determine, if possible, how to make things better.

---

4   Even though I am citing Abhorrence's 2018 release here, I am also drawing on Morton's discussion of the Anthropocene in Morton 2013, 4–5.

Gerry Canavan

Aliens: *District 9* (Blomkamp, 2009)

In *Screening Space: The American Science Fiction Film*, Vivian Sobchack attempts to distinguish between the horror and science fiction genres on film through the distinction she draws between the Monster and the Creature. 'The horror film', Sobchack says, 'is primarily concerned with the individual in conflict with society or with some extension of himself, the science fiction film with society and its institutions in conflict with each other or with some alien other' – or, to put it another way, the horror film deals with 'moral chaos', while the science fiction film deals with 'social chaos' (Sobchack 2001: 29–30). Thus, the Monster of horror 'seems to arise inevitably out of a personal Faustian obsession or the inherent animal nature of Man' (Sobchack 2001: 30), reflected in what she describes as the 'absolutely dramatically necessary ... anthropomorphic form' (Sobchack 2001: 30) of the Monster to register its essentially human character. Where the Creature of science fiction is 'less personalized' and possesses little interiority – simply acting out without malice in accordance with a destructive nature we find mysterious, ineffable, and fundamentally inhuman – 'conversely, in the horror film there is always something sympathetic about the Monster, something which gives us – however briefly – a sense of seeing the world through his eyes, from his point of view' (Sobchack 2001: 32).

Sobchack's thoughts on recognizing the Monster versus the Creature as the dividing line between science fiction and horror provide a useful point of entry to Neill Blomkamp's *District 9*, a hybrid work which, like the films of James Carpenter or David Cronenberg for an earlier generation, hovers indeterminably between the two genres. If we follow Jeffrey Jerome Cohen's method of 'reading cultures from the monsters they engender' (Cohen 2019: 3), what might *District 9*'s pointed inversion of the familiar first-contact science fiction narrative have to tell us about the contemporary South Africa that produced it, and about the larger planetary community that made it such

Monsters of Hybridity

an international success? Although it mostly abandons the narrative frame partway through the film, *District 9* begins in a 'found footage' mode simultaneously reminiscent of horror films like *The Blair Witch Project* (Myrick and Sánchez, 1999) and *Cloverfield* (Reeves, 2008), on the one hand, and cringe pseudo-documentary comedy like *This Is Spinal Tap* (Reiner, 1984) and *The Office* (UK: Gervais and Merchant 2001–2003, US: Gervais, Merchant and Daniels, 2005–2013), on the other; we see the arrival of the spacecraft depicted both through the objective, horrified gaze of news media figures and sober, professorial experts and from the goofy, incompetent perspective of Wikus van de Merwe (Sharlto Copley), a mid-level alien affairs employee for whom dealing with alien refugees is just another day on the job. What has happened is a sort of alternate history of contemporary South Africa, in which everything is different, and nothing has changed.

In 1982, a spaceship arrived over Johannesburg and hovered over the city for months without making contact; when humans finally took the initiative to cut into the spaceship they found not interstellar diplomats greeting them to some universal Federation of Planets but starving, miserable refugees, helplessly huddling in their own filth, apparently unable to fly off or work the ship in any way. Even their technology, coded to their specific extra-terrestrial biology, is completely useless to us; we learn nothing about propulsion or antigravity from studying the spaceship, and cannot commodify or instrumentalize anything they have brought with them. Accordingly, the aliens (derisively nicknamed 'Prawns' for their insectoid appearance) soon become a problem rather than an opportunity, and become consigned to a slum-like refugee camp at the outskirts of the city, a temporary measure that becomes permanent as the decades wear on and no better solution presents itself. This camp is the 'District 9' of the title – which for anyone familiar with the history of South African apartheid will trigger the memory of District Six, a division of Cape Town from which over 60,000 inhabitants were forcibly removed by the government in the name of ethnic cleansing and gentrification.

Rather than inaugurating a science fictional narrative of galactic expansion, à la *Star Trek*, *District 9* instead tells a much more grounded story about weak, desperate visitors coming to humanity in dire need of help, and humans treating them with malice and contempt – our own hackneyed fantasies about the glorious technoutopia to come returned to us as a nauseous vision of mass suffering and social-ecological collapse. The Prawns are monsters in appearance and behaviour – essentially gigantic cockroaches, they respect none of the dietary or sanitary taboos that human society requires – but it is humanity's callous and xenophobic speciesism that truly comes under critique as the narrative unfurls. The ordinary citizens of Johannesburg revile the Prawns, and simply want them gone, in an anti-immigrant panic made all the more disturbing when one remembers that the original *District 9* short, 'Alive in Joburg', was filmed by asking unknowing interview subjects what they thought about *Zimbabwean* refugees, with the science-fictionalized narrative context overlaid only in editing. In contrast, the multinational conglomerate who has been tasked with managing and administering the Prawn encampment, MNU, makes much of its money from the sale and manufacture of weapons. They are ultimately interested in the Prawns insofar as they can figure out a way to make their high-tech weapons available for human use; we discover as the film goes on that they are doing grotesque experiments on the Prawns in secret basement levels of their Johannesburg office park. However, even before we see this we see Wikus and others happily abusing the Prawns, including a scene in which Wikus's team torches discovered Prawn eggs (which seem to scream in pain in response), gleefully calling this grim procedure an 'abortion'. Even putting aside these nightmarish events, though, the entire impetus for the film, a camp-wide eviction notice, callously preformed at the borders of the legal to give a sheen of legitimacy to the raw violence of removal, is disturbing enough: the Prawns are finally being moved from District 9 to a new encampment, District 10, ostensibly intended to be permanent, but looking and feeling more like an carefully constructed concentration camp to District 9's hacked-together shantytown.

As the film goes on, our sympathies become more and more aligned with the Prawns, despite their monstrosity, especially after we meet a Prawn named Christopher Johnson (played by Jason Cope, who along with Sharlto Copley acted in and was one of the producers of the 'Alive in Joburg' short). Christopher Johnson – an aggressively generic white-coded name suggesting just how completely Prawn culture has been subsumed into human society – immediately appears different than the other Prawns: clearly more intelligent, and acting very parentally towards a young Prawn who seems perhaps to be his child, Christopher Johnson has a treasure trove of both human and alien technology that is soon revealed to be part of his plan to retake the ship and leave Earth. (This intelligence is perhaps marked most directly in the film by the introduction of subtitles to depict Christopher Johnson's complex speech, which shows an intertranslatability between human thought and Prawn thought that earlier portions of the film denied, with the humans treating the Prawns more or less as animals acting by instinct.) While it is never revealed what happened on the spaceship to leave it in such disrepair, with scores of starving Prawns in the cargo hold the only survivors, many fans have speculated that Christopher Johnson represents the last surviving member of a different caste than the 'drone' Prawns we otherwise see inhabiting District 9, perhaps something akin to a queen or worker bee in a honey bee colony (and further blurring our sense of what gender and reproduction might mean among the Prawns in the bargain). Or perhaps Christopher Johnson is simply an exceptional Prawn, with genius technological acumen he seems to have passed on to his child as well.

While attempting to serve Christopher Johnson his eviction notice, Wikus discovers his cache of alien technology and becomes splashed with a mysterious black fluid that appears to be fuel for the Prawn's advanced technology. Now the film becomes fully invested in the transgressive, boundary-defying porousness of the monster; if, as Cohen notes, 'the monster polices the borders of the possible', serving as a marker of what is prohibited and 'call[ing] horrid attention to the orders that cannot – *must* not – be crossed' (Cohen 2019: 12–13), Wikus's contamination by the fluid and the horrifying transformation of his body that ensues shows how unstable such prohibitions really are. Over the next few days, Wikus becomes a Prawn, beginning with his extremities and proceeding until his entire body has been transformed; while no explanation for this reaction to the chemical is ever offered by the film, the inescapable implication is that humans and Prawns are not so different after all, sharing some foundational biological similarities (and perhaps that *all* the Prawns were once human beings, transformed by the fluid under unknown circumstances after abduction by aliens and now unable to effectively communicate or advocate for themselves). The interchangeability of human and Prawn – the unexpected possibility that one might suddenly change from one to another – reveals that what separates the two beings is custom of law, not biological essence; once Wikus begins to transform, his rights as a human being and as a citizen of South Africa vanish in an instant, and he becomes part of the same terrifying regime of unprotected statelessness as the Prawns (including subjection to the same secret weapons experiments being undertaken at MNU headquarters). Likewise, forced to occupy their abject subject position at the bottom of the social hierarchy, Wikus becomes forced to pay attention to the Prawns and their needs for the first time in his career – and suddenly the language of clicks and grunts that the Prawns use to communicate becomes a complex language he can use to negotiate complex schemes and mutually beneficial agreements with Christopher Johnson, when previously he dismissed their minds as entirely subhuman, completely unworthy of his respect. It takes Wikus some time to stop identifying with the humans and to begin identifying with the Prawns, but by the end of the film he is in full revolutionary solidarity with them, deploying Prawn weapons against his former co-workers in a desperate bid to allow Christopher Johnson the time he needs to reach the mothership and escape Earth.

Wikus's transformation is simultaneously a personal tragedy for him and an opening of his mind, allowing him to transform himself from a deeply unethical, Eichmannesque functionary of a horrific regime of exclusion and removal to a self-sacrificing hero fully committed to helping the helpless (even if this has all only happened because he is now one of them). Falsely accused of interspecies sex – the government's cover-story for how his transformation happened – at the end of the film Wikus is a figure for this transgressive desire, leaving a metal flower he has crafted with his Prawn claws for his wife as a symbol of his continued love for her, despite her betrayal earlier in the film and everything that has happened since. Cohen notes in 'Monster Culture (Seven Theses)' how the figure of the monster often stands in for transgressive, normatively proscribed sex acts like homosexuality and miscegenation, which the monster narrative frames as objects of both 'fear and attraction' (Cohen 2019: 19). This becomes quite clear in *District 9*, where Wikus's transhuman transformation from 'normal, ordinary' human into one of the hyperbolically racialized and ambiguously gendered Prawns deeply ennobles him, and perhaps even saves his soul. The final shot of the film is of someone we assume is Wikus, now fully Prawn, working on another flower amidst the rubble and open fires of District 9; he briefly glances at the camera, perhaps in search of recognition, but soon returns to his sculpture, admiring his creation.

Figure 67. Wikus's sculpture. *District 9*, directed by Neil Bloomkamp (Sony Pictures Releasing, 2009).

Only as a Prawn is Wikus a better man, and so the initial body horror of Wikus's monstrous becoming gives way to something almost utopian instead. On the level of allegory the message seems clear: it is only through the abandonment of the privileges of whiteness, straightness, maleness, cisness, First-Worldness – indeed, the taking up of arms against them, here depicted literally as violent revolt – that an ethically decent, politically liveable, creatively vibrant life becomes possible. The alternative – the status quo – would not be worth holding on to, even if we could. 'The old world is dying, and the new world struggles to be born', Gramsci tells us. 'Now is the time of monsters' (quoted in Žižek 2010: n.p.). *District 9*, in the end, thus invites us to embrace the fearful possibility of our own monsterization. Or, as Cohen writes:

> Monsters are our children. They can be pushed to the farthest margins of geography and discourse, hidden away at the edges of the world and in the forbidden recesses of our mind, but they always return. And when they come back, they bring not just a fuller knowledge of our place in history and the history of knowing our place, but they bear self-knowledge, human knowledge – and a discourse all the more sacred as it arises from the Outside. (Cohen 2019: 20)

Cohen begins this section of his essay with a epigram from *The Tempest*: 'This thing of darkness I acknowledge mine' – Prospero's final concession that Caliban is not a monster at all, not outside, but inside, a being he owes both responsibility and dignity. *District 9*, with its barely sublimated transformation of the actually existing racism, xenophobia, and state violence that structures contemporary society, seeks to teach the same lesson. It is deeply unfortunate that the film as a whole seems unable to extend this same lesson to the Nigerians who populate its margins: they like the Prawns are depicted as a cruel, monstrous deviation from the human, without the gift of a redemption arc, and their horrific deaths at the hands of Prawn weapons are treated simply as comedic spectacle, played for shock and for laughs. The breakdown in cosmopolitan solidarity here – that it is weirdly easier for the film to recognize the common humanity of cockroach aliens than non-white people – is a regrettable feature of too much genre fiction, which all-too-frequently reinscribes racist assumptions about the immutable nature of identity even as it attempts to allegorize anti-racist struggle and the better possibility of a post-racist, cosmopolitan future. *District 9* ends with another unexpected doubt about the transformative hope it has shown us, with Christopher Johnson and his son the lone inhabitants of the spaceship flying off to get help for the remaining Prawns they have been forced to leave behind. A sequel, often referred to as *District 10*, has been long-expected, but has not yet materialized – so we have still to wonder whether Johnson will return at the head of a medical relief convoy or an invading armada. What if the Prawns, or their masters, return, only to do to us what we have done to them? After enduring *District 9*, there's little doubt we will have earned whatever harsh lesson they will carry back, if and when it ever comes.

Elana Gomel

Zombie: *The Girl with All the Gifts* (Carey, 2014)

During the grand age of utopias and dystopias, the unknown future hurtling towards the present was often imagined as a monster. The famous lines from William Butler Yeats' 'Second Coming' (1919) express the mingled hope and apprehension in the face of the coming millennium:

> Surely the Second Coming is at hand.
> The Second Coming! Hardly are those words out
> When a vast image out of Spiritus Mundi
> Troubles my sight: somewhere in sands of the desert
> A shape with lion body and the head of a man,
> A gaze blank and pitiless as the sun,
> Is moving its slow thighs, while all about it
> Reel shadows of the indignant desert birds.

Utopia and dystopia are structurally the same genre: dystopia is 'utopia's alter ego' (Kumar 1987). Both are predicated on the apocalyptic longing for a decisive transformation, a radical break in history that will usher in something new, something different. Lee Quinby describes this longing as the 'millennial seduction', predicated on the belief that a catastrophe is always a prelude to renewal; that the 'world destruction' will usher in 'a new transformed earth' (Quinby 1999: 4). Violence and horror are inextricably connected with hope and desire, so that a utopian/dystopian mindset is poised between the conviction that 'the crimes and follies of the past could be left behind in an all-encompassing transformation of human life' and the fear of the price this transformation will demand (Gray 2006). The irreducible ambivalence of the utopian impulse is reflected in the monstrous body of the utopian subject. Yeats' chimeric 'shape' is the millennial New Man, 'a politicized version of the archetypal "hero myth"' (Griffin 1993: 35).

The New Man, the utopian subject of the future, was both repulsive and irresistible; both horrifying and sublime. No matter how enticing the millennial seduction he represented, there was a monstrosity hiding inside the steely-eyed heroic images of the Ubermensch or his left-wing equivalents. The monster is always a cultural oxymoron: the 'monstrous lurks somewhere in that ambiguous, primal space between fear and attraction' (Cohen 1996: 19). In the utopias of the 1930s, such as Olaf Stapledon's *Odd John* (1935), the Ubermensch is a sort of divine monster, transcending humanity in his indifference to petty morals and psychological taboos. Indeed, extreme violence often heralded the birth of the utopian/dystopian subject in the last century's visions of the future.

However, both utopia and dystopia have lost their luster. We are living in the age of post-utopia and post-apocalypse (Buell 2013), in which the future is represented as the entropic wasteland of decay rather than 'the new heaven and the new earth' (Rev. 21: 1). Not surprisingly, our signature monster is the zombie: the creature of return and recycling rather than of breakthrough and renewal. Zombies are 'a ubiquitous symbol of any kind of systemic failure, from zombie banks in economics to zombie categories in social theory' (Schmeink 2016: 67). The temporality of the zombie is not the arrow of the apocalypse but rather the stasis of the perpetual 'now', in which things fall apart but are never renewed; drag on but never resolve; are dying but never completely dead. If the Second Coming arrives in the shape of the Walking Dead, no millennium is likely to follow the endless Tribulations.

But can utopia be resurrected in the age of zombiehood? Can the New Man be reborn if the future is no longer radically different but merely the dismal continuation of the present? Gumbrecht described the current episteme as the 'chronotope of the broad present', in which the future is bracketed out rather than viewed with fear or longing (2014). There can be no utopia of the present. It turns out there is. M. R. Carey's *The Girl With All the Gifts* (2014) is both a zombie novel and a classic utopia. It is a tour de force in which the rotten corporeality of the zombie is reconfigured in the utopian shape of the New Man (or at least, the New Human). But because of the irresolvable contradiction at the heart of its conceit, it presents an interesting case study of the way in which popular culture, hampered by what Fredric Jameson called our 'inability to imagine the future' (2005), tries to break through 'the chronotope of the broad present' and offer a glimpse of something different. But since no novel, no matter how accomplished, can escape its cultural matrix, *The Girl with All the Gifts* is a monstrous text revelling in its own monstrosity; a zombie resurrection of dead hopes and dreams that is aware of its own zombiehood; a millennial dream confessing to being a nightmare.

The novel, based on Carey's award-winning short story 'Iphigenia in Aulis', was made into a popular movie of the same title. In this essay, however, I will discuss the original novel, with only few references to the visual aesthetics of the monstrous body in the film. Melanie is a little zombie girl. She lives in the world infected with a mutant fungus *Ophiocordyceps unilateralis*, which transforms human beings into mindless flesh-eaters called 'hungries'. Melanie and other infected children like her, however, retain their mental capacities, while being irresistibly attracted to live human prey. Indeed, Melanie is exceptionally intelligent. She and others like her are locked up in an experimental facility with scientists looking for a cure, while being educated by Melanie's favourite teacher Miss Helen Justineau and being experimented upon by the scientist Dr Caroline Caldwell. The educational process takes place in the classroom where children are chained to their desks while the teacher has to wear a protective suit to mask the flesh smell that can drive her charges into a feeding frenzy. After the facility is breached, Melanie, the teacher and several others escape into the zombie-infested wilderness, still looking for a cure. It turns out, however, that there is no cure. Melanie and other intelligent hungries are a second-generation, born with the fungus in their bodies. They cannot be cured because they *are* the disease. The novel ends with Melanie deliberately releasing the spores of *Ophiocordyceps unilateralis* to infect the rest of the world.

At its publication, the novel was praised for its moral complexity. Torie Bosch's review in *Slate* summarized its main conflict as 'the clash of pragmatism and humanity', in which Dr Caldwell's atrocious research meant to save the human race is juxtaposed with Miss Justineau's dedication to the individual children in her care. But Melanie is more than a helpless victimized child. She is also the perpetrator of the ultimate atrocity: the genocide of the entire human race. In order for the second-generation hungries to inherit the Earth, humanity has to go:

> This way is better. Everybody turns into a hungry all at once, and that means they'll all die, which is really sad. But then the children will grow up, and they won't be the old kind of people but they won't be hungries either. They'll be different. (Carey 2014: 399)

Melanie's genocidal violence is exceptional even by the standards of the quasi-fascist New Man. When Odd John, the Nietzschean superman in Stapledon's novel is faced with a similar dilemma, he chooses to commit suicide rather than destroy humanity. But it fits with the millenarian belief that purification requires suffering and that that 'violence can save the world' (Gray 2007: 103). As Melanie explains: 'There's no cure for the hungry plague, but at the end the plague becomes its own cure' (Carey 2014: 397).

Melanie's corporeal monstrosity reflects the duality of her role as an innocent child and a zombie messiah; a victim and a killer. As opposed to the shambling, decaying bodies of the Walking Dead, she is a pretty little girl, 'like a princess in a fairy tale; skin as white as snow' (Carey 2014: 1). But when she preys on humans, she becomes a cannibalistic predator, swift, unrelenting and deadly. Trying to prevent herself from eating her beloved teacher, 'she wrestles with a wild animal, and the animal is her' (Carey 2014: 115). It is not simply that hungries become obligate meat-eaters but that the smell of human flesh transforms them into the Walking Dead of horror movies, switching off the higher brain functions, so they cannot restrain or control their own behaviour. Melanie is Beauty and the Beast in one body. This is emphasized in the poster for the movie version, in which a child's face is confined in the muzzle of a rabid predator.

In the movie, Melanie is played by a black actress. While meant as a nod to racial equity, this actually weakens the novel's rhetoric of monstrosity, in which black and white are not racial indicators but rather markers of plot functions: saviour and villain; protagonist and antagonist. The juxtaposition of 'black' and 'white' in the opening of the novel emphasizes the oxymoronic duality of Melanie's role: 'Her name is Melanie. It means "black girl", from an ancient Greek word, but her skin is actually very fair so she thinks maybe it's not such a good name for her' (Carey 2014: 1). She would rather be called Pandora, the 'girl with all the gifts', the one who has unleashed all evils upon humanity – or all blessings, depending on what version of the myth one consults (more of the role of Greek mythology below). Black and white, child and beast, victim and murderer, Melanie is a monster of hope, a walking oxymoron, a contradiction made flesh (Carroll 2003).

But can Melanie be seen as posthuman? Can we argue that rather than a zombie New Hu/man, a recycled utopian subject, she is a genuinely new

Figure 68. The two faces of Melanie in one image. *The Girl With All the Gifts*, directed by Colm McCarthy (Warner Brothers Pictures, 2016).

articulation of post/transhuman possibilities of our age? Some critics believe she is (Hale and Dolgoy: 2018). But there are two problems with this view. First, as opposed to the transhuman supermen of contemporary sci-fi, Melanie is not the product of a bio-technological modification. The zombie fungus is a random mutation. The second problem, however, is more interesting. Posthumanism, of whatever variety, always expressed a philosophical and ideological opposition to what Nietzsche contemptuously called 'human, all too human'. Melanie, on the other hand, is a true humanist.

Critical posthumanism is a philosophy based on the rejection of the centralized individualistic subject and 'an enlarged sense of inter-connection between self and others, including the non-human or "earth" others' (Braidotti 2013: 48). Melanie is a super-predator rather than an eco-warrior, and she has no interest in contributing to 'the well-being of an enlarged community, based on environmental inter-connections' (Braidotti 2014: 48). Her genocide of the old human species is based on the evolutionary calculus of competition and survival. Nor does she have any sympathy with other nonhuman animals, convinced that the intelligent hungries belong on top of the food chain by virtue of their intelligence. She is filled with rage at Dr Caldwell for experimenting on the 'feral' hungries 'as though they were just animals' because, being intelligent, they are not (Carey 2014: 365). Critical posthumanism's goal is 'destabilizing or throwing into question the schema of the human' (Wolfe 2009). Melanie's goal is re-establishing these schema – but without the humans themselves.

At the end of the novel, Melanie creates a school for hungries, in which Miss Justineau, kitted out in a sealed-environment suit to protect her from her student's appetite, teaches the Western canon. Passing the baton of the Enlightenment to zombies, she starts with the alphabet, 'Greek myths and quadratic equations will come later' (Carey 2014: 460).

The pervasive influence of Greek mythology in the novel is striking. Not only is Melanie compared, numerous times, to Pandora, 'the girl with all the gifts', but her adoration of Miss Justineau stems from the stories the teacher tells of the Greek gods and heroes. In the story she writes for herself, Melanie is chosen by the gods, like Pandora, and she is also Achilles the monster-slayer. Greek mythology becomes a synecdoche for the values that Melanie embraces: Western tradition; classical education; science and literature. What makes the hungries superior is that they are better at the Enlightenment game than humans themselves. They are smarter, savvier, more technologically astute. So what if Melanie is a cannibal? She can do differential equations in her head. If the critical posthumanism of Braidotti, Wolfe and others attempts to free biological humanity from the shackles of humanism, Carey's novel does the opposite. The zombie is a humanist. The zombie utopia is a classroom. Humanity is dead but the Oxbridge curriculum lives on.

What are we to make of zombies studying Plato? At the end, Carey's novel reads almost as a parody of traditional utopias. Representing the New Humans as zombies, 'walking corpses' (Carey 2014: 104), carries the heavy load of cultural references which cannot be neutralized by classical allusions. The novel tries to resurrect the millennial seduction of the 'new heaven and new earth' but knows it cannot be done. If the unknown future used to be represented by Antichrist, the monster of sublimity, now it can only be represented by the zombie, the monster of second-handedness, repetition and recycling.

When Melanie is about to escape her imprisonment, she contemplates her future and is afraid of it:

> Misgivings are crowding in on her. She's in uncharted territory, and she fears the blank, inscrutable future into which she is being rushed before she is ready. She wants her future to be like her past, but she knows it won't be. (Carey 2014: 94)

Melanie here speaks for our age: the age of Anthropocene, post-utopia and ecological degradation, in which the only vision of the future we can embrace is that of the past.

Patricia MacCormack

Afterword: Becoming Monstrous and the Monster Becoming: *Hannibal* (Fuller, 2013–2015)

NBC's *Hannibal* (2013–15) celebrates death in its many manifestations without abstracting it from flesh and thus defaults to celebrating flesh in ways far stranger than society can manage. Secondly it represents a vision of Vitalistic death through flesh which privileges aesthetics over spectacle and the baroque folding of viewer, perpetrator and victim rather than the oppositional dialectics of perp/victim, detective/psychopath and thus ultimately win/lose, good/evil. Finally, it surmounts the question of subjects entirely through this emphasis on relationality over dialectic. Beginning with creating diversity (the conversion of the novel's male characters into female characters and white characters into minority characters), it continues by presenting a relation of desire – between Hannibal and Will, between spectacle and spectator – that is entirely beyond male hysteria, gender, even sex and death, toward unbound desire, and within this matrix of relations it entirely dismantles all divisions, living in nature beyond morality yet retaining a disdain for the unethical or those who block the flows and ebbs of human flesh and desire. *Hannibal* does not belong to the worlds of Freud or forensics, Foucault and the clinic or Kant and aesthetics. It belongs to Artaud and the Body without Organs, to Deleuze and Guattari and becomings, to Kristeva and the sublime, to Lyotard and the great ephemeral skin.

The Monster Becoming: The Body without Organs

Hannibal is nominally a procedural drama. More than that, it is a tableau of the many and varied manifestations of flesh and the utility of the flesh when life is extinguished, vanquished or considered unworthy. Each killer, as well as Hannibal himself, has an extraordinary motive for their murders which, contrary to actual serial killers, is frequently devoid of aggressive violence, narcissism or nihilism – the Angel-Maker,[1] the Mushroom-Man,[2] the Cotard-Sufferer,[3] the wound-man maker[4] and of course Hannibal just in Season 1 are launched upon their own becomings and launch the flesh of their victims onto becomings – becoming-fungus, becoming-angel, becoming-unmasked, then in Season 2 Randall Tier's becoming-beast, the

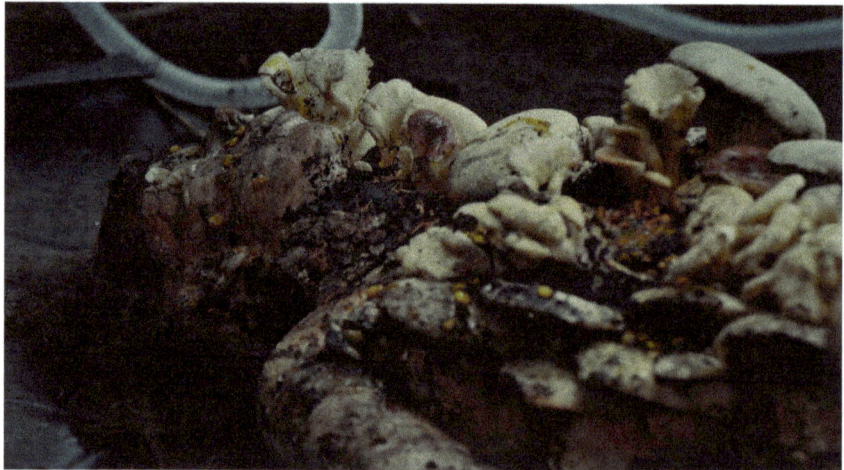

Figure 69. The monstrous becomings of the Mushroom-Man. *Hannibal*, Season 1, Episode 2, created by Bryan Fuller (Sony Pictures Television: 2013–15).

1   Eliot Budish who first appeared in Season 1, Episode 5.
2   Season 1, Episode 2.
3   Georgia Madchen who first appeared in Season 1, Episode 10.
4   Season 1, Episode 7.

Figure 70. Becoming beehive. *Hannibal*, Season 2, Episode 6, created by Bryan Fuller (Sony Pictures Television: 2013–15).

bee lady and her victim's becoming-hive finally coalescing in Season 3 with Francis Dollarhyde's becoming of the families he murders toward his own becoming the great-red-dragon.

Each of these killers and their victims show divergent examples of the killers' becoming not something else – thus not transforming into another thing – but the becoming of an abstracted or fabulated entity which is a trajectory without finitude – a dragon, an enflamed angel, a connective fungal community, a long extinct beast. The angel as abstracted mythic creature, the mushroom as vegetal rhizome, the faceless as the designified body-without-organs, the beast as a prehistoric extinct cave bear with cyborg exoskeleton, the great red dragon as a melange of fine art, body art, inhuman masculinity and an absence of self. Deleuze and Guattari state of becomings:

> These combinations are neither genetic nor structural; they are interkingdoms, unnatural participations. This is the only way nature operates – against itself ... the origin of packs is entirely different from that of families and States; they continually work them from within and trouble them from without, with other forms of content, other forms of expression. The pack is simultaneously an animal reality and the reality of the becoming-animal of the human being ... an entire becoming that implies multiplicity, celerity, ubiquity, metamorphosis, and treason, the power of affect. (242, 243)

The affective potentializations of the killers in *Hannibal* are their divergence from mainstream serial killers, who align themselves rigorously along state and regime lines usually of misogyny but also racism, classism and other signifying traits that far from being a metamorphosis, turn them into totalitarian operators of majoritarian usually white male subjectivity. Theirs has no affect because it hyperrealizes established patterns of power (as imposed, Spinoza's *potestas*). They are humans taken to the extreme, while *Hannibal*'s killers are treacherous to their species and intrigue the audience and the FBI because investigating their motive is its own form of becoming inhuman through entering into an alliance with the strange and imaginative affects of their actions as acts of creation, their power to affect as potentiality (Spinoza's *potentia*). This is why empathy is so crucial to Will Graham's role in the show, as he is forced to empathize with inhuman becomings from animal to vegetal, celestial and cosmic, and it is empathy not opposition which drives his desire.

The victims offer another expression of becoming in their configurations. The corpses in *Hannibal* are rarely buried or discarded. They most frequently are purposefully killed through an abstract and bizarre scheme which perhaps explains the sympathy the show is able to solicit from the viewer upon the revelation of the killer. Few kill for aggressive death drive 'fun'. Deleuze and Guattari state the organism, significance and subjectification are the three enemies of the Body without Organs. The organism organizes the matter of flesh into a hierarchical legible system of the human, significance articulates the symbolic referents of the body – its gender, race, sexuality, etc., subjectification places this articulated body into the social strata at the appropriate level. Failure to fulfil these obligations of turning flesh into text results in the depraved, perverted tramp (Deleuze and Guattari 2004: 159). The victims are configured as Bodies without Organs by which they are reconfigured upon alternate trajectories of signification to become more than and altogether different from what they were before, which is why their dead body status rather than making them defunct, makes them fascinating. The corpses in *Hannibal* are both literally and aesthetically dismantled just as is the body without organs – 'dismantling the organism [is] opening the body to connections that presuppose an entire assemblage, circuits, conjunctions, levels and thresholds, passages and distributions of intensity and territories and deterritorializations measured with the craft of a surveyor' (Deleuze and Guattari 2004: 160). This is a show of art in both senses of the word. In its many examples of aesthetically reconfigured human flesh – be it for food, or for spectacle – the human is honoured as a work of potential plasticity.

Figure 71. Becoming spectacle, becoming art. *Hannibal*, Season 1, Episode 5, created by Bryan Fuller (Sony Pictures Television: 2013–15).

In *Hannibal* one almost forgets that murder must occur in order for these *tableaux mourants* to exist. As spectator's our relationship with these bodies is as plastic as their own unique configurations. It is a baroque relation because it cannot exist in opposition of love/loathing, horror/wonder but is simultaneously as desiring grotesque and undeniably libidinal fascination. We ourselves, to enter into the becomings with these bodies, these killers, must also open ourselves. Lyotard states:

> Open the so-called body and spread out all its surfaces . . . spread out the immense membrane of the libidinal 'body' which is quite different to a frame. It is made from the most heterogeneous textures, bone, epithelium, sheet to write on, charged atmospheres, swords, glass cases, peoples, grasses, canvases to paint ... The interminable band with variable geometry . . . has not got two sides, but only one, and therefore neither exterior nor interior. (Lyotard 1993: 1, 2–3)

Extending the becomings of the killers and their victims is the cinesexuality of *Hannibal*. The spectatorial relationship here is baroque. The image creates with us a territory which is enclosed in a spectatorial event as images puncture and flow within and between the apertures in our soul. The extent to which an image can be experienced as baroque is found in the incommensurable combinations, connections and apertures it creates within our soul and its expression of the world. Within the screen the killers and their victims are already manifold pleats of matter becoming-otherwise without determinism or dialectic. These images puncture us as flesh launching our own Body without Organs as spectators. When punctures are made within folds, holes do not lead from the interior to the exterior, from in to out or from the smooth surface to the damaged, which would be the moral signified codings of these image-events. Holes create tunnels of relation which allow surfaces to encounter each other and certain flows to traverse many sections in a small space. They are the corridors of the labyrinthine fold. These holes can be made through not an emptying excavation but a luminous filling intensity, and their affects are unable to be evaluated via binary options, thus the sumptuous beauty of horror *Hannibal* affords. Sometimes these holes are made when signification becomes duplicitous and few things are more duplicitous than our drooling at cannibal plates and sculptural cadavers. When we see baroque images of ruptured organs on screen which do not destroy but rather reterritorialize a body the organ is no longer its own self.

A certain form we find attractive which repels us or repulsive which attracts us, when fear or disgust comes from desire, the relation between our desire and the image's own dissimilarity from itself creates apertures in the folds, cutting across more planes than would seem immediately likely. The image of an object which looks as itself is no longer itself thus any idea of what it is reminds us that all images are germinal in that we cannot rely on what we expect or think they are to constitute what they can do or will become. Each desiring event is what Deleuze calls larval; the ways in which it unfolds and refolds to new folds comes from the extent to which this larval nature is exploited. The killers have already launched this project upon themselves and their victims – becoming anew without template or destination. Larvae are invertebrate and not yet actualized, thus Deleuze exploits their lack of supporting structure and porous potentiality. The decision taken between habit and difference potentiality creates larvality – the moment of a baroque ethics. It is important to note that the persistent use of the idea of the multiple is not plural in any incongruous or random sense. Proliferations occur through what Deleuze calls passive synthesis, defined not simply by 'receptivity – that is, by means of the capacity to experience sensations – but by virtue of the contractile contemplation which constitutes the organism itself before it constitutes the sensations' (1994b, 78). These are the affective potentials of the images, the affects which occur before the synthesis of representation and meaning. As affect images the killers and victims of *Hannibal* fulfil this baroque spectatorial event to themselves become qualities of affectivity which exceed any forensic or psychological profiling.

Face to Face with the Monster

And the singular most baroque perpetrator of these particular works of art amongst the many offerings is of course Hannibal himself. Beyond the behavioural science of the books and the deferred signifiers of Hannibal's craziness in the texts with his maroon eyes and polydactyl hands this is a Vitalistic Nietzschian Hannibal (but Nietzsche as Deleuze would have read him). Artaud states:

> I think about life. All the systems that I shall ever construct will never equal my cries: the cries of a man engaged in remaking his life. I imagine a system in which all of man would participate, man with his physical flesh and the heights, the intellectual projections of his mind ... But I must inspect the meaning of flesh which is to give me a metaphysics of Being and the definitive understanding of Life. For me the word Flesh above all means apprehension, hair standing on end, flesh laid bare with all the intellectual profundity of this spectacle of pure flesh and all its consequences for the senses, that is, for the sentiments. (Artaud 1988: 110–11)

Once again the world is made elliptical as Hannibal creates these works of alimentary art which are simultaneously abject before they convert to digested waste, but he himself is a work of art, through the deliriously fetishistic cinematography which seems obsessed with his face and makes of it rather than a facial machine which operates via the white wall black hole system, a despotic delirium of unravelling planes, a topography of beauty. Just as the becomings of flesh and killer in *Hannibal* are powers of affect so too for Deleuze the close-up of the face which creates this topographic plane of texture and pressure is an affection image – that is an image which exists before reading, or before the second and third powers of cinema which are perception (secondness) and judgement or conversion to meaning (thirdness).

Figure 72. The beautiful Monster. *Hannibal*, created by Bryan Fuller (Sony Pictures Television: 2013–15).

And just as Artaud calls the conversion of the flesh to an organized organism the Judgement of God, so too making legible and thus legislated the meaning of images is a judgement which closes off the *potentia* of the image. No plane organizes the body and deprives it of its potential more so than the face: Deleuze and Guattari state: 'The faciality machine is not an annexe to the signifier and subject; rather it is subjacent (connexe) to them and their condition of possibility ... The deterritorializion of the body implies a reterritorialization on the face; the decoding of the body implies an overcoding by the face' (Deleuze and Guattari 2004: 180–1). *Hannibal* as a prime example of television made deeply cinematic, holds a particular obsession with two faces in particular, that of Will and Hannibal. It does this so they cannot be subsumed into their white male majoritarian status. It makes their beauty a series of despotic fractal affects which escape and scatter into the light of the unimaginable, cinesexual decolonizations of subjectivity toward facial-affect becomings.

Figure 73. Becoming monster; Hannibal as Will, Will as Hannibal. *Hannibal*, created by Bryan Fuller (Sony Pictures Television: 2013–15).

This technique is crucial in our refusal to read Hannibal's subjectivity and is exacerbated by what Bryan Fuller has called the 'micro-acting' of Mads Mikkelsen, almost imperceptible movements and twitches, extensions and retractions of the tiny facial muscles, so that the skin appears to breathe beneath its surface and meaning comes not from expression but affect from micro-pulsion. Face as form converts to plane of intensive affects. The close-up functions as it closes up the macro movements of the body to intensify the micro movements of the face. The close-up then, is according to Deleuze,

> a series of micro movements on an immobilised plate of nerve. When a part of the body has had to sacrifice its motoricity in order to become the support for organs of reception, the principle feature of these will now only be tendencies to movement or micro-movements which are capable of entering into intensive series … the face is this organ carrying plate of nerves which has sacrificed most of its global mobility and which gathers or expresses in a free way all kinds of tiny local movements which the rest of the body usually keeps hidden. (Deleuze and Guattari 2004: 87–8)

In this way the delirium caused by the face blocks the traditional behavioural reading in the Lomborosian sense of the criminal and this expressive form is vital for the many ambivalent ways in which *Hannibal* demands of its audience an impossible but nonetheless inevitable love and empathy for the cannibal. In cinema Deleuze writes that traditionally the face is a reflecting and reflective unit of measure. In psychoanalytic gaze theory this holds. In order to enter into a cinesexual becoming this oscillation between narcissism and anacliticism must be broken or the characters will remain signified and subjectified, subject and object. In this sense even our desire for Hannibal is not for a signified object but a supplication to a plane of what Guattari calls asignification – the seductive libidinal economy of an image without deferral to meaning or function. This has a second ethical function within the programme and in reference to renegotiating the profiler/profile dyad. Just as Deleuze connects the close-up to the becoming solid, then liquid, then gaseous of the spectator, so too does our Will POV of Hannibal's face compel us into a first solid (we know, they do not know), liquid (we know but are complicit because we are becoming-cannibal) then gaseous (we are now within and of Hannibal's cosmos) cinesexual plane. The defacialization of the face in the close-up is integral to becomings in cinema as it denies opposition and thus even though the premise of the show is profiler/profiled the very regime of this structure is repudiated by the camerawork. The close-up functions as a relational affect – demanding of the audience the creation of unthought relations between incommensurable ideas or objects and powers. Hannibal is rarely active in the entire series – we see him murder very infrequently and his movement goes from stillness to high velocity with alarm. Everything is already found in his face and the close-ups of Will intensify throughout the series and seasons as Will and Hannibal close the dialectic in their relationship, the closure of a gap that only Will really perceived from the beginning, as our becoming Hannibal through the liquification into his face has already altered our view of the world as one with good and evil, killers and catchers.

Ultimately this of course follows the deconstructions of becoming which are beyond gender and race (and it is important to note Fuller refused to utilize any forms of sexual violence for titillation in the show). But it also produces, through the continuing relation between the increasing close-ups of Will and Hannibal a new form of desire, a new form of relationality. Fans who ship Hannigram themselves deny this is any ordinary homoerotics. The relationship which develops between Will and Hannibal, first through the close-ups, then at the end of Season 2 the thanaterotic ritual of Hannibal

Figure 74. Our monster, ourselves. *Hannibal*, created by Bryan Fuller (Sony Pictures Television: 2013–2015).

stabbing Will and finally the mutual forgiveness, the shared reckoning, the redemption, the slaying of the Red Dragon and the Dionysian fall from the cliff, has nothing to do with traditional hetero, homo or even queer erotics and is entirely unique in its intimacy between two bodies melding toward a cosmically complex and differentiated, but ultimately unified, imperceptible consciousness that remains one of the most profound and difficult to interpret relationships ever written for television.

Bibliography

28 Days Later, dir. Danny Boyle (London: DNA Films, 2002).
Abhorrence, *Megalohydrothalassophobic* (Turku, Finland: Svart Records, 2018).
——, *Abhorrence* (Cleveland: Seraphic Decay Records 1991).
——, *Vulgar Necrolatry* (1990).
Aho, Tanja, Liat Ben-Moshe, and Leon J. Hilton, 'Mad Futures: Affect/Theory/Violence', in *American Quarterly*, Vol. 69, No. 2 (June 2017), 291–302.
Alive in Joburg, written and directed by Neill Blomkamp (Spy Films, 2006).
American Horror Story: *Apocalypse*, created by Ryan Murphy and Brad Falchuk (20th Television, 2018).
American Horror Story: *Coven*, created by Ryan Murphy and Brad Falchuk (20th Television, 2014).
American Horror Story: *Murder House*, created by Ryan Murphy and Brad Falchuk (20th Television, 2011).
American Psychological Association Guidelines for Psychological Practice with Boys and Men <https://www.apa.org/about/policy/boys-men-practice-guidelines.pdf>, accessed 30 November 2019.
Anderson, Craig, 'Where Are the Wolves?: With Their Rich History on Screen, We Should be Seeing Lycanthropes There More Often', in *Fangoria*, no. 329 (2014), 74–6.
Anderson, Jennifer L., *Strange Places*: *Illustrating the Otherworldly in Mike Mignola's Hellboy* (Master of Science in Theory, Criticism and History of Art, Design and Architecture. thesis, Pratt Institute, 2007).
Angel Heart, dir. Alan Parker (United States: Carlco Pictures, 1987).
Anon., '*Psycho* revamp changes "transphobic" shower scene', *The Times*, 17 April 2017 <https://www.thetimes.co.uk/article/psycho-revamp-changes-transphobic-shower-scene-025tpcflx> accessed 19 November 2019.
Anon., 'Punished for Hundred Year Old Crime', in *Universal Weekly*, vol. 3, no. 24 (1913): 16–17.
Anzaldúa, Gloria, *Borderlands/La Frontera. The New Mestiza* (San Francisco, CA: Aunt Lute Books, 2007).
Arata, Stephen D., 'The Occidental Tourist: Dracula and the Anxiety of Reverse Colonization', *Victorian Studies* 33:4 (1990), 621–45.

Armknecht, Megan, Jill Terry Rudy, and Sibelan Forrester. 'Identifying Impressions of Baba Yaga Navigating the Uses of Attachment and Wonder on Soviet and American Television' (*Marvels & Tales*, 31, 1, 2017), 62–77.
Arneson, Dave, and Gary Gygax, *Dungeons & Dragons: Single Volume Edition* (Lake Geneva, WI: Tactical System Rules, 1974).
Artaud, Antonin, *Antonin Artaud: Selected Writings* (Berkeley: University of California Press, 1988).
Auerbach, Nina, *Our Vampires, Ourselves* (Chicago: University of Chicago, 1996).
Bacchilega, Cristina, and Marie Alohalani Brown, *The Penguin Book of Mermaids* (New York: Penguin, 2019).
Balina, Marina, Helena Goscilo, and Mark Lipovetsky, eds, *Politicizing Magic: An Anthology of Russian and Soviet Fairy Tales* (Evanston, IL: Northwestern University Press, 2005).
Bane, Theresa, *Encyclopedia of Beasts and Monsters in Myth, Legend and Folklore* (Jefferson, NC: McFarland, 2016).
Banivanua-Mar, Tracey, *Violence and Colonial Dialogue* (Honolulu: University of Hawaii Press, 2007).
Barker, Martin, Ernest Mathijs, and Xavier Mendik, 'Menstrual Monsters: The Reception of the *Ginger Snaps* Cult Horror Franchise', in Ernest Mathijs and Xavier Mendik, eds, *The Cult Film Reader* (Maidenhead: Open University Press, 2009), 482–94.
Barnouw, Erik, *The Magician and the Cinema* (New York: Oxford University Press, 1981).
'Bart's Inner Child', *The Simpsons*. Season 5, Episode 7. 11 November (Fox Television, 1993).
Bastian, Adolf, *Reiser in Siam im Jahre 1863* (Jena: H. Costenoble, 1867).
Bates Motel, created by Carlton Cuse, Kerry Ehrin, and Anthony Cipriano (A&E 2013–2017).
Baumann, Benjamin, 'Tamnan Krasue: Constructing a Khmer Ghost for a Thai Film', *Kyoto Review of Southeast Asia*, 14 (2013).
———, 'From Filth-Ghost to Khmer-Witch: Phi Krasue's Changing Cinematic Construction and its Symbolism', *Horror Studies*, 5, 2 (2014), 183–96.
———, 'The Khmer Witch Project: Demonizing the Khmer by Khmerizing a Demon', in Peter J. Bräunlein and Andrea Lauser, eds, *Ghost Movies in Southeast Asia and Beyond: Narratives, Cultural Contexts, Audiences* (Leiden: Brill, 2016), 141–83.
———, 'Ghosts of Belonging. Searching for Khmerness in Rural Buriram', *Dissertation* (Humboldt-Universität zu Berlin, 2017).
Baumann, Benjamin, and Nicolas Verstappen, 'Ein thailändischer Bram Stoker', *Südostasien,*, 3 (2018).
Beal, Timothy K., *Religion and its Monsters* (New York: Routledge, 2002).
Bedazzaled, dir. Harold Ramis (United States: Regency Enterprises, 2000).

Beller, Steven, *Antisemitism: A Very Short Introduction*, 2nd edition (Oxford: Oxford University Press, 2015).
Benn Michaels, Walter. *The Beauty of a Social Problem: Photography, Autonomy, Economy* (London: The University of Chicago Press, 2015).
Benshoff, Harry M., *Monsters in the Closet: Homosexuality and the Horror Film* (Manchester: Manchester University Press, 1997).
Benshoff, Harry M., and Sean Griffin, *America on Film: Representing Race, Class, Gender, and Sexuality at the Movies* (Malden, MA: Wiley-Blackwell, 2004).
Bierhorst, John, *The Hungry Woman. Myths and Legends of the Aztecs* (New York: Quill, 1984).
Bill & Ted's Bogus Journey, dir. Peter Hewitt (Nelson Entertainment/Interscope, 1991).
Billson, Anne, 'The Werewolf Howls Again', in *The Guardian Film & Music* (5 February 2010), 7.
Bourgault du Coudray, Chantal, *The Curse of the Werewolf: Fantasy, Horror and the Beast Within* (London: I.B. Tauris, 2010).
Bishop, Kyle William, *American Zombie Gothic* (Jefferson, NC: McFarland & Company, 2010).
Bizzaca, Chris, 'The World of *Cleverman*', in *Screen Australia.gov.au*, 1 June 2016. <https://www.screenaustralia.gov.au/sa/screen-news/2016/06-01-the-world-of-cleverman> accessed 12 August 2019.
Black Sunday, dir. Mario Bava (Italy: Galatea Film/Jolly Film, 1960).
Blair Witch Project, The, dir. Eduardo Sánchez and Daniel Myrick (Orlando, FL: Haxan Films, 1999).
Blake, Linnie, *The Wounds of Nations: Horror Cinema, Historical Trauma and National Identity* (Manchester: Manchester University Press, 2008).
Bloomer, Jeffrey, 'Why are Goats Associated with the Devil, Like Black Philip in *The Witch*'?, *Slate*, 26 February 2016. <https://slate.com/culture/2016/02/goats-and-the-devil-origins-black-phillip-in-the-witch-isnt-alone.html> accessed 15 December 2019.
Bobako, Monika, *Islamofobia jako technologia władzy. Studium z antropologii politycznej* (Cracow: Universitas, 2017).
Bosch, T. (2014). *Review of The Girl With All the Gifts*, July. Retrieved from Slate.com: <https://slate.com/culture/2014/07/mike-careys-zombie-novel-the-girl-with-all-the-gifts-reviewed.html>.
Botting, Fred, *Gothic* (London: Routledge, 1996).
Bradbury, Ray, 'Skeleton', *Weird Tales* (September 1945), 32–40.
Braidotti, Rosi, *The Posthuman* (London: Polity Press, 2013).
Brooks, Max, *World War Z* (New York: Crown Publishing Group, 2006).

Browning, John Edgar, 'Disability and Slasher Cinema's Unsung "Children"', in *Monstrous Children and Childish Monsters: Essays on Cinema's Holy Terrors*, eds Ed. Markus Bohlmann and Sean Moreland (Jefferson, NC: McFarland, 2015).

Brunvand, Jan Harold, *Encyclopedia of Urban Legends* (Santa Barbara, CA: ABC-CLIO, 2001).

Buell, F., 'Post-Apocalypse: A New US Cultural Dominant', *Frame: Journal of Literary Studies*, 26.1 (May 2013), 9–31.

Bukatman, Scott, 'Sculpture, Stasis, the Comics, and Hellboy', *Critical Inquiry*, Vol. 40, No. 3, Comics & Media, eds Hillary Chute and Patrick Jagoda (Spring 2014), 104–17.

Burnell, A. C., *The Voyage of J. H. van Linschoten*, Vol. 1 (London: Hakluyt Society, 1885).

Byron, Glennis, 'La Llorona and *KM31*', *The Gothic Imagination. University of Stirling*, 13 March 2011 <http://www.gothic.stir.ac.uk/blog/la-llorona-and-km31/> accessed 15 October 2019.

Calautti, Katie, 'The Secrets Behind the *Game of Thrones* Fighting Skeletons', *Vanity Fair*, 17 June 2014, <https://www.vanityfair.com/hollywood/2014/06/game-of-thrones-fighting-skeletons> accessed 26 September 2019.

Candyman, dir. Bernard Rose (Los Angeles, CA: Propaganda Films/PolyGram Filmed Entertainment, 1992).

Cano, Alfonso, *El pueblo del sol* (Mexico City: Fondo de cultura económica, 2004).

Carey, M. R., *The Girl with All the Gifts* (New York: Orbit Books, 2014).

Carlsen, Per Juul, 'The Werewolf Within', *Danish Film Institute*, 9 May 2014. <https://www.dfi.dk/en/english/werewolf-within> accessed 18 December 2019.

Carroll, Noël, 'Horror and Humor', in *The Journal of Aesthetics and Art Criticism*, vol. 57, no. 2 (1999), 145–60.

———, *The Philosophy of Horror; or Paradoxes of the Heart* (London: Routledge, 2003).

Carved: The Slit-Mouthed Woman (Kuchisake-onna), dir. Kōji Shiraishi (Tokyo: Twin Co. Ltd./Tornado Film/Memory Tech/Earl Grey Film, 2007).

Cat People, dir. Jacques Tourneur (RKO Radio Pictures, 1942).

Chapman, Aimée, *Spooky House* (New York: Priddy Books 2015).

Charteris-Black, Jonathan, 'Britain as a Container: Immigration Metaphors in the 2005 Election Campaign', *Discourse and Society* 17:5 (September 2006), 563–81.

Cherry, Brigid, *Horror* (New York: Routledge, 2009).

Cherry Falls, dir. Geoffrey Wright (Los Angeles, CA: Rogue Pictures, 2000).

Cisneros, Sandra, *Woman Hollering Creek and Other Stories* (New York: Random House, 2011).

Clemens, Valdine, *The Return of the Repressed: Gothic Horror from The Castle of Ortranto to Alien* (Albany: State University of New York Press, 2009).

Cleverman, dir. Wayne Blair and Leah Purcell (Sundance TV, 2016–17).

Click, Melissa A, Lee Hyungji, and Holly Wilson Hollady, 'Making Monsters: Lady Gaga, Fan Identification, and Social Media', *Popular Music and Society*. Vol. 36:3 (2013), 360–79.

Cohen, Jeffrey Jerome, 'Monster Culture: Seven Theses', in Jeffrey Jerome Cohen, ed., *Monster Theory: Reading Culture* (Minneapolis: University of Minnesota Press, 1996/2019), 3–25.

Coleman, Robin R. Means, *Horror Noire: Blacks in American Horror Films from the 1890s to Present* (New York: Routledge, 2011).

Contagion, dir. Steven Soderbergh (Burbank: Warner Bros, 2011).

Cook, David 'Zeb', et al., *Monstrous Compendium Volume* (Lake Geneva, WI: TSR, 1989).

Cooke, Jennifer, *Legacies of Plague in Literature, Theory, and Film* (New York: Palgrave Macmillan, 2009).

Coombe, Kirk, and Brenda Boyle, *Masculinity and Monstrosity in Contemporary Hollywood Cinema* (New York: Palgrave Macmillan, 2013).

Cooper, Erin. 'Tasmania Proving to be Perfect Backdrop for Gothic Horror, with The Nightingale the Latest Addition', ABC News, 20 August 2019, <https://www.abc.net.au/news/2019-08-21/the-nightingale-the-latest-in-tasmanian-noir-genre/11430480> accessed 20 August 2019.

Corrin, Lisa G., *Mining the Museum: An Installation Confronting History* (Baltimore, MD: W.W. Norton, 1994).

Cowan, Douglas E., 'Horror and the Demonic' in John Lyden, ed., *The Routledge Companion to Religion and Film* (London: Routledge, 2009) 403–19.

Creed, Barbara, *The Monstrous-Feminine: Film, Feminism, Psychoanalysis* (London: Routledge, 1993a)

———, 'Dark Desires, Male Masochism in the Horror Film', in Steve Cohen and Ina Hark, eds, *Screening the Male* (London: Routledge, 1993b)

———, *Phallic Panic* (Melbourne: Melbourne University Press, 2005)

———, 'Forward', in David Baker, Stephanie Green and Agńieszka, Stasiewicz-Bieńkowska, eds, *Hospitality, Rape and Consent in Vampire Popular Culture: Letting the Wrong One In* (Cham: MacMillan, 2017), v–ix.

Crofts, Penny, and Anthea Vogl, 'Dehumanized and Demonized Refugees, Zombies and World War Z', *Law and Humanities* 13:1 (March 2019), 29–51.

Cropsy, dir. Joshua Zeman and Barbara Brancaccio (New York: Afterhours Productions/Ghost Robot, 2009).

Cry of the Werewolf, dir. Henry Levin (Columbia Pictures, 1944).

Cultural Cutouts, Interview of Wangechi Mutu (New York, 2014), produced by Kasper Bech Dyg (Louisiana Channel, Louisiana Museum of Modern Art, 2015), <https://channel.louisiana.dk/video/wangechi-mutu-cultural-cutouts.> accessed 14 December 2019.

Curse of La Llorona, The, dir. Michael Chaves (Los Angeles, CA: Atomic Monster, 2019).
De Vos, G. 1996. *Tales, Rumors and Gossip: Exploring Contemporary Folk Literature in Grades 7–12* (Westport, CT: Libraries Unlimited, 1996), 58.
Deep Blue Sea, dir. Renny Harlin (Los Angeles, CA: Warner Brothers, 1999).
Deleuze, Gilles, and Félix Guattari, *A Thousand Plateaus: Capitalism and Schizophrenia*, trans. Brian Massumi (London: Continuum, 2004).
Demos, John, *Entertaining Satan: Witchcraft and the Culture of Early New England* (Oxford: Oxford University Press, 1982).
De-Valle Arizpe, Artemio, 'La Llorona' in Bernardo Esquinca and Vicente Quirarte, eds, *Ciudad fantasma: relato fantástico de la Ciudad de México (XIX-XXI): antología* (Mexico City: Almandía, 2017),16–23.
Devil and Max Devlin, The, dir. Steven Hilliard Stern (United States: Walt Disney Productions, 1981).
Devil's Advocate, The, dir. Taylor Hackford (United States: Regency Enterprises, 1997).
Dickson, E. J., 'What Is the Momo Challenge'?, *Rolling Stone*, 26 February 2019. <https://www.rollingstone.com/culture/culture-news/what-is-momo-challenge-800470/> accessed 1 June 2019.
District 9, dir. Neill Blomkamp (Sony Tristar Pictures, 2009).
Dove, Shawn Michael. *The Hidden Monster – Pedafilia* (Bloomington, IN: Authorhouse, 2002).
Dressed to Kill, dir. Brian De Palma (Los Angeles, CA: Universal Studios, 1980).
Douglas, Mary, *Purity and Danger: An Analysis of Concepts of Pollution and Taboo* (Abingdon on Thames: Routledge and Keegan Paul, 1966).
Dworkin, Andrea, *Intercourse* (United States: Free Press, 1987).
Dwyer, Phillip, and Amanda Nettlebeck, ' "Savage Wars of Peace": Violence, Colonialism and Empire in the Modern World', in Phillip Dwyer and Amanda Nettlebeck, eds, *Violence, Colonialism and Empire* (Cham: Palgrave Macmillan, 2018).
El grito de la muerte, dir. Fernando Méndez (Mexico City: Alameda films, 1959).
Eljaiek-Rodríguez, Gabriel, *The Migration and Politics of Monsters in Latin American Cinema* (Cham: Palgrave Macmillan, 2018).
Ellis, Emma Grey, 'Trump's Presidency has spawned a New Generation of Witches', *Wired.com*, 30 November 2019, <https://www.wired.com/story/trump-witches> accessed 31 October 2019.
End of Days, dir. Peter Hyams (United States: Beacon Pictures, 1999).
Enright, Robert, 'Resonant Surgeries: The Collaged World of Wangechi Mutu', Border Crossings, no. 105 (Feburary, 2008), <https://bordercrossingsmag.com/article/resonant-surgeries-the-collaged-world-of-wangechi-mutu> accessed 14 December 2019.

Estes, Clarissa Pinkola, *Women who run with the wolves: Myths and stories of the Wild Woman Archetype* (New York: Ballantine, 1992).
Exorcist, The, dir. William Friedkin (United States: Warner Bros Pictures, 1973).
Fay, Jennifer and Justus Nieland, *Film Noir* (New York: Routledge, 2010).
Ferris, William R. *The Storied South: Voices of Writers and Artists* (Chapel Hill: The University of North Carolina Press, 2013).
Forrester, Sibelan, Helena Goscilo, and Martin Skoro, eds, *Baba Yaga: The Wild Witch of the East in Russian Fairy Tales* (Jackson: University Press of Mississippi, 2013).
Foster, Michael Dylan, *Pandemonium and Parade: Japanese Monsters and the Culture of Yokai* (Berkeley: University of California Press, 2009).
Foucault, Michel, *Abnormal: Lectures at the Collège de France 1974–1975*, trans. Graham Burchell (London: Verso, 2003).
——, *The Spectacle of the Scaffold* (London: Penguin, 2006).
Freud, Sigmund, 'The Uncanny', 1919, in James Strachey, ed. and trans., *The Standard Edition of the Complete Psychological Works of Sigmund Freud: Vol. XVII* (London: Hogarth Press, 1953), 219–52.
——, *The Penguin Freud Reader*, ed. Adam Phillips (London: Penguin, 2006).
Game of Thrones, created by David Benioff and D. B. Weiss (HBO, 2011–19).
Garber, Marjorie, *Vested Interests: Cross Dressing and Cultural Anxiety* (New York: Routledge, 1992).
Gelder, Ken, 'Australian Gothic', in David Punter, ed., *A New Companion to the Gothic* (Oxford: Blackwell, 2012).
Gilbert, Sandra, and Susan Gubar, *The Madwoman in the Attic: The Woman Writer and the Nineteenth-Century Literary Imagination* [1979] (New Haven, CT: Yale University Press, 2000).
Gilman, Charlotte Perkins, *The Yellow Wallpaper* [1892] (Wisehouse Classics, 2016).
Gilman, Sander, *Seeing the Insane* (Battleboro, VT: Echo Point, 1982).
Gingold, Michael, 'Exclusive interview: Director Agnieszka Smoczynska on the Allure of "The Lure"', *Rue-Morgue.com*, 8 February 2017, <https://www.rue-morgue.com/exclusive-interview-director-agnieszka-smoczynska-on-the-allure-of-the-lure/> accessed 1 December 2019.
Ginsburg, Faye, 'The Indigenous Uncanny: Accounting for Ghosts in Recent Indigenous Australian Experimental Media' in *Visual Anthropology Review*, Vol. 34, Iss. 1 (2018), 67–76.
Gombrich, Ernst H., *Art and Illusion: A Study in the Psychology of Pictorial Representation* (London: Phaidon Press, 1960).
Gore, Ariel, *Hexing the Patriarchy, 26 Potions, Spells and Magical Elixirs to Embolden Resistance* (New York: Seal Press, 2019)

Grafius, Brandon, 'Securing the Borders: Isolation and Anxiety in *The Witch*, *It Comes at Night*, and Trump's America', in Victoria McCollum, ed., *Make America Hate Again: Trump-Era Horror and the Politics of Fear* (London: Routledge, 2019), 119–28.

Grannell, Craig. 'An interview with Mike Mignola, Part Two', <http://reverttosaved.com/2008/08/13/an-interview-with-mike-mignola-part-two/> accessed 14 December 2019.

Gray, J., *Black Mass: Apocalyptic Religion and the Death of Utopia* (New York: Farrar, Straus and Giroux, 2007).

Gray, Kishonna L., *Race, Gender, and Deviance in Xbox Live: Theoretical Perspectives from the Virtual Margins* (Waltham, MA: Anderson Publishing, 2014).

Griffin, Casey, and Nina Nessith, *The Science of Orphan Black* (Toronto: ECW Press, 2017).

Griffin, R., *The Nature of Fascism* (New York: Routledge, 1993).

Grotesque (*Gurotesuku*), dir. Kōji Shiraishi (Ace Deuce Entertainment/Tornado Film, 2009).

Gumbrecht, H. U., *Our Broad Present: Time and Contemporary Culture* (New York: Columbia University Press, 2014).

Gupta, Richa, 'How Certain Horror Movies Propagate the Mental Health Stigma', *Huffington Post*, 18 March 2017 <https://www.huffpost.com/entry/horror-movies-and-the-mental-health-stigma_b_58ccbe8ae4b07112b6472dc9?guccounter=1> accessed 26 August 2019.

Halberstam, Jack, 'Technologies of Monstrosity: Bram Stoker's Dracula', Victorian Studies, 36/ 3 *Victorian Sexualities* (1993), 333–52.

———, *Skin Shows: Gothic Horror and the Technology of Monsters* (Durham, NC: Duke University Press, 1995).

Hale Kimberly Hurd, E. D., 'Humanity in a Posthuman World: M. R. Carey's The Girl with All the Gifts', *Utopian Studies*, Vol. 29, No. 3 (2018), 343–61.

Hall, Jake, 'Lady Gaga Pioneered Online Fandom Culture As We Know It', *Vice*, 29 September 2018, <https://www.vice.com/en_uk/article/pakq59/lady-gaga-online-fandom-culture-little-monsters> accessed 18 July 2019.

Hallpike, C. R., 'Social Hair', in *Man, New Series*, Vol. 4, No. 2 (1969): 256–64.

Hanks, Jane, 'Maternity and its Rituals in Bang Chan', *Cornell Thailand Project Interim Reports Series No. 6* (Ithaca, NY: Southeast Asia Program, Dept of Asian Studies, Cornell University, 1963).

Hansen, William, *Handbook of Classical Mythology*. World Mythology. Santa Barbara, CA: ABC-CLIO, 2004).

Hardouin, Charles, 'Traditions et superstitions siamoises', *Revue Indo-Chinoise* (1904), 415–5.

Harman, Graham, *Weird Realism: Lovecraft and Philosophy* (Washington, DC: Zero Books, 2012).
─────, *Object-Oriented Ontology: A New Theory of Everything* (New York: Pelican, 2018).
Hastings, Chris, 'It's political correctness gone *Psycho*! Remake won't show the killer cross-dressing in a shower scene in order to avoid "transphobia"', *Daily Mail*, 15 April 2017 <http://www.dailymail.co.uk/news/article-4415278/Psycho-remake-won-t-cross-dressing-scene.html> accessed 19 November 2019.
Hegel, G. W. F., *Aesthetics: Lectures on Fine Art*, trans. T. M. Knox (Oxford: Oxford University Press, 1975).
Heller-Nicholas, Alexandra, *Found Footage Horror Films: Fear and the Appearance of Reality* (Jefferson, NC: McFarland & Co., 2014).
Henderson, Dion, 'Ed Gein Laughed When Friends Joked About Missing People'. *Wisconsin State Journal* (24 November 1957).
Hill, Frances, ed., *The Salem Witch Trials Reader* (Boston, MA: DaCapo Press, 2000).
History of Westeros podcast, 'Game of Thrones: S8E2 – Book to Show', >https://play.acast.com/s/westeroshistory> accessed 27 April 2019.
Hood, Robert, 'Killer Koalas: Australian and New Zealand Horror Films: A History', *The Scream Factory* 12 June 1994, <http://www.tabula-rasa.info/AusHorror/OzHorrorFilms1.html> accessed 5 December 2019.
Host, The, dir. Bong Joon-ho (Seoul: Showbox Entertainment, 2006).
House on the End of the Street, dir. Mark Tonderai (New York: FilmNation Entertainment, 2012).
Hovitz, Helaina, 'Horror Movies Misrepresent Mental Illness in Every Way', *Vice*, 7 November 2017. <https://www.vice.com/en_us/article/mb3bjb/horror-movies-misrepresent-mental-illness-in-every-way> accessed 26 August 2019.
Howling II: Your Sister is a Werewolf, dir. Phillipe Mora (Hemdale Film Corporation, 1985).
Huba, Jackie. *Monster Loyalty: How Lady Gaga Turns Followers into Fanatics* (New York: Portfolio/Penguin, 2013).
I Am Legend, dir. Francis Lawrence (Burbank: Warner Bros, 2007).
Inagi, Yoki, 'Kuchisake Onna (2007)' in Salvador Murguia ed., *The Encyclopedia of Japanese Horror Films* (Lanham, MD: Rowman & Littlefield., 2007), 176–8.
Ingham, Toby, '*The Babadook*', in *Psychodynamic Practice*, Vol. 21, No. 3 (2015), 269–70.
Inhuman Kiss, dir. Sitisiri Mongkolsiri (Boontamcharoen, 2019).
Inside My Studio: Wangechi Mutu, dir. Dennis Scholl (Anderson Ranch Art Center, *Cultured Magazine*, 28 April 2018, <https://www.culturedmag.com/wangechi-mutu-video/> accessed 14 December 2019).
Insidious, dir. James Wan (Los Angeles, CA: Blumhouse Productions, 2010).
Insidious: Chapter 2, dir. James Wan (Los Angeles, CA: Blumhouse Productions, 2013).

Jacobsen, Pamela, 'Eye on Fiction: *The Babadook* and Maternal Depression', *The Psychologist* Vol. 29, November 2016, <thepsychologist.bps.org.uk/volume-29/november-2016/babadook-and-maternal-depression> accessed 26 July 2018.

Jameson, F., *Archaelogies of the Future: the Desire Called Utopia and Other Science Fictions* (London: Verso, 2005).

Jancovich, Mark, 'Phantom Ladies: the War Worker, the Slacker and the Femme Fatale', in *New Review of Film and Television Studies*, vol. 8, no. 2 (2010): 164–78.

Jaskułowski, Krzysztof, *The Everyday Politics of Migration Crisis in Poland: Between Nationalism, Fear and Empathy* (Cham: Palgrave Macmillan, 2019).

Jentsch, Ernst, 'On the Psychology of the Uncanny' [1906], in Jo Collins and John Jervis, eds, Roy Sellars, trans., *Uncanny Modernity: Cultural Theories, Modern Anxieties* (Hampshire: Palgrave Macmillan, 2008), 216–28.

Jesus of Montreal, dir. Denys Arcand (Canada/France: Cineplex and Orion, 1989).

Johns, Andreas, *Baba Yaga: The Ambiguous Mother and Witch of the Russian Folktale* (New York: Peter Lang, 2004).

Jones, Abigail, 'The Girls Who Tried to Kill for Slender Man', *Newsweek*, 13 August 2014, <https://www.newsweek.com/2014/08/22/girls-who-tried-kill-slenderman-264218.html> accessed 1 June 2019.

Jones, Ernest, *On the Nightmare* (London: Hogarth Press, 1951).

Jones, Stephen, ed., *Clive Barker's A-Z of Horror* (New York: HarperPrism, 1997).

Ju-On: The Grudge, dir. Takashi Shimizu's (Tokyo: Pioneer LDC, 2002).

Kainz, Lena, 'People Can't Flood, Flow or Stream: Diverting Dominant Media Discourses on Migration', 2016, at: <https://www.law.ox.ac.uk/research-subject-groups/centre-criminology/centreborder-criminologies/blog/2016/02/people-can't> accessed 1 December 2019.

Kay, Jeremy, 'Sundance Directors: Agnieszka Smoczynska, *The Lure*', January 2016, <https://www.screendaily.com/sundance/sundance-directors-agnieszka-smoczynska-the-lure/5099031.article> accessed 1 December 2019.

Kellner, Douglas, *Cinema Wars* (West Sussex: Wiley Blackwell, 2010).

Kettering Incident, The, dir. Tony Krawitz (Sydney: Foxtel Showcase, 2016).

King, Nicholas B., 'The Scale Politics of Emerging Diseases', *Osiris*, 2.19 (2004), 62–76.

KM31, dir. Rigoberto Castañeda (Mexico City: Lemon Studios, 2006).

Kotwasińska, Agnieszka, '"We Won't Eat You, Dear": The Collision of Class, Scales, and Body Horror in The Lure' *Frames Cinema Journal*, 11 May 2017, <http://framescinemajournal.com/> accessed 1 December 2019.

Koven, Mikel J., *Film, Folklore, and Urban Legends* (Lanham, MD: The Scarecrow Press, 2008).

Krasue Sao, dir. S. Naowarat (Sanit Kosarot, 1973),

Thawee Witsanukorn, *Krasue Sao* (Nonthaburi: Borisat E.P., 2017).

Kristeva, Julia, *Powers of Horror: An Essay on Abjection*, trans. Leon S. Roudiez (New York: Columbia University Press, 1982).
Krutnik, Frank, *In a Lonely Street: Film Noir, Genre, Masculinity* (New York: Routledge, 1991).
Kumar, K., *Utopia and Anti-utopia in Modern Times* (Oxford: Basil Blackwell, 1987).
Kumar, K., 'Utopia and Anti-Utopia in the Twentieth Century', <http://cas2.umkc.edu/ECON/economics/faculty/Lee/courses/488/reading/utopia7.pdf> accessed May 2018.
Kungl, Carla T., '"The Secret of My Mother's Madness": Mary Elizabeth Braddon and Gothic Instability', in Ruth Bienstock Analik, ed., *Demons of the Body and Mind: Essays on Disability and Gothic Literature* (Jefferson, NC: McFarland, 2010), 170–80.
La Llorona, dir. Ramón Peón (Mexico City: Eco Films, 1933).
La Llorona, dir. René Cardona (Mexico City: Producciones Bueno, 1960).
'La llorona: habitación del desahogo', *Feminicidio.net*, 2 March 2012, <http://feminicidio.net/printpdf/articulo/la-llorona-habitaci%C3%B3n-del-desahogo-0> accessed 1 November 2019.
La maldición de La Llorona, dir Rafael Baledón (Mexico City: Churubusco Studios, 1963).
Lady Gaga, 'Born This Way', *Born This Way*, Track 1 (Interscope, 2011), CD.
Landon, Perceval, 'Thurnley Abbey' in Scott Allie, ed., *The Dark Horse Book of Hauntings* (Milwaukie, OR: Dark Horse). 32–46.
Lawson, Tom. *The Last Man: A British Genocide in Tasmania* (London: I.B. Taurus, 2014).
Leach, Edmund, 'Magical Hair', in *The Journal of the Royal Anthropological Institute of Great Britain and Ireland*, Vol. 88, No. 2 (1958): 147–64.
Leddon, Alan, *A Child's Eye View of Ghosts and Hauntings* (Madison, WI: Spero Publishing, 2014).
Leeder, Murray, *The Modern Supernatural and the Beginnings of Cinema* (New York: Palgrave Macmillan, 2017).
LeFrançois, Brenda A., and Robert Menzies, eds, *Mad Matters: A Critical Reader in Canadian Mad Studies* (Toronto: Canadian Scholars Press, 2013).
LeFrançois, Brenda, Peter Beresford, and Jasna Russo, 'Editorial: Destination Mad Studies', in *Intersectionalities: A Global Journal of Social Work Analysis, Research, Polity, and Practice*, Vol. 5, No. 3 (2016), 1–10.
Legend, dir. Ridley Scott (United States: Embassy International Pictures, 1985).
Lemonick, Michael D., 'The Killers All Around', *Time*, 12 September 1994, <http://content.time.com/time/magazine/article/0,9171,981430,00.html> accessed 4 November 2015.

León-Portilla, Miguel, *Visión de los vencidos: Relaciones indígenas de la conquista* (México City: Universidad Nacional Autónoma de México, 1959).
Levina, Marina, and Diem-My T. Bui, *Monster Culture in the 21st Century: A Reader* (London: Bloomsbury Academic, 2013).
Limón, José E., 'La Llorona, The Third Greater Legend of Greater Mexico: Cultural Symbols, Women, and the Political Unconscious', in Adelaida R. del Castillo, ed., *Between Borders: Essays on Mexicaca/Chicana History* (Encino, CA: Floricanto Press), 399–32.
Lindquist, Sherry C. M., *Monster Marks* (Memphis, TN: Art Museum of the University of Memphis, 2018), <https://www.memphis.edu/amum/exhibitions/monstermarks_galleryguide.php> accessed 14 December 2019.
'Lisa Goes Gaga'. *The Simpsons*. Season 23. Episode 22, 20 May (Fox Television, 2012).
Little Nicky, dir. Steven Brill (United States: Robert Simonds/Happy Madison, 2000).
Lorenz, Taylor, 'Momo Is Not Trying to Kill Children', *The Atlantic*, 28 February 2019, <https://www.theatlantic.com/technology/archive/2019/02/momo-challenge-hoax/583825/> accessed 14 December 2019.
Lure, The [Córki dansingu], dir. Agnieszka Smoczyńska (Kino Świat, 2015).
Lyotard, Jean-François, *The Postmodern Explained: Correspondence, 1982–1985*, trans. Don Barry, Bernadette Maher, Julian Pefanis, Virginia Spate, and Morgan Thomas (Minneapolis: University of Minnesota Press, 1993).
McCollum, Victoria, *Make America Hate Again: Trump-Era Horror and the Politics of Fear* (Abingdon: Routledge, 2019).
MacCormack, Patricia, 'The Queer Ethics of Monstrosity', in Caroline Joan S. Picart and John Edgar Browning, eds, *Speaking of Monsters: A Teratological Anthology* (New York: Palgrave Macmillan, 2012), 255–65.
McGrath, Roberta, *Seeing Her Sex: Medical Archives and the Female Body* (New York: Manchester University Press, 2002).
Mack, Robert L., *The Wonderful and Surprising History of Sweeney Todd: The Life and Times of an Urban Legend* (London: Continuum, 2007).
McRuer, Robert, *Crip Theory: Cultural Signs of Queerness and Disability* (New York: New York University Press, 2006).
Maddox, Jessica, 'Of Internet born: idolatry, the Slender Man meme, and the feminization of digital spaces', *Feminist Media Studies*, Vol. 18, 2 (2018): 235–48.
Malone, Peter, in Rhonda Burnette-Bletsch, ed., *The Bible in Motion* (Berlin: De Gruyter, 2016), 327–40.
Mama, dir. Andy Muschietti (Universal City: Universal Pictures, 2013).
Mann, William E., 'Augustine on Evil and Original Sin' in David Vincent Meconi and Eleonore Stump, eds, *The Cambridge Companion to Augustine* (Cambridge: University of Cambridge Press, 2014).
Marble Hornets, dir. Joseph DeLage Troy Wagner (Alabama: Grampo Co., 2009–14).

Mark of the Devil, dir. Michael Armstrong (West Germany: HIFI-Stero-70/Filmvertrieb KG, 1970).

Mathijs, Ernest, *John Fawcett's* Ginger Snaps (Toronto: University of Toronto Press, 2013).

May, Josephine, *Reel Schools: Schooling and the Nation in Australian Cinema* (New York: Peter Lang, 2013).

Means Coleman, Robin R., *Horror Noire: Blacks in American Horror Films from the 1890s to the Present* (Oxford: Routledge, 2011).

Mignola, Mike. 'Epilogue' in *Hellboy: Wake the Devil* (Milwaukie, OR: Dark Horse, 1997).

——, 'The Baba Yaga' in *Hellboy: The Chained Coffin and Others* (Milwaukie, OR: Dark Horse, 1998).

——, 'Baba Yaga's Feast' in *Hellboy: The Wild Hunt* (Milwaukie, OR: Dark Horse, #4, 2009).

Millard, Anna 'The Internet Thinks Alyssa Milano Is Casting A Spell On Brett Kavanaugh', <https://www.refinery29.com/en-us/2018/09/212682/alyssa-milano-witch-kavanaugh-hearing-viral-photo> accessed 30 October 2019.

Miller, Sam J., 'Assimilation and the Queer Monster', in Aviva Briefel and Sam J. Miller, eds, *Horror after 9/11: World of Fear, Cinema of Terror* (Austin: University of Texas Press, 2011), 220–33.

Mitter, Partha, *Much Maligned Monsters: a History of European Reactions to Indian Art* (Oxford: Clarendon Press, 1977).

Mittman, Asa Simon, and Peter J. Dendle, eds, *The Ashgate Research Companion to Monsters and the Monstrous* (London: Routledge, 2017).

Moers, Ellen, 'Female Gothic: The Monster's Mother', in *The New York Review of Books* (21 March 1974), <https://www.nybooks.com/articles/1974/03/21/female-gothic-the-monsters-mother/> accessed 21 August 2019.

Moos, David, *Wangechi Mutu: This You Call Civilization?* (Toronto: Art Gallery of Ontario, 2010).

Moraga, Cherríe, *The Hungry Woman: A Mexican Medea and Heart of the Earth : a Popul Vuh Story* (Albuquerque, NM: West End Press).

Moreno, Caroline, 'Guillermo Del Toro On How He Balances The Dark With The Good: "I'm Mexican"', *Huff Post*, 9 January 2018. <https://www.huffpost.com/entry/guillermo-del-toro- mexican_n_5a551394e4b0efe47ebdaa32> accessed 29 November 2019.

Morton, Timothy, *The Ecological Thought* (Cambridge, MA: Harvard University Press, 2010).

——, *Hyperobjects: Philosophy and Ecology after the End of the World* (Minneapolis: University of Minnesota Press, 2013).

Muir, John Kenneth, *Horror Films of the 1980s* (Jefferson, NC: McFarland, 2007).

Murphy, Carole, 'Rivers of Blood, Sea of Bodies: An Analysis of Media Coverage of Migration and Trafficking on the High Seas', in Jon Hackett and Seán Harrington, eds, *Beasts of the Deep: Sea Creatures and Popular Culture* (Bloomington: Indiana University Press, 2018), 154–70.

Musharbash, Yasmine, 'Introduction: Monsters, Anthropology, and Monster Studies', in Yasmine Musharbash and Geir Henning Presterudstuen, eds, *Monster Anthropology in Australasia and Beyond* (New York: Palgrave Macmillan, 2014), 1–24.

——, 'Pangkarlangu, Wonder, Extinction', in Yasmine Musharbash and Geir Henning Presterudstuen, eds, *Monster Anthropology. Ethnographic Explorations of Transforming Social Worlds Through Monsters* (London: Bloomsbury, 2020), 59–73.

Musolf, Andreas, *Mirror Images of Europe: Metaphors in the Public Debate about Europe in Britain and Germany* (Munich: Iudicium Verlag, 2000).

——, 'Dehumanizing Metaphors in UK Immigrant Debates in Press and Online Media', *Journal of Language Aggression and Conflict* 3:1 (2015), 41–56.

My Mom's a Werewolf, dir. Michael Fischa (Crown International Pictures, 1989).

Mystics in Bali, dir. Djalil, H. Tjut (Video Tape Corp, 1981).

Needful Things, dir. Fraser Clarke Heston (United States: Castle Rock/New Line Cinema 1993).

Nicholls, Christine, 'Monster Mash: What Happens when Aboriginal Monsters are Co-Opted into the Mainstream', in Yasmine Musharbash and Geir Henning Presterudstuen, eds, *Monster Anthropology. Ethnographic Explorations of Transforming Social Worlds Through Monsters* (London: Bloomsbury, 2020), 89–111.

Night of the Living Dead, dir. George Romero (Pittsburgh, PA: Image Ten, 1968).

Nightingale, The, dir. Jennifer Kent (Adelaide: Causeway Films, 2019).

Nightmare on Elm Street, dir. Wes Craven (Los Angeles, CA: New Line Cinema Media Home Entertainment, 1984).

Norman, Joseph S., ' "[...] tentacular invisible mother divine"!: (The) Weird (in) Metal as convergence of sonic extremities and literary margins', in *Metal Music Studies* 5.2 (2019): 225–42.

——, ' "Sounds Which Filled Me with an Indefinable Dread": The Cthulhu Mythopoeia of H. P. Lovecraft in "Extreme" Metal', in David Simmons, ed., *New Critical Essays on H. P. Lovecraft* (New York: Palgrave, 2013), 193–208.

Noroi: The Curse, dir. Kōji Shiraishi (Tokyo: Xanadeux Company, 2005).

Nosferatu, dir. F. W. Murnau (Berlin: Jofa-Atelier, 1922).

Occult (Okaruto), dir. Kōji Shiraishi (Tokyo: Creative Axa/Company Ltd. Image Rings, 2009).

Omen, The, dir. Richard Donner (United States: Mace Neifeld Productions, 1976).

On the End of Eating Everything, Interview with Wangechi Mutu (Louisiana Channel: Louisiana Museum of Modern Art, Humlebæk, Denmark, 2015). <https://channel.louisiana.dk/video/wangechi-mutu-end-eating-everything> accessed 14 December 2019.

O'Regan, Tom. *Australian National Cinema* (London: Routledge, 1996).

Orphan Black, starring Tatiana Maslany, created by Graeme Manson and John Fawcett (Toronto: Temple Street Productions, 2013–2017).

Outbreak, dir. Wolfgang Petersen (Burbank: Warner Bros, 1995).

Parker, Charlie, 'PC GONE PSYCHO: Remake of Hitchcock classic *Psycho* axes cross-dressing killer in shower scene over 'transphobia' fears', *The Sun*, 16 April 2017 <https://www.thesun.co.uk/news/3343599/remake-of-hitchcock-classic-psycho-axes-cross-dressing-killer-in-shower-scene-over-transphobia-fears/> accessed 19 November 2019.

Paz, Octavio, 'The Sons of La Malinche', in Gilbert Joseph and Timothy Henderson, ed., *The Mexico Reader* (Durham, NC: Duke University Press, 2002), 20–7.

Pence, Gregory E., *What We Talk About When We Talk About Clone Club: Bioethics and Philosophy in Orphan Black* (Dallas, TX: Smart Pop, 2016).

Perez, Domino Renee, *There Was a Woman. La Llorona from Folklore to Popular Culture* (Austin: University of Texas Press, 2008).

Perry, Sarah, *Melmoth* (New York: Custom House, William Morrow: 2018).

Phillips, Shawn M., 'The Most Dangerous Deviants in America: Why the Disabled are Depicted as Deranged Killers', in Lawrence C. Rubin, ed., *Mental Illness in Popular Media: Essays on the Representation of Disorders* (Jefferson, NC: McFarland, 2012).

Picnic at Hanging Rock, dir. Peter Weir (Adelaide: British Empire Films, 1975).

Pilinovsky, Helen, 'Russian Fairy Tales: Baba Yaga's Domain' in *The Journal of Mythic Arts*, <https://endicottstudio.typepad.com/articleslist/baba-yagas-domain-by-helen-pilinovsky.html> accessed 14 December 2019.

Planet Terror, dir. Robert Rodriguez (New York: Dimension Films, 2007).

Poole, Jennifer M., and Jennifer Ward, '"Breaking Open the Bone": Storying, Sanism, and Mad Grief"', in Brenda A. LeFrançois and Robert Menzies, eds, *Mad Matters: A Critical Reader in Canadian Mad Studies* (Toronto: Canadian Scholars Press, 2013), 94–104.

Preston, Richard, 'Crisis in The Hot Zone', *New Yorker*, 26 October (1992), 80–1.

―――, 'The Vaccine Debacle', *The New York Times*, 2 October (1994).

Price, Margaret, *Mad at School: Rhetorics of Mental Disability and Academic Life* (Ann Arbor: University of Michigan Press, 2011).

Psycho, dir. Alfred Hitchcock (Los Angeles, CA: Paramount Pictures, 1960).

Pyzik, Agata, *Poor but Sexy: Culture Clashes in Europe East and West* (Zero Books: 2014).

Quinby, L., *Millennial Seduction: A Skeptic Confronts Apocalyptic Culture* (Ithaca, NY: Cornell University Press, 1999).
Rajadhon, Phya Anuman, 'The Phi', *The Journal of the Siam Society*, 41, 2 (1954), 153–78.
———, *Life and Ritual in Old Siam. Three Studies of Thai Life and Custom*, trans. William Gedney (New Haven, CT: HRAF Press, 1961).
Ramji, Rubina, 'An Interview with Agnieszka Smoczynska, Director of The Lure', *Journal of Religion & Film* 20:2, article 31 (2016) <https://digitalcommons.unomaha.edu/jrf/vol20/iss2/31> accessed 1 December 2019.
Reisigl, Martin, and Ruth Wodak, *Discourse and Discrimination: Rhetorics of Racism and Antisemitism* (London: Routledge, 2001).
Resident Evil 2: Apocalypse, dir. Alexander Witt (West Hollywood: Impact Pictures, 2004).
Resident Evil: Extinction, dir. Russell Mulcahy (Culver City: Screen Gems, 2007).
Riddle, Tohby, *Yahoo Creek* (Crows Nest: Allen & Unwin, 2019).
Riggs, Elizabeth E., 'Mental Illness and the Monstrous Mother: A Comparison of Representation in *The Babadook* and *Lights Out*', in *Film Matters*, Vol. 9, No. 1 (Spring 2018), 30–8.
Ring (Ringu), dir. Hideo Nakata (Tokyo: Ringu/Rasen Production Committee, 1998).
Rogerius, Abraham, *De Open-Deure tot het verborgen Heydendom* (Gravenhage: Nijhof, 1917).
Rosemary's Baby, dir. Roman Polanski (United States: Paramount Pictures, 1968).
Rosewarne, Lauren, *Cyberbullies, Cyberactivists, Cyberpredators: Film, TV, and Internet Stereotypes* (Santa Barbara, CA: Praeger, 2016a).
———, *Intimacy on the Internet: Media Representations of Online Connections.* (New York: Routledge, 2016b).
———, 'Cinema and Cyberphobia: Internet Clichés in Film and Television', in *Australian Journal of Telecommunications and the Digital Economy*, Vol. 4, 1 (2016c), 36–53.
———, '"Nothing Crueler than High School Students": The Cyberbully in Film and Television', in *International Journal of Technoethics*, Vol. 8, 1 (2017): 1–17.
Rothberg, Michael, *Multidirectional Memory: Remembering the Holocaust in an Age of Decolonialsation* (Stanford, CA: Stanford University Press, 2009).
Rousseau, Jean-Jacques, *Dialogues*, eds Roger D. Masters and Christopher Kelly, trans. Judith R. Bush, Christopher Kelly, and Roger D. Masters. In *The Collected Writings of Rousseau*, Vol. 1. (Hanover, NH: University Press of New England, 1990).
Rowlands Alison, 'Not "the Usual Suspects"? Male Witches, Witchcraft and Masculinities in Early Modern Europe in Witchcraft and Masculinities in Early Modern Europe' (New York: Palgrave Macmillan, 2009).
Rude, Mey Valdivia, 'Who's Afraid of the Big, Bad Trans Woman? On Horror and Transfemininity', *Autostraddle*, 8 October 2013, <https://www.

autostraddle.com/whos-afraid-of-the-big-bad-trans-woman-on-horror-and-transfemininity-198212/> accessed 28 November 2019.
Rudy, Jill Terry, and Jarom Lyle McDonald, 'Baba Yaga, Monsters of the Week, and Pop Culture's Formation of Wonder and Families through Monstrosity' (*Humanities*, 5, 40, <http://www.mdpi.com/journal/humanities>, 2016).
Ruskin, J. 'Lecture 1, 'Conventional Art', *The Two Paths*, in E. T. Cook and A. Wedderburn, eds, *The Works of John Ruskin*, Vol. 16 (London: George Allen, 1905), 265.
Russo, Jasna, and Angela Sweeney, eds, *Searching for a Rose Garden: Challenging Psychiatry, Fostering Mad Studies* (Monmouth: PCCS Books Ltd., 2016).
Salvatore, R. A., *Canticle* (Lake Geneva, WI: TSR, 1991).
Sandahl, Carrie, 'Queering the Crip or Cripping the Queer? Intersections of Queer and Crip Identities in Solo Autobiographical Performance', in *GLQ: A Journal of Lesbian and Gay Studies*, Vol. 9, Nos 1–2 (2003), 25–56.
Sanna, Antonio, 'Silent Homosexuality in Oscar Wilde's *Teleny* and *The Picture of Dorian Gray* and Robert Louis Stevenson's *Dr. Jekyll and Mr. Hyde*', *Law & Literature*, Vol. 24, No. 1 (March 2012), 21–39.
Santa Ana, Otto, 'Like an Animal I Was Treated: Anti-immigrant Metaphor in U.S. Public Discourse' *Discourse and Society* 10:2 (1999), 191–224.
Santos, Cristina, *Unbecoming Female Monsters: Witches, Vampires, and Virgins* (Lanham, MD: Lexington, 2016).
Sastry, Keertana, 'What The Heck Are Those Skeleton Guys on "Game of Thrones"? You Know, Besides Trouble', *Bustle*, 15 June 2014. <https://www.bustle.com/articles/28191-what-the-heck-are-these-skeleton-guys-on-game-of-thrones-you-know-besides-trouble> accessed 14 December 2019.
Schaefer, David, *Urban Legends and the Japanese Tale* (London: The Institute for Cultural Research, 1990).
Schalk, Sami, *Bodyminds Reimagined: (Dis)ability, Race, and Gender in Black Women's Speculative Fiction* (Durham, NC: Duke University Press, 2018).
Schmeink, L., '"Scavenge, Slay, Survive": The Zombie Apocalypse, Exploration, and Lived Experience in DayZ', *Science Fiction Studies*, Vol. 43, No. 1 (March 2016), 67–84.
Schmidt, Francis, 'Introduction: les polythéismes: dégénérescence ou progrès'?, in *L'Impensable polythéisme: Etudes d'historiographie religieuse*, ed. Francis Schmidt (Paris: éditions des archives contemporaines, 1988), 13–91.
Schneck, Robert Damon, *President's Vampire: Strange-but-True Tales of the United States of America* (San Antonio, TX: Anomalist Books, 2005).
Schoonmaker, Trevor, 'A Conversation: Wangechi Mutu and Trevor Schoonmaker', in Trevor Schoonmaker, ed., *Wangechi Mutu: A Fantastic Journey* (Durham, NC: Nasher Museum of Art, Duke University, 2013), 95–117.

Schwab, Raymond, *La Renaissance orientale* (Paris: Payot, 1950).
Schweitzer, Dahlia, *Going Viral: Zombies, Viruses, and the End of the World* (New Brunswick, NJ: Rutgers University Press, 2018).
Scott, Mathew, 'Oscars: Thailand Selects "Inhuman Kiss" for International Feature Film Category', <https://www.hollywoodreporter.com/news/2020-oscars-thailand-selects-inhuman-kiss-international-feature-film-category-1244184>, accessed 25 October 2019.
Sederholm, Carl H., 'H. P. Lovecraft, Heavy Metal, and Cosmicism', *Rock Music Studies* 3.3 (2016): 1–15.
Sederholm, Carl H., and Jeffrey Andrew Weinstock, 'Introduction: Lovecraft Rising', in Sederholm and Weinstock, eds, *The Age of Lovecraft* (Minneapolis: University of Minnesota Press, 2016), 1–42.
Shapira, Tom. 'Red in Fang and Claw', in S. G. Hammond, ed., *The Mignolaverse: Hellboy and the Comic Art of Mike Mignola* (Edwardsville, IL: Sequart Organization, 2019), 43–56.
Shelley, Mary, *Frankenstein, or the Modern Prometheus* [1831] (New York: Penguin, 1992).
She-Wolf of London, dir. Jean Yarbrough (Universal Pictures, 1946).
Shirome, dir. Kōji Shiraishi (Tokyo: Shirome Project Partners Stardust Promotion, 2010).
Showalter, Elaine, *Sexual Anarchy: Gender and Culture at the Fin de Siècle* (New York: Viking, 1990/1992).
Silence of the Lambs, The, dir. Jonathan Demme (Los Angeles, CA: Orion Pictures, 1991).
Sinacola, Dom, 'The Witch' in 'The 25 Best Movies About Witches'. *Paste Magazine*, 3 February 2019, <https://www.pastemagazine.com/articles/2019/01/the-25-best-movies-about-witches.html> accessed 14 December 2019.
Sleepaway Camp, dir. Robert Hiltzik (American Eagle Productions, 1983).
Slender Man, dir. Sylvian White (Sony Pictures Releasing, 2010).
Smith, Andrew, and Diana Wallace, 'The Female Gothic: Then and Now', in *Gothic Studies*, Vol. 25 (August 2004), 1–7.
Smith, Angela M., *Hideous Progeny: Disability, Eugenics, and Classic Horror Cinema* (New York: Columbia University Press, 2011).
Snelson, Tim, *Phantom Ladies: Hollywood Horror and the Home Front* (New Brunswick, NJ: Rutgers University Press, 2015).
Snyder, Midori, 'In Praise of the Cook', *Labyrinth*, 2005, <https://www.midorisnyder.com/essays/in-praise-of-the-cook-ii.html> accessed 14 December 2019.
Sobchack, Vivian, *Screening Space: The American Science Fiction Film* (New Brunswick, NJ: Rutgers University Press, 2001).
Sontag, Susan, *Regarding the Pain of Others* (New York: Picador, 2003).
South Park: Bigger, Longer & Uncut, dir. Trey Parker (Paramount/Warner Bros/Comedy Central, 1999).

Squires, John, 'The Urban Legend That Inspired "The Bye Bye Man" is Pretty Damn Creepy', *Bloody Disgusting*, 19 January 2017. <https://bloody-disgusting.com/news/3421740/urban-legend-inspired-bye-bye-man-pretty-damn-creepy/> accessed 22 March 2019.

Stevenson, Robert Louis, *The Strange Case of Dr. Jekyll and Mr. Hyde*, 1886, ed. Katherine Linehan (London: W.W. Norton, 2003).

Strain, The, created by Guillermo del Toro and Chuck Hogan (Century City: FX, 2014–2017).

Strause, Jackie, 'American Horror Story's Antichrist Responds to Church of Satan Criticism: "He's a Righteous Character"', *The Hollywood Reporter*, 2 November 2018.

Sundance TV, *Cleverman/ Creating the Hairies' Behind the Scenes* on YouTube, 23 June 2016. <https://www.youtube.com/watch?v=l_AaoSoY9Fo> accessed 7 October 2019.

Suspiria, dir. Dario Argento (Italy: Seda Spettacoli, 1977).

Suspiria, dir. Luca Guadagnino (United States: Amazon Studios, 2018).

Synnott, Anthony, 'Shame and Glory: A Sociology of Hair', in *The British Journal of Sociology* Vol. 38, No. 3 (1987): 381–413.

Tambiah, Stanley, *Buddhism and the Spirit Cults in North-East Thailand* (Cambridge: Cambridge University Press, 1970).

Taussig, Michael, *Mimesis and Alterity: A Particular History of the Senses* (New York: Routledge, 1992).

Tenacious D in the Pick of Destiny, dir. Liam Lynch (United States: Red Hour Films, 2006).

Textor, Robert, *Roster of the Gods: An Ethnography of the Supernatural in a Thai Village* (New Haven, CT: Human Relations Area Files, 1973).

Thacker, Eugene, *In the Dust of this Planet: Horror of Philosophy Vol. 1* (Washington, DC: Zero Books, 2011).

This is the End, dir. Seth Rogen and Evan Goldberg (Columbia Pictures/Mandate Pictures/Point Grey Pictures, 2013).

Thompson, Kirsten Moana, *Apocalyptic Dread: American Film at the Turn of the Millennium* (Albany: State University of New York Press, 2007).

Transhumanist Declaration, Humanity +, n.d. <https://humanityplus.org/philosophy/transhumanist-declaration/> accessed 28 October 2019.

Travers, Ben, '*Psycho* Gets Woke: Rihanna's *Bates Motel* Shower Scene is a Progressive Twist on Hitchcock – Showrunner Interview', *IndieWire*, 27 March 2017 <http://www.indiewire.com/2017/03/bates-motel-psycho-episode-6-recap-rihanna-shower-spoilers-1201797019/> accessed 19 November 2019.

Trometta, Jim, *The Horror! The Horror!: Comic Books the Government Didn't Want You to Read!* (New York: Abrams ComicArts, 2010).

Tudor, Andrew, *Monsters and Mad Scientists*: *A Cultural History of the Horror Movie* (Oxford: Blackwell, 1989).
Urban Legend, dir. Jamie Blanks (Los Angeles, CA: Original Film/Phoenix Pictures, 1998).
Varthema, Ludovico di, *Itinerario di Ludovico di Varthema Bolognese* (published in Rome in 1510). English translation by John Winter Jones, *The Itinerary of Ludovico di Varthema of Bologna* (London: Hakluyt Society, 1863).
Witch, The: *A New England Folktale/The Witch*, dir. Robert Eggers (A24, 2015).
Waid, Mark, and Alex Ross, *Kingdom Come* (New York: D.C. Comics, 1997).
Walking Dead, The, created by Frank Darabont and Angela King (New York: AMC, 2010-present).
Wallace, Molly, *Risk Criticism*: *Precautionary Reading in an Age of Environmental Uncertainty* (Ann Arbor: University of Michigan Press, 2016).
Wang, Lin, 'Skeleton', in Jeffery Andrew Weinstock, ed., *The Ashgate Encyclopedia of Literary and Cinematic Monsters* (Farnham: Ashgate, 2014).
Warme, Gordon, 'Removing Civil Rights: How Dare We'? in Brenda A. LeFrançois and Robert Menzies, eds, *Mad Matters*: *A Critical Reader in Canadian Mad Studies* (Toronto: Canadian Scholars Press, 2013), 210–20.
Warner, Kate, 'Relationships with the Past: How Australian Television Dramas Talk about Indigenous History' in *M/C Journal. A Journal of Media and Culture*, Vol. 20, No. 5, 2017, <http://journal.media-culture.org.au/index.php/mcjournal/article/view/1302> accessed 1 October 2019.
Warner, Marina, *No Go the Bogeyman*: *Scaring, Lulling, and Making Mock* (New York: Farrar, Strauss, and Giroux, 1999).
Wehler, Melissa, 'Revising Ophelia: Representing Madwomen in Baillie's *Orra* and *Witchcraft*', in Ruth Bienstock Analik, ed., *Demons of the Body and Mind*: *Essays on Disability and Gothic Literature* (Jefferson, NC: McFarland, 2010), 110–18.
Weinstock, Jeffrey Andrew, 'Invisible Monsters: Vision, Horror, and Contemporary Culture', in Asa Simon Mittman, and Peter J. Dendle, eds, *The Ashgate Research Companion to Monsters and the Monstrous* (London: Routledge, 2017). 275–92.
Weisman, Alan, *The World Without Us* (New York: St Martin's Press, 2007).
Wells, H. G., *The Invisible Man*: *A Grotesque Romance* [1896] (Project Gutenberg, 2004), <https://www.gutenberg.org/files/5230/5230-h/5230-h.htm> accessed 12 December 2019.
Werewolf, The, dir. Henry MacRae (Bison Film Company, 1913).
Werewolf Woman, dir. Rino di Silvestro (Rome: Dialchi Film, 1976).
Westfahl, Gary, 'Skeletons', in Gary Westfahl, ed., *The Greenwood Encyclopedia of Science Fiction and Fantasy*: *Themes, Works, and Wonders* (Westport, CT: Greenwood Press, 2005), 722–4.

Wexman, Virginia Wright, 'Horrors of the Body: Hollywood's Discourse on Beauty and Rouben Mamoulian's *Dr. Jekyll and Mr. Hyde*', in William Veeder and Gordon Hirsch, eds, *Dr. Jekyll and Mr. Hyde After One Hundred Years* (Chicago: University of Chicago Press, 1988), 282–312.

When Animals Dream, dir. Jonas Alexander Arnby (AlphaVille Pictures, 2014).

Williams, Linda, 'Film Madness: The Uncanny Return of the Repressed in Polanski's *The Tenant*', in *Cinema Journal*, Vol. 20, No. 1 (Spring 1981), 63–73.

Williams, Skip, et al. *Monster Manual* (Renton, WA: Wizards of the Coast, 2003).

Williams, Tony, *Hearths of Darkness: The Family in the American Horror Film* (Mississippi: University of Mississippi Press, 1996).

Willis, Deborah. 'Wangechi Mutu', *Bomb*. Published electronically 28 February 2014, <https://bombmagazine.org/articles/wangechi-mutu/> accessed 14 December 2019.

Witches of Eastwick, The, dir. George Miller (United States: Guber-Peters Co./Kennedy Miller, 1987).

Witchfinder General, dir. Michael Reeves (Tigon/AIP, 1968).

Wittkower, R., 'Marvels of the East: A Study in the History of Monsters', *Journal of the Warburg and Courtauld Institutes*, Vol. 5 (1942) 159–97.

Wolfe, C., 'Human, All Too Human: "Animal Studies" and the Humanities', *PMLA*, Vol. 124, No. 2 (March 2009), 564–75.

Wood, Juliette, *Fantastic Creatures in Mythology and Folklore: From Medieval Times to the Present Day* (London: Bloomsbury, 2018).

Wood, Robin, *Hollywood from Vietnam to Reagan ... and Beyond*, expanded and revised edition [1989] (New York: Columbia University Press, 2003).

Woodbridge, Karl Bell, *The Legend of Spring-heeled Jack: Victorian Urban Folklore and Popular Cultures* (Martlesham: The Boydell Press, 2012).

World War Z, dir. Marc Foster (Paramount Pictures, 2013).

Wright, Kristen, ed., *Disgust and Desire: The Paradox of the Monster* (Leiden: Brill, 2018).

Young, Elizabeth, *Black Frankenstein: The Making of an American Metaphor* (London: New York University Press, 2008).

Zimmerman, Jacqueline Noll, *People Like Ourselves: Portrayals of Mental Illness in the Movies* (Oxford: Scarecrow Press, 2003).

Zipes, Jack, *The Irresistible Fairy Tale: The Cultural and Social History of a Genre* (Princeton, NJ: Princeton University Press, 2012).

Žižek, Slavoj. 'A Permanent Economic Emergency'. *New Left Review 64* (July/August 2010), <https://newleftreview.org/issues/II64/articles/slavoj-zizek-a-permanent-economic-emergency> accessed 14 December 2019.

Notes on Contributors

ANTHONY CURTIS ADLER is Professor of German and Comparative Literature at Yonsei University's Underwood International College, where he has taught since 2006. His research focuses on the intersections of political theory, media studies, literary studies, and continental philosophy, and he has published articles, in edited volumes and journals such as *Diacritics, Continental Philosophy Review, Cultural Critique,* and *Angelaki,* on topics ranging from Fichte, Kant, Hölderlin, and Agamben to the revival of the phonograph, esoteric apophaticism in the work of P. K. Dick, and H. C. Andersen's abject things. In his *Celebricities: Media Culture and the Phenomenology of Gadget Commodity Life* (Fordham University Press, 2016) he combines traditional academic prose with fragmentary forms, and Marxist materialism with Heidegger, to offer a phenomenological analysis of the modes of experience of late capitalism.

SIMON BACON is an independent scholar based in Poznan, Poland. He has edited books on various subjects including *Undead Memory: Vampires and Human Memory in Popular Culture* (2014), and *Growing Up with Vampires: Essays on the Undead in Children's Media* (2018), both with Katarzyna Bronk, and *Gothic: A Reader* (2018), *Horror: A Companion (2019),* and *Transmedia: A Companion* (forthcoming). He has published monographs on *Becoming Vampire: Difference and the Vampire in Popular Culture* (2016), *Dracula as Absolute Other: The Troubling and Distracting Specter of Stoker's Vampire on Screen* (2019), and *Eco-Vampires: The Vampire as Environmentalist and Undead Eco-activist* (2020), and is currently working on *Invasion of Vampires From Another World: The Cinematic Alien Progeny of War of the Worlds and Dracula.*

BENJAMIN BAUMANN is a postdoctoral associate at Heidelberg University's Institute of Anthropology. Before joining Heidelberg University in April 2020, he was research associate at the Department of Southeast Asian

Studies at Humboldt-Universität zu Berlin's Institute of Asian and African Studies. Trained as a socio-cultural anthropologist, his multidisciplinary work examines rural lifeworlds, socio-cultural identities, and local language games, while focusing on the ghostly aspects of collective belonging in contemporary Thailand.

EMILY BRICK is Senior Lecturer in Film and Media at Manchester Metropolitan University. Her work focuses on gender and monstrosity and she is currently working on all things witchy.

JOHN EDGAR BROWNING is Professor of Liberal Arts at the Savannah College of Art and Design. He has over fifteen contracted or published books and over seventy-five shorter works, including *The Forgotten Writings of Bram Stoker* (Palgrave, 2012) and *Zombie Talk: Culture, History, Politics* (Palgrave, 2015; with David Castillo, et al.), as well as *Dracula – An Anthology: Critical Reviews and Reactions, 1897–1920* (Edinburgh University Press, forthcoming) and *New Queer Horror Film and TV* (Horror Studies) (University of Wales Press, forthcoming; with Darren Elliott-Smith). He is also co-editing, with David J. Skal, the second Norton Critical Edition of Dracula.

GERRY CANAVAN is an associate professor in the English Department at Marquette University, specializing in twentieth- and twenty-first-century literature. An editor at *Extrapolation* and *Science Fiction Film and Television*, he has also co-edited *Green Planets: Ecology and Science Fiction* (2014), *The Cambridge Companion to American Science Fiction* (2015) and *The Cambridge History of Science Fiction* (2019). His first monograph, *Octavia E. Butler*, appeared in 2016 in the Modern Masters of Science Fiction series at University of Illinois Press.

GAIL DE VOS is an adjunct associate professor for the School of Library and Information Studies at the University of Alberta in Edmonton, Alberta, Canada, developing and teaching online courses on storytelling, Canadian children's literature, and graphic novels and comic books. She also teaches an online course on First Nations Children's Books for ATEP (Aboriginal Teaching Education Program) in the Faculty of Education. She is the author of nine award-winning books on folklore, literature, and popular culture, as well as numerous chapters for academic monographs. She has presented her research in conferences across North America and Europe. She is a professional storyteller who specializes in telling contemporary legends to young adults. Her major research focus is on exploring connections between folklore and comic books.

EDDIE FALVEY completed his AHRC-funded PhD project on the early films of New York at University of Exeter. Since finishing his PhD, he has been Lecturer in Contextual Studies at Plymouth College of Art and is developing his thesis into a monograph for University of Amsterdam Press. Moreover, he is the author of an upcoming volume, *Re-Animator* (Auteur), co-editor of a forthcoming edited collection on contemporary horror, and has published on various topics, including horror film, adaptation studies, reception studies, and animation.

PHIL FITZSIMMONS is currently an independent research and educational consultant. Prior to this he was Assistant Dean of Research (Faculty of Education, Business and Science) at Avondale University College and Director of Research (San Roque Research Institute, California).

ELANA GOMEL is an associate professor at the Department of English and American Studies at Tel-Aviv University. She has taught and researched at Princeton, Stanford, University of Hong Kong, and Venice International University. She is the author of six academic books and numerous articles on subjects such as narrative theory, posthumanism, science fiction, Dickens, and Victorian culture. As a fiction writer, she has published more than fifty fantasy and science fiction stories and three novels.

ALEXANDRA HELLER-NICHOLAS is a film critic, programming consultant and academic from Australia. She has written eight books on cult, horror and exploitation cinema with an emphasis on gender politics, including *Rape-Revenge Films: A Critical Study* (2011), *Found Footage Horror Film: Fear and the Appearance of Reality* (2014) and *Masks in Horror Cinema: Eyes Without Faces* (2019). She is an Adjunct Professor at Deakin University with a PhD in Screen Studies from the University of Melbourne, and a film programmer for Fantastic Fest in Austin.

AGNIESZKA KOTWASIŃSKA is an assistant professor at the American Studies Center, University of Warsaw. She specializes in Gothic and horror studies, gender studies and queer theory, and feminist new materialism(s). Her current research interests centre on embodiment in the so-called low genres, death, illness and mourning in horror, and schizoanalysis. She has published articles in *Somatechnics*, *Polish Journal of American Studies*, *Praktyka Teoretyczna*, and *Women, Gender and Research*, among others. She is currently working on her first monograph exploring horror fiction by American women writers.

MURRAY LEEDER is a research affiliate at the University of Manitoba and holds a PhD from Carleton University. He the author of *Horror Film: A Critical Introduction* (Bloomsbury, 2018), *The Modern Supernatural and the Beginnings of Cinema* (Palgrave Macmillan, 2017) and *Halloween* (Auteur, 2014), editor of *Cinematic Ghosts: Haunting and Spectrality from Silent Cinema to the Digital Era* (Bloomsbury, 2015) and *ReFocus: The Films of William Castle* (Edinburgh University Press, 2018), as well as numerous articles and book chapters.

SHERRY C. M. LINDQUIST is Associate Professor of Art History at Western Illinois University. Her publications include *Agency, Visuality and Society at the Chartreuse de Champmol* (2008), *Meanings of Nudity in Medieval Art* (2012), and articles in numerous journals and anthologies. Her awards include grants from Fulbright, Getty, Kress, Mellon, and the British Academy. *Medieval Monsters: Terrors, Aliens, Wonders* (2018), with Asa Mittman, accompanies the exhibit they curated at the Morgan Library, the Cleveland Museum of Art, and the Blanton Museum.

PATRICIA MACCORMACK is Professor of Continental Philosophy at Anglia Ruskin University Cambridge. She has published extensively on philosophy, feminism, queer and monster theory, animal abolitionist activism, ethics, art and horror cinema. She is the author of *Cinesexuality* (Routledge

2008) and *Posthuman Ethics* (Routledge 2012) and the editor of *The Animal Catalyst* (Bloomsbury 2014), *Deleuze and the Animal* (Edinburgh University Press 2017), *Deleuze and the Schizoanalysis of Cinema* (Continuum 2008) and *Ecosophical Aesthetics* (Bloomsbury 2018). Her new book is *The Ahuman Manifesto: Activisms for the End of the Anthropocene* (Bloomsbury 2020).

CRAIG IAN MANN is Associate Lecturer in Film and Media at Sheffield Hallam University. He has a particular interest in the cultural significance of popular genres; his first monograph, *Phases of the Moon: A Cultural History of the Werewolf Film*, is forthcoming from Edinburgh University Press. He has contributed to *Horror Studies* and the *Journal of Popular Film and Television*, as well as several edited collections, and is co-organizer of the Fear 2000 conference series on contemporary horror media.

PARTHA MITTER is an art and cultural historian. At present, he is Emeritus Professor at the University of Sussex. Formerly, he was a research fellow at Clare Hall, Cambridge. He has lectured internationally and has held visiting fellowships in the United States. He is the author of *Much Maligned Monsters: History of European Reactions to Indian Art* (1977), which studies western misrepresentations of ancient Indian art. He has also written extensively on modern art and national identity in colonial India. More recently he has been writing on western modernism and the globalization of art.

YASMINE MUSHARBASH is Senior Lecturer in Anthropology at the Australian National University. She conducts participant observation-based research with Warlpiri people in central Australia on social relations among Warlpiri people and between Warlpiri people and Others, including non-Indigenous people, dogs, birds, and monsters. Her work is concerned with the everyday and themes such as neo-colonialism, fear, the night, boredom and death. She has co-edited *Monster Anthropology from Australasia and Beyond* (2014) and *Monster Anthropology: Ethnographic Explorations of Transforming Social Relations through Monsters* (2020).

INÉS ORDIZ is Lecturer in Spanish and Latin American Studies at the University of Stirling (UK). She holds a PhD in Modern Languages from the University of León (Spain), with a specialization in Comparative Pan-American Gothic Literature. She is the co-editor of the volume *La (ir)realidad imaginada: Aproximaciones a lo insólito en la ficción hispanoamericana* (Universidad de León, 2014) and *Latin American Gothic in Literature and Culture* (Routledge, 2018), which focus on the various manifestations of fantasy and the Gothic in Latin American literature and film.

W. SCOTT POOLE is the author of the 2018 *Wasteland: The Great War and The Origin of Modern Horror* and the award-winning *Monsters in America* (2011; revised 2018). His biography of H. P. Lovecraft, *In the Mountains of Madness* (2016), was a Bram Stoker award nominee. He has authored numerous other books and contributed to a significant number of essay collections along with publishing hundreds of reviews and op-eds. He is a historian at the College of Charleston, where he teaches courses in the history of horror, politics, and pop culture.

LEAH RICHARDS is Associate Professor of English at LaGuardia Community College, City University of New York. Publications include 'This *Land* was Made for You and Me: The Rise of the Oppressed in *Land of the Dead*' in the *Journal of Popular Culture* (2018) and 'Mass Production and the Spread of Information in *Dracula*: "Proofs of so wild a story"' in *English Literature in Transition, 1880–1920* (2009). She is the co-editor of *Supernatural Studies* and *Representation in* Steven Universe (2020).

LAUREN ROSEWARNE is a senior lecturer at the University of Melbourne, Australia. She has published and commented widely on issues of sex, gender, film and television. Her eleventh book, Why We Remake: The Politics, Economics and Emotions of Film and TV Remakes, has recently been published by Routledge. More information is available at <http://www.laurenrosewarne.com>.

DAHLIA SCHWEITZER is an associate professor at the Fashion Institute of Technology. Her latest book, *L.A. Private Eyes* (2019), examines the tradition of the private eye as it evolves in films, book, and television shows set in Los Angeles. Her previous works include *Going Viral: Zombies, Viruses, and the End of the World* (2018), *Cindy Sherman's Office Killer: Another Kind of Monster* (2014), as well as essays in publications including *Journal of Popular Film and Television*, *Jump Cut*, and *Journal of Popular Culture*.

CARL H. SEDERHOLM is Professor of Interdisciplinary Humanities at Brigham Young University and chair of the Department of Comparative Arts and Letters. He is the editor of *The Journal of American Culture* and co-editor (with Jeffrey Weinstock) of *The Age of Lovecraft*. His other work includes the co-edited volume *Adapting Poe: Re-Imaginings in Popular Culture* (with Dennis Perry) and the co-authored book (also with Dennis Perry) *Poe, the 'House of Usher', and the American Gothic*. He has also published multiple essays on authors such as Edgar Allan Poe, H. P. Lovecraft, Stephen King, Jonathan Edwards, Lydia Maria Child, and Nathaniel Hawthorne.

DANIEL SHEPPARD is a PhD candidate at Birmingham City University, UK. His thesis is called 'Gays, Women and Chainsaws: Queer Approaches to Characterisation and Identification in Contemporary Slasher Film and Television, 1996–2019' and is fully funded by the AHRC (Arts and Humanities Research Council) Midlands4Cities Doctoral Training Partnership.

ANGELA M. SMITH is Associate Professor in English and Gender Studies and Director of the Disability Studies Initiative at the University of Utah. Her research focuses on disability representation in American cinema and popular culture. She is the author of *Hideous Progeny: Disability, Eugenics, and Classic Horror Cinema* (Columbia University Press, 2011) and articles in the journals *Post Script*, *College Literature*, and *Literature and Medicine* and in the essay collections *Horror Zone* and *Popular Eugenics*.

Index

abject xiii, 6, 7, 22, 35, 46, 150, 158, 179, 221, 239
Abortion 116, 169, 219
abuse 23–4, 27, 29–30, 46, 48, 53, 91, 115, 156, 159, 170, 178, 198
African xiii, xv, xvii, 202, 207, 218
    American xiv, xii, 88
alien xii, 82, 217–20, 223
allegory 98, 111, 223
America 4, 16, 25, 42, 45, 51, 56, 58, 67, 88, 89, 94, 168–9, 172, 176, 202, 207, 209
animal xi, xii, 42, 98, 101, 105, 126, 129, 152, 158, 160, 168, 217, 220, 228, 230, 235, 236
anthropocene 137, 143, 214, 217, 231
Antichrist 130, 132, 150, 151, 157, 160, 231
anti-Semitism
archetype 69, 161, 225
Asia 101–3, 107, 113, 202, 207
Australia 15, 32, 34–5, 37, 38, 137–9, 141–3

beast xviii, 15, 19, 32, 43, 167, 168, 174, 228, 234, 235
black magic 104, 109
blood xii, 3, 10, 34, 51, 90, 93, 107, 112, 141, 150, 172, 203, 205, 211
body xii–xiii, xviii, 7, 8, 9, 15, 19, 29, 31, 35, 38, 43, 46, 52, 89, 101, 104, 122, 139, 150, 152, 156, 193, 198, 201, 203, 220, 222, 225, 227, 228, 232, 235–7, 240–1
Bogey Man (boogey) 16, 19, 69–70, 86, 88
bully 29, 69, 72, 73, 81
    cyber- 69–74

cannibal 44, 46, 122, 123, 126, 137, 143, 160, 205, 228, 231, 238, 242
capitalism 84, 157, 158, 164–5, 176
child 16, 59, 81, 84, 87, 90, 91, 115, 151, 154, 177, 179, 184, 186, 219, 220, 227, 228
    -hood 4, 15, 34, 75, 82, 160
    loss of 20, 86, 101, 111, 123, 143
Christian xviii, 9, 130, 132, 134, 150, 153, 168, 207
cis 178, 179, 222
Cohen, Jeffrey Jerome xi, xiv, 1–2, 4, 36, 43, 142, 211, 217, 220, 221–3, 226
colonial 3, 8, 9, 32, 33–4, 36, 37, 96, 104, 113, 115, 129, 130, 138, 142
contagion 9, 10, 106, 107, 108, 201, 205, 206, 208
contamination 10, 220
corpse 141, 211, 231, 236
Creed, Barbara 20, 27, 38, 150, 152, 158, 178
curse 4–5, 89, 95, 113, 170, 174

death 7, 20, 34, 36, 87, 91, 97, 102, 103, 112, 116, 122, 123, 138, 158, 174, 176, 179, 183, 184, 186, 188, 193, 206, 207, 211, 213, 215, 223, 233, 236
destabilize 46, 91, 114, 115, 117, 230
devil 106, 119, 126, 129, 132–3, 149, 150, 154, 161, 163
disability 15, 17–8, 22, 53, 158, 186
disease 10, 19, 42, 196, 201, 206–7, 209, 227
documentary 51, 86, 87, 90, 218
domestic 23–4, 26, 91, 123, 159, 168, 180, 203
double/Doppelgänger 180, 181, 193

Dracula 2–4, 18, 41, 53, 203
dream 29, 45, 73, 81, 139, 143, 154, 155, 167, 214, 227
dystopia 114, 138, 201, 205, 225–6

embody 1, 26, 27, 43, 69, 70, 93, 112, 122, 142, 150, 152, 187–8, 195, 196, 199
   dis- 71, 188, 189
emotion 7, 19, 23, 24, 53, 94, 161, 181
environment xv, xvii, 28, 34, 35, 45, 197, 202, 212–13, 230
erotic 37, 47, 160, 242, 244
ethnicity 176, 218
eugenics 41, 42, 163, 193, 194
evil xiv, 15, 17, 75, 82–3, 93, 95–7, 98, 106, 121, 122, 126, 149, 150, 152, 154, 156, 160, 204, 228, 233, 242
excess 7, 17, 28, 34, 161
exorcism 17
Exorcist, The 18, 72, 150, 151
exploitation xiii, 16, 46, 73, 115, 116, 176, 238

fantastic xiv, 123
fantasy 27, 28, 47, 71, 73, 91, 94, 129, 161, 186, 187, 190, 218
father 28, 45, 83, 103, 111, 112, 150, 172, 174, 178, 180–1, 194
feminine 10, 36, 46, 53, 153, 158, 161, 165, 175
feminism xi, xvii, 20, 29, 114, 115, 157, 160, 169, 170, 172, 178
filth 33, 101, 218
folklore 15, 101, 122, 124, 127
forest 32, 33, 35, 104, 122, 123, 154, 183
forgive xv, 112, 143
Frankenstein 2, 19, 20, 186, 193, 194, 197, 199, 209
Freud, Sigmund 6, 7, 16, 138, 180, 234

gaslighting 8, 29
gaze 23, 35, 95, 98, 218, 225, 242

gender xiii, 9–10, 20, 43, 53, 74, 88, 102, 105, 111, 113, 114, 116, 121, 158, 161, 168, 175, 179, 181, 220, 221, 232, 236, 242
ghost xiv, 27, 28, 72, 88, 89, 101, 102, 104, 106–7, 111, 113, 115, 123, 158, 186, 187–8
   lore 101, 104
globalization xvii, 4, 5, 9, 42, 87, 102, 107, 113, 114, 115, 172, 201–2, 210, 212, 213, 216, 242
God/god 119, 130–2, 134–5, 168, 194, 195, 231, 240
goddess 112, 129, 168
gory 51, 90, 211
Gothic 2, 15, 18–9, 20, 22, 32, 33–4, 35, 41, 43, 95, 96, 98, 107, 142
guilt xv, 55, 98

Hairy 5, 10, 16, 18, 25, 27, 81, 91, 115, 137–44, 203, 239
Halberstam, Jack 1–2, 6, 35, 38, 41, 45, 46, 141, 142
haunt 16, 29, 35, 58, 70, 86, 88, 96, 111, 116, 129, 137, 143, 179, 188
hero 5, 38, 121–2, 158, 160, 188, 190, 212, 221, 225, 225, 231
hetero
   -normative 19, 46, 175
   -patriarchal 114, 176, 177, 178, 179, 181
   -sexual 178, 191, 244
homo
   -erotic 242
   -phobia 2, 114
   -sexual 176, 221, 244
horror xv, 15, 18, 19, 22, 37, 41–3, 46, 52, 53, 56, 58, 72, 75, 85–7, 88, 89–90, 91, 93–4, 97–8, 103, 112, 113, 115, 116, 142, 150, 152, 153, 158, 168, 174, 176, 177, 180, 186, 189, 190, 208, 210, 211, 214, 215, 217, 218, 222, 225, 228, 237

Index

humanism
   post- xi, xvii, 230, 231
   trans- 198, 199
hybrid xii, xiii, xv, xvii, xix, 34, 41, 59, 114, 217

identity xi, xiii, 10, 31, 36, 38, 41, 53, 73, 74, 102, 112, 114, 142, 175, 178, 179, 181, 193, 197, 223
immigrant 3, 8, 41–3, 44, 46, 47, 168, 169, 219
India 9, 129–31, 134, 136
Indigenous 32, 112, 137–9, 142–3, 168
infected 42, 44, 46, 109, 169, 201, 203–4, 205, 208, 227
internet 69, 70–3, 75, 79, 85, 86, 114, 208
Islam 134
   -ophobia 46

Kristeva, Julia 6, 36, 150, 234

Latin America 41, 115
legend xviii, 86, 87, 89, 111, 113, 114–5, 119, 122, 137
   urban 84–7, 88, 89–91
lore 114, 193, 203
love 3, 4, 7, 22, 25, 37, 45, 74, 79, 84, 87, 106, 112, 160, 163, 164, 170, 193, 195, 221, 237, 242
Lovecraft, H. P. 41, 96, 210, 212–3, 214

madness 8, 15, 18–9, 22, 23, 83, 154
magic 21, 22, 79, 82, 102, 106, 109, 122, 126, 149, 155, 157, 160, 162–4, 168, 183
malevolent 24, 102, 106, 160
masculinity 26, 28, 33, 35, 37, 53, 152, 157, 158, 160, 161, 163, 164, 165, 167, 174, 178, 235
mask 8, 29, 52–3, 55–8, 67, 90–1, 227, 234
maternal 21, 47, 180

memory 6, 29, 31, 70, 91, 119, 180, 186, 209, 218
mental illness 15–6, 19, 21–2, 29, 35, 41, 45
mermaid 8, 41, 43–7
metaphor 3, 36, 42, 43, 46, 102, 140, 167, 173, 174, 206, 213
military 94, 97, 167, 202, 209
Millennial 81, 225–6, 227, 231
millennium 52, 69, 79, 130, 170, 175, 179, 225
miscegenation 3, 10, 46, 221
misogyny 2, 46, 153, 178–9, 189, 236
monster xviii, xix, 1–7, 11, 15, 18, 19, 23, 29, 31, 34, 38–9, 42–3, 53, 69–72, 74, 77–8, 80–2, 84, 85, 87, 91, 93, 96, 97, 101, 106, 113, 116, 119, 121, 126, 129, 130, 134, 136, 137, 141, 142, 149, 157–8, 160, 163, 165, 167, 174, 175, 176–8, 183, 186, 188, 190, 293–4, 199, 205, 208, 209–11, 214, 216, 217, 221, 222, 226, 228, 231
   culture xiv
monstrosity xiv, 9, 15, 19, 24, 38, 45, 77, 81, 84, 112, 115, 143, 149, 151–3, 155, 161, 164–5, 174, 176, 219, 228
monstrous xi, xii, xviii, 4, 7, 11, 18, 21, 31, 34, 36, 41–3, 46, 47, 58, 101, 113, 116, 127, 129, 133, 136, 157, 158–9, 186, 193–5, 199, 210, 213, 222, 224, 226–7
mother xvii, 18, 20, 34, 47, 72, 77, 81–3, 91, 111, 112, 114, 160, 164, 170, 172–3, 174, 176, 178–81, 194, 197
mouth 16, 17, 91, 93, 97, 106, 132, 203
murder 15, 35–6, 46, 47, 53, 56, 58, 59, 67, 87, 88, 94, 98, 111, 112, 114, 115, 154, 155–6, 179, 180, 207, 228, 234, 235, 237, 242
myth 37, 83, 104, 131, 137, 143, 225, 228, 230
mythical xviii, 8, 36, 70, 83, 112, 138, 149, 162, 235
mythology 23, 43, 67, 87, 106, 121, 142, 178, 179, 194

narcissism 77, 234, 242
nightmare 7, 19, 69, 73, 87, 94, 177, 205, 227
Nightmare on Elm Street, A 59, 62, 73, 74, 186
nihilism 163, 234

Other xiv, xviii, 32, 38, 42, 46, 48, 52, 82, 123, 139, 141, 142, 158, 168, 176, 177, 217
outsider 3, 6, 206

paedophilia 32, 34, 35, 37, 38, 159
paranoia 16, 138
parent 16, 59, 89, 194, 219
patriarchy 9, 20, 28, 32, 46, 111, 114, 116, 117, 152, 153, 156, 159, 164, 170, 172, 175
plague 206–7, 228
pornography xii, xiii, 27, 52, 169
possession 15, 17, 18, 25, 27, 150, 154, 155, 181
Psycho 58, 65, 74, 175–6, 179–80, 186
psychoanalysis 6, 7, 84, 158, 176–7, 242
psychological 15, 16, 17, 19, 22, 34, 53, 69, 181, 202, 226, 239
psychopath 19, 29, 85, 178, 233
psychosexual 51

queer 10, 19, 22, 175–8, 181, 197, 244

racism xi, xiv, xvii, 18, 41, 45, 46, 88, 223, 236
religion 106, 112, 131, 132, 134, 135, 152, 157, 164
resurrection 7, 95, 226, 227, 231
ritual 46, 90, 143, 242
rural 41, 102, 109, 172, 202
Russia 4, 9, 16, 121, 123, 126, 127, 163

Satan 4, 133, 149–56, 160, 161, 163, 164
sexual 7, 10, 25, 27, 28, 31, 34, 36, 41, 47, 59, 81, 115, 116, 151, 152, 160, 169, 242
  bi- 3, 176, 197

trans- 179
sexuality 1, 37, 44, 46, 58, 169, 176, 197, 236
sexualized xiii, 26, 45, 170, 171
skin 18, 27, 38, 46, 56, 58, 120, 203, 228, 233, 241
soul 17, 34, 122, 123, 132, 150, 163, 164, 211, 221, 238
spectre 152, 194
spirits 27, 28, 44, 102, 106, 122, 132
spiritual 152, 207
Stoker, Bram 2–3, 18, 42, 96, 203
sublime 214, 226, 232
supernatural 7, 16, 18, 19, 34, 36, 88, 91, 96, 113, 153, 154, 163, 164, 190
superstition 15, 16

taboo 6, 43, 104, 106, 219, 226
technology 5, 45, 48, 69, 70–3, 75, 133, 164, 198, 218, 220, 230, 231
technophobia 73
teeth 122, 123, 132, 133, 187
threshold 37, 38, 123, 236
torture 95, 114, 133
toxic masculinity 26, 28, 157, 160
traces 2, 6, 11, 31, 86
transcend xviii, 79, 98, 119, 121, 226
transcultural 9, 41, 42, 87, 111, 113, 114, 119, 149
transform xiii, xiv, xviii, 1, 31, 37, 38, 43, 46, 79, 81, 89, 102, 106, 107, 108, 123, 169, 170, 173, 203, 210, 213–15, 221–3, 225, 227, 235
transgressive 6, 7, 37, 43, 53, 55, 59, 111, 113, 117, 152, 164, 220
transphobic 176
trauma xv, xviii, 15, 19–21, 24, 31, 53, 55, 59, 72, 74, 91, 170, 180–1
treacherous 22, 44, 122, 236
trope 17, 42, 43, 96, 158, 159, 160, 163, 177–8, 195, 197, 201, 205

uncanny xi, xiv, 16, 82, 102, 103–4, 106, 138, 158, 194, 195, 198, 199
urban 41, 88, 90, 202
utopia xvii, 218, 222, 225–6, 228, 231

vampire 1–3, 5, 6, 7, 88, 107, 138, 158, 160, 186, 201, 203, 204, 205
villain 15, 53, 58, 67, 69, 121, 140, 154, 183, 187, 203, 204, 228
violence xii, xvii, 8, 15, 19, 20, 23, 24, 26–8, 42, 83, 87, 91, 93, 94, 111, 113, 115, 116, 138, 150, 151, 157, 159–61, 179, 180, 188, 205, 219, 222, 225, 226, 228, 234, 242

witch 10, 87, 91, 102, 104, 106–7, 119, 121–3, 126–7, 152–6, 157, 159–64, 218
wolf
    Big Bad 16
    -man 158
    she- 10, 168–74
    were- 167–74
Wood, Robin 176–7
woods 126, 155, 172

xenophobia 2, 41–3, 219, 223

zombie 1, 4, 42, 43, 183, 186, 188, 201, 204, 205, 226–7, 228, 230, 231

Genre Fiction and Film Companions

Series Editor: Simon Bacon

The *Genre Fiction and Film Companions* provide accessible introductions to key texts within the most popular genres of our time. Written by leading scholars in the field, brief essays on individual texts offer innovative ways of understanding, interpreting and reading the topics in question. Invaluable for students, teachers and fans alike, these surveys offer new insights into the most important literary works, films, music, events and more within genre fiction and film.

We welcome proposals for edited collections on new genres and topics. Please contact baconetti@googlemail.com or oxford@peterlang.com.

Published Volumes

The Gothic
Edited by Simon Bacon

Cli-Fi
Edited by Axel Goodbody and Adeline Johns-Putra

Horror
Edited by Simon Bacon

Sci-Fi
Edited by Jack Fennell

Monsters
Edited by Simon Bacon

Lightning Source UK Ltd.
Milton Keynes UK
UKHW021843211220
375658UK00004B/24